Music in the Western

Music in the Western: Notes from the Frontier presents essays from both film studies scholars and musicologists on core issues in western film scores: their history, their generic conventions, their operation as part of a narrative system, their functioning within individual filmic texts and their ideological import, especially in terms of the western's construction of gender, sexuality, race, and ethnicity. The Hollywood western is marked as uniquely American by its geographic setting, prototypical male protagonist and core American values. *Music in the Western* examines these conventions and the scores that have shaped them. But the western also had a resounding international impact, from Europe to Asia, and this volume distinguishes itself by its careful consideration of music in non-Hollywood westerns, such as *Ravenous* and *The Good, the Bad, and the Ugly* and in the "easterns" which influenced them, such as *Yojimbo*. Other films discussed include *Wagon Master*, *High Noon*, *Calamity Jane*, *The Big Country*, *The Unforgiven*, *Dead Man*, *Wild Bill*, *There Will Be Blood*, and *No Country for Old Men*.

Contributors: Ross Care, Corey K. Creekmur, Yuna de Lannoy, K. J. Donnelly, Caryl Flinn, Claudia Gorbman, Kathryn Kalinak, Charles Leinberger, Matthew McDonald, Peter Stanfield, Mariana Whitmer, and Ben Winters

The *Routledge Music and Screen Media Series* offers edited collections of original essays on music, in particular genres of cinema, television, video games, and new media. These edited essay collections are written for an interdisciplinary audience of students and scholars of music and film and media studies.

Kathryn Kalinak is Professor of English and Film Studies at Rhode Island College. She is the author of *Settling the Score: Music in the Classical Hollywood Film* (1992), *How the West Was Sung: Music in the Westerns of John Ford* (2007), and *Film Music: A Very Short Introduction* (2010). In 2011, she received RIC's Thorp Award for Distinguished Scholarship and Creative Activity.

Routledge Music and Screen Media Series
Series Editor: Neil Lerner

The **Routledge Music and Screen Media Series** offers edited collections of original essays on music in particular genres of cinema, television, video games, and new media. These edited essay collections are written for an interdisciplinary audience of students and scholars of music and film and media studies.

Music in the Western: Notes from the Frontier
Edited by Kathryn Kalinak

Music in Television: Channels of Listening
Edited by James Deaville

Music in the Horror Film: Listening to Fear
Edited by Neil Lerner

Music in the Western

Notes from the Frontier

Edited by Kathryn Kalinak

Routledge
Taylor & Francis Group

NEW YORK AND LONDON

First published 2012
by Routledge
711 Third Avenue, New York, NY 10017

Simultaneously published in the UK
by Routledge
2 Park Square, Milton Park, Abingdon, Oxon OX14 4RN

Routledge is an imprint of the Taylor & Francis Group, an informa business

Library of Congress Cataloging-in-Publication Data
Music in the Western : notes from the frontier / edited by Kathryn Kalinak.
     p. cm.—(Routledge music and screen media series)
     Includes bibliographical references and index.
     1. Motion picture music—History and criticism. 2. Western films—
History and criticism. I. Kalinak, Kathryn Marie, 1952–
ML2075.M876 2011
781.5′42—dc22   2011016963

ISBN: 978–0–415–88226–2 (hbk)
ISBN: 978–0–415–88227–9 (pbk)
ISBN: 978–0–203–68003–2 (ebk)

Typeset in Goudy
by Keystroke, Station Road, Codsall, Wolverhampton
Printed and bound in the United States of America on acid-free paper by
Edwards Brothers, Inc.

Senior Editor: Constance Ditzel
Senior Editorial Assistant: Mike Andrews
Production Manager: Sarah Stone
Marketing Manager: Joon Won Moon
Copy Editor: Janice Baiton
Proofreader: Jane Canvin
Cover Design: Salamander Hill Design

SUSTAINABLE FORESTRY INITIATIVE
Certified Fiber Sourcing
www.sfiprogram.org

Contents

Series Foreword   vii
Acknowledgments   ix

Introduction   1
KATHRYN KALINAK

PART I
Music in the Classical Hollywood Studio Film   19

1 The Cowboy Chorus: Narrative and Cultural Functions
   of the Western Title Song   21
   COREY K. CREEKMUR

2 "A Cowboy Has to Sing": John Ford, Walt Disney, and
   Sons of the Pioneers   37
   ROSS CARE

3 Reinventing the Western Film Score: Jerome Moross and
   The Big Country   51
   MARIANA WHITMER

4 Silencing the Truth: Music and Identity in *The Unforgiven*   77
   BEN WINTERS

5 A Tale of Two Cowgirls: Songs, Western Novelty Acts,
   and 1950s Hollywood   94
   CARYL FLINN

PART II
Westerns Outside Hollywood   115

6 Innovation and Imitation: An Analysis of the
   Soundscape of Akira Kurosawa's *Chambara* Westerns   117
   YUNA DE LANNOY

7 The Dollars Trilogy: "There are two kinds of western
   heroes, my friend!"   131
   CHARLES LEINBERGER

8 Europe Cannibalizes the Western: *Ravenous*   148
   K. J. DONNELLY

9 "How . . . were we going to make a picture that's better
   than this?": Crossing Borders from East to West in
   Rashomon and *The Outrage*   165
   KATHRYN KALINAK

PART III
The Contemporary Western   181

10 From the Barroom Floor: American Song, Saloon
   Culture, Stack O'Lee, and *Wild Bill*, or "Did you
   touch my hat?"   183
   PETER STANFIELD

11 Musical Worlds of the Millennial Western: *Dead Man*
   and *The Three Burials of Melquiades Estrada*   203
   CLAUDIA GORBMAN

12 Mountains, Music, and Murder: Scoring the American
   West in *There Will Be Blood* and *No Country For Old Men*   214
   MATTHEW MCDONALD

   Notes on Contributors   228
   Index   230

Series Foreword

While the scholarly conversations about music in film and visual media have been expanding prodigiously since the last quarter of the twentieth century, a need remains for focused, specialized studies of particular films as they relate more broadly to genres. This series includes scholars from across the disciplines of music and film and media studies, of specialists in both the audible as well as the visual, who share the goal of broadening and deepening these scholarly dialogues about music in particular genres of cinema, television, videogames, and new media. Claiming a chronological arc from the birth of cinema in the 1890s to the most recent releases, the *Music and Screen Media* series offers collections of original essays written for an interdisciplinary audience of students and scholars of music, film and media studies in general, and inter-disciplinary humanists who give strong attention to music. Driving the study of music here are the underlying assumptions that music together with screen media (understood broadly to accommodate rapidly developing new tech-nologies) participates in important ways in the creation of meaning and that including music in an analysis opens up the possibility for interpretations that remain invisible when only using the eye.

The series was designed with the goal of providing a thematically unified group of supplemental essays in a single volume that can be assigned in a variety of undergraduate and graduate courses (including courses in film studies, in film music, and other interdisciplinary topics). We look forward to adding future volumes addressing emerging technologies and reflecting the growth of the academic study of screen media. Rather than attempting an exhaustive history or unified theory, these studies—persuasive explications supported by textual and contextual evidence—will pose questions of musical style, strategies of rhetoric, and critical cultural analysis as they help us to see, to hear, and ultimately to understand these texts in new ways.

Neil Lerner
Series Editor

Acknowledgments

The quality of an anthology is the product of its contributors. First and foremost I would like to thank the scholars whose work is represented here. I feel honored that each of them agreed to participate, often when it was extremely difficult to do so. A "yip-pee-i-ay i-ay, yip-pee-i-oh" (as Pecos Bill would say) to Claudia Gorbman for suggesting the book's subtitle. Of course, this anthology would not have been possible without the vision of Neil Lerner who inaugurated the series and serves as its general editor. His guidance and support have played no small part in helping me through the process of editing this volume. At Routledge, Constance Ditzel was always ready to answer any question, large or small, and Michael Andrews handled a further onslaught with a combination of good cheer and patience. I am grateful to Dean Earl Simson and the Faculty Research Fund at Rhode Island College for their support of this project and to the staff of Adams Library, particularly Lisa Maine, for help above and beyond the call of duty. Finally, I want to thank my husband Ralph and my daughter Emily, who continue to indulge my passion for westerns and who have contributed, more than they know, to making my journey to this book's completion a happy trail.

Introduction

Kathryn Kalinak

Music in the Western: Notes from the Frontier presents a series of essays exploring music for the western. As the field of film music begins to emerge from the disciplinary specificity which has marked its development, film studies scholars and musicologists have begun to learn from one another's perspective. It is my hope that this anthology will be an example of the fruitful insights that can be gained from such interdisciplinarity. In fact, some readers may be surprised by who authored what: musicologists concerned with the history of the western and including detailed analyses of *mise-en-scène* and editing; film studies scholars quoting and analyzing musical passages and contextualizing western scores in terms of music history; and scholars from both fields concerned with the film score in both narratological and ideological terms. Although the western has been marked as a typically American genre, it has been adopted and adapted by filmmakers around the world. Part of the project of this anthology is to consider the global reach of the Hollywood western and investigate both its effect on filmmaking traditions internationally and the effect of these traditions on its development. Music is no small part in this process. Finally, some notes about the frontier. On the most obvious level, the essays here treat music as part of the western's representation of the frontier. But the frontier signifies in other ways as well. The anthology is positioned on the frontier of genre studies, extending the boundaries of what constitutes the proper study of the western and it presents cutting-edge essays which represent the frontier of film music scholarship.

"Typically American"

When producer C. V. Whitney fielded a complaint from composer Max Steiner about the editing of the score for John Ford's *The Searchers* (1956), Whitney pointed out that by cutting some of Steiner's music, Ford produced a "typically American" score.[1] Of all Hollywood's genres, the western has always had the closest connection to America itself, given its emphasis on a specific moment in American history (roughly 1860–1900) and its focus on a specific American space (the western frontier of the US). Contemporary westerns fiddle with the time period but depend upon the traditional western's narrative formulas and geographic locales. Westerns of either variety have much to say about America, the American character, and American values, and they do it not only through narrative and visual style, but also through music.

The western in the US has a long history that begins with cinema's first blockbuster, *The Great Train Robbery* (1903). It would prove to be one of silent film's most durable genres. The silent western as it developed in the first three decades of the twentieth century set the parameters, generating narrative formulas, iconic characters, and representative settings that have informed the genre ever since. And, as for all of silent film, musical accompaniment played an important role. To the best of my knowledge, no complete scores for US silent westerns survive. However, musical encyclopedias and cue sheets of the era reveal that some of the genre's musical conventions, specifically for the cowboy hero (and his horse) and for Indians, were already in place by the 1910s. In Erno Rapée's encyclopedic *Motion Picture Moods*, we find "Western Allegro" and "Western Scene" which incorporate the loping rhythms perceived to be characteristic of a horse's leisurely gait (a pattern of four beats, usually with syncopation on the second and fourth beats).[2] Rapée also includes "Indian Agitato," "Indian War-Dance," and "Sun-Dance" all of which utilize the tom-tom rhythm (four equal beats with the accent on the first). Cue sheets reveal some of the same conventions: the tom-tom rhythm when an Indian shoots a young woman in the epic western *The Covered Wagon* (1923) or the horse rhythm for Silver King, cowboy star Fred Thomson's famous horse, in *Hands Across the Border* (1926). By the sound era, such musical conventions would be completely familiar to audiences of the western.

Such familiarity was not created by silent film accompaniment alone. Musical encyclopedias and cue sheets drew upon musical conventions already circulating in the culture. Michael Pisani has demonstrated that musical stereotypes for Indians appropriated the tropes of nineteenth-century art music for exoticism and Otherness. By the 1910s, as Claudia Gorbman has documented, these musical stereotypes for Indians were firmly in place. Folk and traditional music as well as period songs were also harnessed to the genre and began to appear in silent westerns by the 1910s—via song lyrics printed in the intertitles: "Home Sweet Home" in *Bucking Broadway* (1917), "Sweet Genevieve" in *Hellbent* (1918), "Oh! Susanna" in *The Covered Wagon*, "Drill, Ye Terriers, Drill" in *The Iron Horse* (1924).

The Sound Western's Two Paths

The western forks into two separate paths with the advent of sound film, trajectories largely defined by the use of music: 1930s B westerns, also known as series westerns, which exploited the new country-and-western music developing on the radio and in the recording industry; and A westerns, top-of-the-line studio product exploding onto screens in the late 1930s, which eschewed country-and-western music, and tapped into cultural currents in American art music.

Both varieties depended upon music that their core audiences recognized as American and even specifically western. Cowboy songs figured prominently in the country-and-western repertoire that formed the backbone of B westerns, and many country-and-western recording artists dressed in cowboy attire on and off stage. Although A westerns were more informed by developments in the concert hall than on the radio, here too the landscape of the American West and the character of the cowboy found musical expression.

B westerns, as Peter Stanfield has demonstrated, addressed the working class, and country-and-western music was part of these films' "class specific address."[3] Emerging from southern vernacular hillbilly music in the 1920s, country-and-western music quickly became associated with the cowboy. Many of its earliest recording stars, such as Jimmie Rodgers and Gene Autry, recorded cowboy songs. In fact, Autry billed himself early on as "Oklahoma's Singing Cowboy." Country-and-western music was spurred on by the growth of the radio and recording industries in the 1930s but it found its most visible outlet in the series westerns that lured country-and-western artists such as Autry, Roy Rogers, and Tex Ritter to perform in the movies. (Jimmie Rodgers, perhaps the greatest country-and-western performer, had died by 1933.) The B western would dead-end on the big screen by the late 1940s, but found a home on the small screen, becoming a staple of television in the 1950s and 1960s. But country-and-western's legacy may well be its introduction of contemporary popular music into the western score.

A westerns followed a different musical trail. A defining movement in American art music occurred in the 1930s when composers turned away from the abstraction of European Modernism, the urbanity of jazz, and even the elitism of the concert hall to embrace a new source of inspiration for an authentic American sound—Anglo-American folk song, period music, and hymnody—and the uncomplicated melodies, simple harmonies, characteristic rhythms, and sparse orchestrations derived from them. This is a music that found its audience, and its particular definition of American-ness continues to be a powerful determinant on what sounds American in music to this day.

This music had a primal connection to the West: to its mythic archetypes—the cowboy, the rancher, the farmer—and to its distinctive geography of wide open space. Composers such as Roy Harris, Virgil Thomson, and Aaron Copland shaped this new aesthetic, often by invoking hymns or folk tunes and exploiting their distinctive melodies, rhythms, harmonies, and textures: Harris's *Folksong Symphony* (1940); Thomson's *Symphony on a Hymn Tune* (1928); and Copland's *Billy the Kid* (1939), *Rodeo* (1942), and *Appalachian Spring* (1944), which famously quotes the Shaker hymn "Tis the Gift to Be Simple." These composers, some of whom actually worked in Hollywood, proved extremely influential, none more so than Copland.

Copland followed Thomson to Hollywood in the late 1930s where both composers embraced the new medium of sound film. Copland's scores, few though they were, garnered critical acclaim and provided a model for original composition in a distinctly American idiom. He would become especially influential on composers of the western. Although Copland never scored a traditional western (the contemporary western *The Red Pony* (1949), set on a ranch in California, is as close as he got), Andre Previn would write of him: "I doubt whether any film composer faced with pictures of the Great American Outdoors, or any western story, has been able to withstand the lure of trying to imitate some aspects of Copland's peculiar and personal harmony."[4] Neil Lerner points to the sense of wide open space in Copland's music, resulting from the composer's "disjunct melodies and widely spaced voicings . . . parallel diatonic harmonies, wind and brass timbres [and] a fondness for fourths and fifths, both harmonically and melodically."[5] Copland resonated with composers of the western. While there are clearly exceptions to his influence (post-war psychological westerns such as *Naked Spur* (1953), for example), Copland exerted something of a gravitational pull on composers of the genre and his influence is particularly pronounced in the musical evocation of landscape in scores such as Dimitri Tiomkin's for *Red River* (1948), Hugo Friedhofer's for *Broken Arrow* (1950), Emil Newman and Hugo Friedhofer's for *Hondo* (1953), Jerome Moross's for *The Big Country* (1958), Elmer Bernstein's for *The Magnificent Seven* (1960), and Frank De Vol's for *McLintock!* (1963).

John Ford and the Use of Traditional Music

John Ford, arguably the greatest director of westerns, had a strong predilection for folk music, period song, and hymnody in his films. The score for *Stagecoach* (1939), described in the credits as "Based on American folk song," quotes fourteen different pieces of traditional American music, heard either as source music or as part of the background score. These pieces include: the Protestant hymn "Shall We Gather at the River," the cowboy tune "O Bury Me Not on the Lone Prairie," the Civil War anthem "The Battle-Cry of Freedom," Stephen Foster's parlor ballads "Jeanie with the Light Brown Hair" and "Gentle Annie," and the minstrel song "Carry Me Back to Old Virginny." Soon Ford began to feature performances of western songs to great effect, especially in the cavalry trilogy, where soldiers sing the traditional "The Girl I Left Behind Me" in *She Wore a Yellow Ribbon* (1949) and dance to the hymn "All Praise to St. Patrick" in *Fort Apache* (1948). Anticipating the theme-song craze of the 1950s, Ford featured the country-and-western songs of Sons of the Pioneers in *Rio Grande* (1950), and had the Sons actually don cavalry uniforms and sing on-screen.

Let's note here that much folk music and many traditional songs, especially those connected with the West, are not authentic in the way we have supposed them to be. Many turn out to be composed by Easterners with little or no experience of the frontier. And some, such as "Oh! Susanna" by Stephen Foster, are minstrel songs. Despite their provenance, these songs were assumed to be genuine and they lent authenticity to the genre's depiction of the historical past. Music also carries ideological meaning, evoking emotionally laden and culturally determined responses which position the audience to accept the underlying ideologies of the genre, especially in terms of race, ethnicity, gender, and class. (See the section following on Indian music as an example of how ideologies of race become embedded in the western film score.) Songs, because of their lyrics, are an especially potent form of cultural transmission, working powerfully, and often on a less than conscious level, to convince us that the genre taps into the wellspring of authentic American values.

This use of traditional music in the western film score often triggered the use of instruments, such as the guitar, harmonica, and banjo, widely perceived as authentically western. While it is important to point out that some of these instruments did not typically appear in the historical West (the guitar, for instance, was much more common in Mexico than in the nineteenth-century American frontier) and some that did, such as the mandolin and jaw harp, rarely make an appearance in Hollywood westerns. Yet like folk music itself, these instruments were perceived to be genuine and added to the authenticity of a score. Tiomkin's orchestral pallette in *Red River*, for instance, includes banjo, harmonica, and guitar which we can even glimpse at moments in the film.

A westerns are not exceptional in their use of traditional music and instruments, however. Peter Stanfield points out that folk song was also heard in B westerns where singing cowboys, steering clear of the "cultural dissonance" of jazz, [6] exploited folk song (and the guitar) to create a distinctly country musical identity in films such as the Gene Autry vehicle *Carolina Moon* (1940) where we hear "Old Folks at Home." The inclusion of folk, hymnody, and traditional music, however, would become practically *de rigueur* in A westerns of the studio era. Although sometimes heard in overblown symphonic arrangements, this music could also be very simply performed, a cappella or with minimal accompaniment: Robert Mitchum singing "The Streets of Laredo" in *Pursued* (1947); Harry Carey, Jr. singing "I Ride an Old Paint" in *Red River*; Lillian Gish singing "Beautiful Dreamer" in *Duel in the Sun* (1946); Ricky Nelson singing "[Get Along Home] Cindy, Cindy" accompanied by guitar in *Rio Bravo* (1959); and Myrna Loy playing "Shall We Gather at the River" on the piano in *The Red Pony* (1949).

Revisionist westerns of the post-studio era which eschewed the perceived romanticism of earlier studio output, aimed for a more authentic rendering of western history, settings, and characters. Yet the iconically revisionist western, *The Wild Bunch* (1968), employs "Shall We Gather at the River." The 1887 hymn "Leaning on the Everlasting Arms" (aka "Leaning on Jesus") turns up evocatively in both *Wild Bill* (1995) and *True Grit* (2010). Even *There Will Be Blood* (2007), set in the California oil fields, cannot resist including a hymn.

Many composers working in Hollywood in the post-studio era, in the 1960s, 1970s and beyond, were drawn to new ways of scoring westerns. (More on this below.) But even scores that gravitated to new musical aesthetics, such as Lennie Niehaus's for *Pale Rider* (1985) and Jerry Fielding's for *The Outlaw Josey Wales* (1976), include cues that harken back to the distinctive use of the harmonic and melodic model of folk song and hymnody that characterized Copland's music.

The Musical Representation of Indians

The musical representation of Indians operated differently. Although Native American music had been transcribed or recorded by ethnographers as early as the 1910s, Native American music does not find its way into the accompaniment for on-screen Indians in any significant way in the studio era. Instead, Indian music exploits powerful musical codes that reinforce cultural stereotypes about Otherness: Indians are positioned outside American-ness. The use of music to define ethnic and racial boundaries, what K. J. Donnelly describes as "expelling that which you disown and reconfiguring the outside to fit your fears"[7] was a staple of classical Hollywood scoring.

As Michael Pisani has demonstrated, Indian music was derived from musical stereotypes for the representation of western Europe's exotic Others—Turks, Chinese, and Arabs, in particular—that developed concurrently with European Imperialism including: unusual repetitive rhythms, modal melodies, short descending motifs, a tendency to veer away from conventional major and minor tonalities and toward chromaticism, and unusual instrumentation, especially involving percussion. These stereotypes were ready at hand for composers and performers looking for ways to accompany Indians on the stage and in Wild West entertainments. Extant music from *Buffalo Bill's Wild West and Congress of Rough Riders of the World*, for instance, includes clear examples of these stereotypes, in compositions such as "On the Warpath" and "The Passing of the Red Man."

Not surprisingly, the stereotypes found their way into film. As Claudia Gorbman has documented, Hollywood developed a musical vocabulary for representing Indians which connoted the primitive and the savage. Composer Dimitri Tiomkin described it as a "telegraphic code that audiences recognize."[8] This code frequently included the tom-tom rhythm, what Gorbman terms the "Indian-on-the-warpath cliché,"[9] often played by drums or low bass instruments, perfect fifths and fourths in the harmonic design, and modal melody. Indian music was so generic that Max Steiner could recycle the same Indian cue from *They Died With Their Boots On* (1941) in *The Searchers* (1956). Even post-war liberal westerns, whose project was to humanize the Indian, recycle these stereotypes.

In the post-studio era, some westerns began to explore the possibilities of Native American music. Alex North incorporated some authentic Cheyenne chanting and rhythms in his score for *Cheyenne Autumn* (1964) and Leonard Rosenman did field work collecting Sioux songs before composing his score for *A Man Called Horse* (1970). Nevertheless, both scores approach Native American music cautiously and both filter their sources through Hollywood scoring conventions. John Barry's score for *Dances With Wolves* (1990) manages to avoid the stereotypes of Indian music for the Sioux. The score's sweeping melodies incorporate authentic Sioux chanting and rhythms enfolded in Romantic orchestrations, as Claudia Gorbman notes, "the same lush musical language as the good white protagonist."[10] Similarly, Timothy E. Scheurer points out that for "Buffalo Hunt," Barry exploits the classical western scoring practices "we generally associate with the forces of civilization" to accompany the Sioux.[11] However, both Gorbman and Scheurer note that the Pawnees, the film's bad Indians, receive the brunt of the score's exoticism. Although the Pawnee escape stereotypical Indian music, they are represented by an angular modernist idiom, in the words of Gorbman, "a less hackneyed means to replicate Indian otherness."[12] Scheurer notes the more conventional use of tremolo strings and the "half-step descending pattern to suggest menace" when Pawnees are on-screen.[13]

The Western Outside Hollywood

Although the western was "typically American," it would soon prove of interest to filmmakers around the world who adopted, co-opted, transformed, or displaced the western's generative narratives, characters, and settings. Mexico produced numerous westerns throughout its golden era of the 1940s and 1950s and produced the surrealist cult western *El Topo* in 1970. But it was mid-century before the western was discovered in East Germany (with *Indianerfilms* such as *The Sons of the Great Bear* in 1965), West Germany (many of which were based on the novels of German writer Karl May, such as the *Winnetou* series 1963–65 and *Old Shatterhand* in 1964), India (*Sholay* in 1975, which proved one of the highest grossing films ever to come out of Bollywood), and Brazil (Glauber Rochas's 1969 *Antonio das Mortes* which won at Cannes). Throughout the USSR and its satellite nations, so-called red westerns were popular: *A Man from the Boulevard des Capucines* (USSR, 1987), *Lemonade Joe* (Czechoslovakia, 1964), and *The Oil, the Baby, and the Transylvanians* (Romania, 1981). In Japan, the samurai films of Akira Kurosawa have strong links to the western (and have sometimes been labeled "easterns"), and indeed, three have been famously remade as westerns in Hollywood and elsewhere: *Rashomon* (1950) as *The Outrage* (1964), *The Seven Samurai* (1954) as *The Magnificent Seven* (1960), and *Yojimbo* (1961) as *A Fistful of Dollars* (1964).

These non-American westerns sometimes critiqued American core values and even America itself, but more often they spoke to the particular histories, value systems, and narrative conventions of the countries in which they were produced. Although their musical scores sometimes appropriate tropes of the Hollywood western, often with irony, more typically non-American westerns make use of indigenous rather than Anglo-American folk and traditional music.

It would be difficult to find a better example of the innovative and iconoclastic approach of filmmakers outside Hollywood to this American genre than the westerns produced in Italy mid-century, often referred to as spaghetti westerns. The most notable ones, directed by Sergio Leone and starring Clint Eastwood, continue to influence westerns inside and outside Hollywood to this day. *A Fistful of Dollars*, *For a Few Dollars More* (1965), and *The Good, the Bad, and the Ugly* (1966) stand as monuments to the western, un-American as they are. Leone recast the genre through the sensibility of the 1960s and helped to shape the revisionist western, profoundly altering notions of the American

West and the western hero. Their scores by Ennio Morricone share in the films' revisionary aesthetic: scoring is sparse, melodies are few, harmonies are uncomplicated, orchestrations are unconventional, and emotional triggers for the audience are avoided. In *The Good, the Bad, and the Ugly*, as Charles Leinberger has shown, Morricone enlists an electric guitar, an ocarina (an ancient flute), and a harmonica, along with whistling, yodeling, grunting, vocalizations (at times unrecognizable as human), whipcracks, and gunshots. Morricone effectively turned his back on the Hollywood conventions for western scoring and in the process provided a new model, more appealing to younger audiences and infused with the aesthetics of popular music. And, as Leinberger points out, "many of the same qualities that made rock-and-roll of the 1960s commercially successful did the same for Morricone's film music."[14] The scores for a series of Hollywood westerns starring Clint Eastwood and sometimes directed by him are clearly influenced by Morricone, from *Two Mules for Sister Sara* (1970, actually scored by Morricone) to the lean, jazz-inflected and sparsely orchestrated *Unforgiven* (1992, scored by Lennie Niehaus). Alan Silvestri's score for *The Quick and the Dead* (1995), Mario Beltrami's score for *3:10 to Yuma* (2007), and Hans Zimmer's score for the animated feature *Rango* (2011) are more recent examples of Morricone's influence, as are Koji Endo's score for the Japanese *Sukiyaki Western Django* (2007) and Chan Young-gyu's score for the South Korean *The Good, the Bad, the Weird* (2008).

Popular Music and the Western

Popular music took aim at Hollywood westerns at about the same time that westerns made their initial global impact. The use of originally composed western songs can be heard in *Red River* (1948) and *Wagon Master* (1950). But they became a distinctive feature of the genre with the success of Dimitri Tiomkin's song "Do Not Forsake Me, Oh My Darlin'" (with lyricist Ned Washington) for *High Noon* (1952). The song was marketed before the film's release, pioneering the practice, which continues to the present day, of preselling a film by promoting its music beforehand. Other examples include Marlene Dietrich singing Ken Darby's "Gypsy Davey" in *Rancho Notorious* (1952) and Ricky Nelson and Dean Martin singing "My Rifle, My Pony, and Me" in *Rio Bravo* (1959). But it was the 1960s that saw the advent of decidedly un-western contemporary songs infusing western film scores: "Raindrops Keep Fallin' on My Head," for instance, was prominently featured in *Butch Cassidy and the Sundance Kid* (1969). Revisionist westerns were especially drawn to this aesthetic: Leonard Cohen's songs provide the score for *McCabe and Mrs. Miller* (1971) and Bob Dylan's for *Pat Garrett & Billy the Kid* (1973).

The Contemporary Western

Although reports of the western's demise are regularly circulated, the genre continues to thrive both in Hollywood and outside it. In the last decade,

Hollywood has released several high-profile westerns including: *Open Range* in 2003; a remake of *The Alamo* in 2004; *The Three Burials of Melquiades Estrada* and *Brokeback Mountain*, both in 2005; *Bandidas* in 2006; and *There Will Be Blood*, *3:10 to Yuma*, *The Assassination of Jesse James By the Coward Robert Ford*, and the Oscar winner for Best Picture *No Country for Old Men* all in 2007, which proved a banner year for westerns. *Appaloosa* appeared in 2008, *Jonah Hex* and *True Grit* in 2010, and the animated western *Rango* in 2011. Internationally, the western continues to be a vital genre with the German *Manitou's Shoe* in 2001; the Australian films *The Proposition* in 2005 and *Australia* in 2008; the Polish *Summer Love* in 2006; the Japanese *Sukiyaki Western Django* in 2007; and the South Korean *The Good, The Bad, the Weird* in 2008.

The western score in contemporary Hollywood is indebted to a complicated legacy. The gravitational pulls of the classic Hollywood A western film score, the B western's appropriation of popular music, and Morricone's spaghetti western scores have created a force field through which contemporary western film scores pass. A quick listen to *3:10 to Yuma* and *There Will Be Blood* suggests how two very high-profile westerns negotiate these influences quite differently.

The Academic Study of the Western Film Score

Film studies has concerned itself intimately with the western for over half a century. The French critics of the post-war period, for example, developed their notions of film artistry based on hundreds of American films that flooded France after the wartime drought, and their intellectual leader, André Bazin, called the western "the American film genre par excellence." Ever since then, British and American film scholars have analyzed the western, its histories, and its meanings. Until recently, however, such scholarship has concerned itself little with the music, which arguably carries much of the meaning and feeling that passionately engaged these critics. Some notable exceptions include several entries in the BFI monograph series including Edward Buscombe's *Stagecoach* and *The Searchers* and Jonathan Rosenbaums's *Dead Man* and studies of Sergio Leone's westerns by Christopher Frayling and Robert Cumbow, all of which attend, in some depth, to the score; Phil Hardy's entry on "Music" in *The BFI Companion to the Western*; William Darby's article on musical links among several John Ford westerns; and a special issue of *The Cue Sheet* devoted to the western film score with articles by Warren Sherk on Hans Salter, Linda Danly on Hugo Friedhofer, and Alfred Cochran on Copland.

As criticism of the western has emerged from the paradigms of auteurism, structuralism and genre theory, a generation of scholars from musicology, film and media studies, and popular culture has brought new post-structural perspectives (such as critical musicology, semiotics, Marxism, psychoanalysis, feminist theory, masculinity studies, and cultural studies) to bear on the western and its scores. At the turn of the century, Claudia Gorbman, from film studies, and Michael Pisani, from musicology, wrote extremely influential articles about the musical representation of Indians. Since then, several important studies of western film scores have been published by musicologists: Charles Leinberger's *Ennio Morricone's The Good, The Bad, and The Ugly*, the first and only score for a western to be included in the Scarecrow Film Guide series; Neil Lerner's articles on Copland's relationship to the western film score and on music in *High Noon*. In 2009, the *Journal of Film Music* published a special issue on the western film score including a dialogue between Michael Beckerman and editor William Rosar on the pastoral in western film scoring as well as essays by Beth E. Levy on Copland's *The Red Pony* and Ildar Khannanov on the Russian sources for Tiomkin's *High Noon* ballad. Philip Tagg and Bob Clarida's opus, *Ten Little Title Tunes*, contains a chapter on the theme for the television series *The Virginian*, with much information on and detailed analysis of the theme's antecedents in the western film score. And the country-and-western singer and songwriter Douglas B. Green has written *Singing in the Saddle: The History of the Singing Cowboy*.

Important studies of the western film score have also emerged from the fields of film and media studies: Jeff Smith's chapter on Morricone in his book *The Sounds of Commerce* (1998); Peter Stanfield's work on music for series westerns which culminated in his book *Horse Opera: The Strange History of the Singing Cowboy* (2002); David Arnold's article on the music in *Rio Bravo* (2006); K. J. Donnelly's chapter on American ethnicity in the western film score (2005); and Timothy Scheurer's chapter on the western film score (2008). And I wrote *How the West was Sung: Music in the Westerns of John Ford* (2007).

About this Volume

The essays presented here, each for the first time, contribute to this growing body of scholarship. Some, such as the essays by Ben Winters, Mariana Whitmer, Ross Care, Charles Leinberger, and Matthew McDonald, are written by musicologists; the rest are written by film and media studies scholars. All the essays, however, are concerned with the interactions between music and filmic narrative. Whether focusing on a musical analysis of a score, or concentrating on a score's generic, historical, or ideological import, all of the essays collected here treat the music we hear in westerns as an active participant in the creation of a film's meaning.

The first set of essays treat westerns produced in Hollywood during the studio era, roughly from the 1930s through the early 1960s. This period, often described as classical Hollywood narrative cinema, gave definitive shape to the western genre and set the conventions for its musical scores. In one way or another, each addresses a feature common to many of these westerns, the performance of song.

Corey K. Creekmur's "The Cowboy Chorus: Narrative and Cultural Functions of the Western Title Song" focuses on song, in particular the western title song that developed in the 1950s and became, for a time, *de rigeur* in the genre. Beginning with the obvious commercial value of the originally composed western-sounding title song but quickly moving beyond it, Creekmur investigates the overlooked history of the practice (and reminds us that *High Noon* was not the first western to use one!). Creekmur argues that the western title song functions as a kind of Greek chorus: many westerns, in fact, feature a chorus, a detail that Creekmur points out is in diametric opposition to the realist aesthetic of Hollywood film. Thus title songs "emphasize the films they introduce as narration, or lyric, rather than narrative, or drama." And from this position, title songs often give vent to what the characters cannot express, functioning as "a displacement of the silent cowboy's thoughts and emotions." Title songs also speak to our experience of the genre itself, inviting us to enter the space of the western and conveying the essence of the genre. Unlike diegetic source music and especially folk song, however, title songs do not present that essence through historical artifact but rather through "a crafted work of art and entertainment." Finally, Creekmur takes us full circle to the place of western songs today: "once too lowbrow and blatantly commercial to be included in major studio westerns, and then briefly available as affirmations of historical authenticity, [now they have] simply become too corny and old-fashioned for revisionist Vietnam-era and later westerns."

Ross Care, in "'A Cowboy Has to Sing': John Ford, Walt Disney, and Sons of the Pioneers," focuses on song in the western and unearths a fascinating connection between the scores for Walt Disney's "Pecos Bill" segment from the animated feature *Melody Time* (1948) and John Ford's live-action *Wagon Master* (1950). The country-and-western singing group Sons of the Pioneers recorded songs for both. Care argues that Disney's use of country-and-western song in "Pecos Bill," as well as the particular use to which it was put, constituted a new musical mode for the A feature western. Songs are more tied to the narrative in "Pecos Bill" than in other A westerns of the period where songs usually provide atmosphere. In "Pecos Bill," lyrics drive the plot forward, and, in fact, function as a kind of voice-over narration for the tall tales of the Texas cowboy. And, Care demonstrates, this is how music works in Ford's *Wagon Master* as well. As Care argues, once Ford had determined to use Sons of the Pioneers, he was committed to a more self-conscious use of song to showcase them. Like *Melody Time* before it, *Wagon Master* uses country-and-western songs as an important facet of narrative exposition.

Mariana Whitmer, in "Reinventing the Western Film Score: Jerome Moross and *The Big Country*," demonstrates how Jerome Moross's iconic score harkens back to the roots of western film scoring, his symphonic approach ignoring a trend that by the late 1950s had become a virtual requirement: using an originally composed western song as the score's theme. Moross's background in theater and ballet, Whitmer argues, also positions his music in a somewhat unorthodox relation to the image. Eschewing the scoring of on-screen action, the bread and butter of the western film composer, Moross stepped back from the image to take in the long view, as Whitmer argues, "aurally describing and accompanying the film's most important locations and emotional content, rather than its action." In this way, Whitmer points out, Moross is allied with his friend and mentor Aaron Copland who similarly privileged atmosphere over action.

The commercial pressure to include a song impacted even socially conscious westerns such as John Huston's neglected *The Unforgiven* (1960). As Ben Winters shows us in "Silencing the Truth: Music and Identity in *The Unforgiven*," Dimitri Tiomkin turned a theme for one of the characters, Rachel (Audrey Hepburn), into the song, "The Need for Love," a process not without import for the representation of her character. Based on a novel by Alan LeMay about an Indian girl raised by white Texans, *The Unforgiven* is the inverse of LeMay's more famous captivity narrative and John Ford's filmic adaptation, *The Searchers*. Its equally neglected score, as Winters compellingly argues, is a crucial component of *The Unforgiven*'s complicated and contradictory message about race. At the heart of the conflict surrounding the racial identity of the Indian girl, Rachel, is music. Rachel, who is ignorant of her heritage and is passing as white, is accompanied by a musical theme that "seems to erase her identity as threatening racial other, and replace it . . . [a] sanitized and eroticized fantasy of the exotic." Intriguingly, Winters suggests that Huston's legendary dislike of the film may be traced at least in part to the score's treatment of Rachel. And yet, as Winters shows us, Rachel's theme may be just as much a reflection of other characters' perceptions as it is a simple "whitewashing" of her racial complexity. Thus Winters sees the score contributing to a more complex and ambivalent reading of the film.

Caryl Flinn, in "A Tale of Two Cowgirls: Song, Western Novelty Acts, and 1950s Hollywood," writes about westerns that are filled with so many songs that they constitute a genre of their own: the western musical. Here women hold center stage. Focusing on *Annie Get Your Gun* (1950) and *Calamity Jane* (1953), based on actual historical figures, Flinn shows us that when two blonde cowgirls performed the work of frontier men, the traditional masculinities that peopled the A western as well as the genre's very seriousness seemed suddenly at risk. Drawing upon representations of masculinity in silent westerns and femininity in the B series westerns, the history of song in A westerns, and the major studios' interest in pursuing genre- and gender-bending alternatives in the 1950s, Flinn argues that these films' odd meshings of girl gunslingers and gender impersonations might not have posed the kind of "ideological dislocation" that we might think. Song plays a crucial role in this process, working to balance conflicting demands for mainstream conformity and off-kilter novelty. Flinn ends with an exploration of *Calamity Jane* through the lens of queer theory, considering how the musical score functions in "a film which openly depicts gender as an unstable category."

The second set of essays examines westerns produced outside Hollywood. Westerns developed around the world mid-century in response to the global popularity of the Hollywood western and some of these films, including some which are not actually westerns, have had a determining effect on Hollywood westerns themselves. The essays here trace the mutual influences going back and forth between Hollywood westerns, non-Hollywood westerns, and internationally produced genre films, such as the samurai film, on the score. In "Innovation and Imitation: An Analysis of the Soundscape of Akira Kurosawa's *Chambara* Westerns," Yuna de Lannoy examines two Akira Kurosawa "easterns," and analyzes how Kurosawa established the genre of *chambara* (period films with sword fights) in *Yojimbo* and *Sanjuro* by exploiting "the audio and visual grammar of the American western." De Lannoy then takes us through both scores and traces the influence of Jerome Moross's *The Big Country* and Dimitri Tiomkin's *Rio Bravo*, two scores that Kurosawa and his composer Masuro Sato used as models (who knew?). De Lannoy shows us how steeped in the western Kurosawa was as he was making these films, at one point complaining to Sato, "If only Mifune [the star of these films] could play the guitar!" In fact, we hear a banjo in *Yojimbo* and a *quijada*, a Mexican instrument made from a donkey jaw, in *Sanjuro*, not to mention the use of syncopated rhythms in Yojimbo's own leitmotif. Ultimately de Lannoy demonstrates "how the music of the western served as an aesthetic model on which Kurosawa and Sato constructed their own musical ideas." *Yojimbo*, of course, famously inspired Sergio Leone who remade it in Italy as *A Fistful of Dollars*.

Charles Leinberger in "The Dollars Trilogy: 'There are two kinds of western heroes, my friend!'" traces the influence of a group of spaghetti westerns, including *A Fistful of Dollars*, produced in Italy during the 1960s, which were directed by Sergio Leone and scored by Ennio Morricone. Morricone approached the western score in a different way, ignoring many of the conventions of the genre (in terms of instrumentation, he was drawn to aerophones, for instance, such as the recorder, English horn, harmonica, trumpet, and, in one film, the bass ocarina) and composing in musical modalities outside conventional western harmonics (permutations of the Aeolean and Dorian modes). Leinberger shows us both the links between the classical Hollywood western film score and Morricone (who, like Kurosawa and Sato before him was influenced by aspects of Dimitri Tiomkin's score for *Rio Bravo*), and between Morricone and later composers of the western around the world. As Leinberger so cogently argues of the paradigm shift in western film scoring, "Ennio Morricone is arguably the composer most responsible for accelerating this shift through his innovative scores for the westerns of Sergio Leone."

In "Europe Cannibalizes the Western: *Ravenous*," K. J. Donnelly points out that because of "the dominance of US films abroad . . . Europe feels it knows American culture only too well, and is able unproblematically to fabricate as quintessentially an American film genre as the western." It is through the music, argues Donnelly, that the British production *Ravenous* (1999) "endeavours to negotiate the minefield of film and cultural tradition" through a confrontation with the powerful influence of the classical Hollywood western score. *Ravenous* blends Native American musical elements, Minimalism's repetitive structures, additive construction and modular development, period music and an avant-garde approach to its performance with out-of-tune instruments and deliber-ately amateurish playing. Donnelly point outs the score would be "exceptional in any film let alone in a western." Ultimately, Donnelly makes the case that despite the film's typically western setting, time frame, characters, and even its (strikingly original) use of period music, there is something "stoically and determinedly European" about the score. The music's refusal to be typically American opens up a reading of the film as a critique of Manifest Destiny and of America itself.

The final selection in this section is my own "'How . . . were we going to make a picture that's better than this?': Crossing Borders from East to West in *Rashomon* and *The Outrage*." I begin with the questions: "What happens when a 'typically American' western doesn't begin its life as either a western or an American film?" and "What can a film score tell us then about crossing borders between genres and across national cinemas?" I consider another remake which successfully negotiates this terrain: *The Magnificent Seven* based on *Seven Samurai* (1954). The scores for both films are firmly embedded in genre traditions. On the other hand, *Rashomon*'s composer, Fumio Hayasaka, produced a genre-bending score for this *jidaigeki* or period drama. Alex North, the composer of *The Outrage*, envisioned a similarly convention-defying score for this post-studio western. Ultimately I argue that "the failure of *The Outrage* to successfully adapt *Rashomon* as a western may be less the result of incompatible genres steeped in national and cultural idioms untranslatable outside the nation and more the result of the pressures of institutional practices both within and outside the nation that figured into the production of both films."

In the final section, scholars address contemporary westerns produced in Hollywood in the post-studio era. Peter Stanfield in "From the Barroom Floor: American Song, Saloon Culture, Stack O'Lee, and *Wild Bill*, or 'Did you touch my hat?'" returns us to one of the overriding concerns of this anthology: the centrality of song in the Hollywood western. Stanfield argues that through the performance of song, a film "imbues itself with a sense of historical verisimilitude" that is historically and culturally specific, determined by shifting notions of authenticity across the genre. The essay is rooted in westerns of the classical Hollywood studio era, ranges through B westerns of the 1930s and 1940s, revisionist westerns of the 1960s and 1970s, and ultimately focuses on the contemporary western *Wild Bill* (1995) and the concert saloon, a drinking establishment with staged entertainment. These saloons, removed from both the realm of domesticity and the world of productive labor, proved a "natural home for minstrelsy" which, in its restaging of slavery in the South for audiences in the North, was like the frontier saloon, built upon "a sense of dislocation." Part of the pleasure of *Wild Bill*'s score is its liberal use of saloon songs, both a return to and an updating of an earlier model, and through it renewed claims to authenticity.

Claudia Gorbman in "Musical Worlds of the Millennial Western: *Dead Man* and *The Three Burials of Melquiades Estrada*" reminds us that westerns have as much to say about the era in which they were produced as they do of the historical West. Gorbman is concerned with two films, each positioned within five years of the millennium, and which share both an awareness of the mythic power of the western and a critique of America at the millennium. Gorbman takes us through the sonic worlds of both films to show us how sound and especially music participates in this critique. The score for *Dead Man* (1995), for instance, "a postmodern version of western masculinity on steroids" is out of synch with the anti-heroic protagonist William Blake (Johnny Depp). Similarly a lone guitar connecting to earlier traditions of western scoring is "electrified, fuzzed out, fragmented, its pedigree weakened, attenuated, and exaggerated." As Gorbman demonstrates, the score's deconstruction of both the western protagonist and the western film score mirrors the film's deconstruction of the genre itself. The score for *The Three Burials of Melquiades Estrada* (2005) comprises both orchestral scoring and pre-existing popular songs. It is those songs that constitute a dialectic between Mexico and the US as it is played out across the West and across the border, although as Gorbman demonstrates, a song which may seem to function as an "ethnic signpost . . . can surprise and complicate our mental categories."

Matthew McDonald, in his essay, "Mountains, Music, and Murder: Scoring the American West in *There Will Be Blood* and *No Country for Old Men*," argues that the completely contrasting scores for these films reflect divergent ideas about the American West and its place in contemporary American culture. Johnny Greenwood's score for *There Will Be Blood* (2007), which was singled out at the film's release for its intensity, seemingly contrasts with Carter Burwell's score for *No Country for Old Men* (2007) filled with barely audible drones "virtually unrecognizable" as music. And yet, McDonald points out, "[i]n each film, a crucial function of the music is to establish and comment upon the physical setting, not merely via stereotyped musical associations . . . but by investing the locale with a sonic presence, which at times takes on an omniscient quality or in some cases even seems to function as an agent guiding the action." Readers will be fascinated by McDonald's comparison of both films to *Kubrick's 2001: A Space Odyssey* (1968) in terms of visual and aural depictions of frontiers.

All the essays you are about to read treat the score as a crucial element of the western and remind us what we miss when we ignore the music. *Music in the Western: Notes from the Frontier* ultimately moves into new territory for the study of the western, establishing a new frontier in genre studies. These essays will also, I trust, spark renewed interest in the genre as it is practiced both inside and outside of Hollywood, and spur others to consider the myriad ways that music is central to the western.

Notes

1 C. V. Whitney, letter to Max Steiner, December 9, 1955, Max Steiner Archive, Brigham Young University, Provo, Utah.
2 Philip Tag and Bob Clarida have actually studied horses' gaits to determine whether the rhythms supposedly derived from them are "stylized onomatopoeia" or "culturally arbitrary." Ultimately they decide that it is more "a matter of musical context and stylistic convention" than horse kinesiology. See Tagg and Clarida, *Ten Little Title Tunes* (New York: The Mass Media Scholars Press, 2003), 292–97.

3 Peter Stanfield, *Horse Opera: The Strange History of the Singing Cowboy* (Urbana: University of Illinois Press, 2002), 154.
4 Previn quoted in Neil Lerner, "Copland's Music of Wide Open Spaces: Surveying the Pastoral Trope in Hollywood," *The Musical Quarterly* 85, 3 (2001), 481.
5 Lerner, 482–83.
6 Stanfield, 57.
7 K. J. Donnelly, *The Spectre of Sound: Music in Film and Television* (London: BFI, 2005), 57.
8 Dimitri Tiomkin, "Composing for Films," in *Dimitri Tiomkin: The Man and His Music* (London: National Film Archive, 1986), 72.
9 Claudia Gorbman, "Drums Along the L.A. River: Scoring the Indian" in *Westerns: Films Through History*, ed. Janet Walker (New York: Routledge, 2001), 178.
10 Gorbman, 192.
11 Timothy Scheurer, *Music and Mythmaking in Film: Genre and the Role of the Composer* (Jefferson, NC: McFarland, 2008), 170.
12 Gorbman, 191.
13 Scheurer, 171.
14 Charles Leinberger, *Ennio Morricone's The Good, the Bad, and the Ugly: A Film Score Guide* (Lanham, MD: Scarecrow Press, 2004), 19.

Select Bibliography

Arnold, David L. G. "My Rifle, My Pony, and Feathers: Music and the Making of Men in Howard Hawks' *Rio Bravo*," *Quarterly Review of Film and Video* 23, 3 (2006), 267–79.
Beckerman, Michael and William H. Rosar. "The Idyllic Sublime: A Dialog on the Pastoral Style in Westerns," *Journal of Film Music* 2, 2–4 (2009), 251–62.
Buscombe, Edward. *The Searchers*. London: BFI, 2000.
———. *Stagecoach*. London: BFI, 1992.
Cochran, Alfred. "*The Red Pony*," *The Cue Sheet: Quarterly Journal of The Film Music Society* 11, 2 (1995), 25–35.
Cumbow, Robert C. *Once Upon a Time: The Films of Sergio Leone*. Metuchen, NJ: Scarecrow Press, 1987.
Danly, Linda. "Hugo Friedhofer's Westerns," *The Cue Sheet: Quarterly Journal of The Film Music Society* 11, 2 (1995), 19–24.
Donnelly, Kevin J. "The Accented Voice: Ethnic Signposts of British, Irish, and American Film Music" in Donnelly, *The Spectre of Sound: Music in Film and Television*, 55–87. London: BFI, 2005.
Frayling, Christopher. *Spaghetti Westerns: Cowboys and Europeans from Karl May to Sergio Leone*. London and Boston: Routledge and Kegan Paul, 1981; London: Taurus, 2006.
Gorbman, Claudia. "Scoring the Indian: Music in the Liberal Western," in *Western Music and Its Others: Difference, Representation, and Appropriation in Music*, ed. Georgina Born and David Hesmondhalgh, 234–53. Berkeley: University of California Press, 2000; rev. and rpt. as "Drums Along the L.A. River: Scoring the Indian," *Westerns: Films Through History*, ed. Janet Walker, 177–95. New York: Routledge, 2001.
Green, Douglas B. *Singing in the Saddle: The History of the Singing Cowboy*. Nashville: Country Music Foundation Press and Vanderbilt University, 2002.
Kalinak, Kathryn. *How the West Was Sung: Music in the Westerns of John Ford*. Berkeley: University of California Press, 2007.

Khannanov, Ildar. "*High Noon*: Dimitri Tiomkin's Oscar-Winning Ballad and its Russian Sources," *Journal of Film Music* 2, 2–4 (2009), 225–48.

Leinberger, Charles. *Ennio Morricone's The Good, the Bad, and the Ugly: A Film Score Guide*. Lanham, MD: Scarecrow Press, 2004.

Lerner, Neil. "Copland's Music of Wide Open Spaces: Surveying the Pastoral Trope in Hollywood," *The Musical Quarterly* 85, 3 (2001), 477–515.

———. "'Look at that big hand move along': Clocks, Containment, and Music in *High Noon*," *South Atlantic Quarterly* 104, 1 (2005), 151–73.

Levy, Beth E. "The Great Crossing: Nostalgia and Manifest Destiny in Aaron Copland's *The Red Pony*," *Journal of Film Music* 2, 2–4 (2009), 201–23.

Pisani, Michael. "'I'm an Indian, too': Creating Native American Identities in Nineteenth-and Early Twentieth-Century Music," *The Exotic in Western Music*, ed. Jonathan Bellman, 218–57. Boston: Northeastern University Press, 1998.

Rosenbaum, Jonathan. *Dead Man*. London: BFI, 2000.

Scheurer, Timothy E. "Rhythm on the Range: The Western Film Score," in Scheurer, *Music and Mythmaking in Film: Genre and the Role of the Composer*, 140–75. Jefferson, NC: McFarland, 2008.

Sherk, Warren. "The Western Film Scores of Hans Salter," *The Cue Sheet: Quarterly Journal of The Film Music Society* 11, 2 (1995), 12–18.

Smith, Jeff. "Every Gun Makes Its Own Tune: Ennio Morricone, *The Good, the Bad, and the Ugly* and 'L'Esthetique du Scorpione'," in Smith, *The Sounds of Commerce: Marketing Popular Film Music*, 131–53. New York: Columbia University Press, 1998.

Stanfield, Peter. *Horse Opera: The Strange History of the Singing Cowboy*. Urbana: University of Illinois Press, 2002.

Tagg, Philip and Bob Clarida. "*The Virginian*: Life, Liberty and the US Pursuit of Happiness," in Tagg and Clarida, *Ten Little Title Tunes*, 277–396. New York: The Mass Media Scholars Press, 2003.

Part I

Music in the Classical Hollywood Studio Film

The Cowboy Chorus

Narrative and Cultural Functions of the Western Title Song

Corey K. Creekmur

Major Hollywood genres can be appreciated through concepts that also apply to works of music. Westerns, for instance, may be enjoyed as variations on a theme, with fans welcoming the pleasurable recurrence of familiar motifs in ways similar to the enjoyment of many repetitive musical patterns and forms.[1] Furthermore, the basic components of the western, like fundamental musical elements, can seem comfortably stable, even as the demands of sheer novelty and aesthetic innovation encourage stylistic changes in response to shifting social contexts and cultural tastes. Thus, critics of the film western simultaneously emphasize its continuity as a narrative or mythic form repeating familiar elements while tracing the genre's historical development from classic examples towards self-critical revision. Aficionados of popular musical forms such as the blues or jazz engage in similar forms of subtle negotiation, taking pleasure in reassuring continuity and tradition while excited by challenging alteration and experimentation. In addition to the larger analogy of genres to musical forms, the role of music itself within the western can concretely demonstrate the regular, creative tension between stability and change characterizing the genre overall. While links might be drawn between the musical scores composed for westerns across the genre's entire history, at a moment in the 1950s—a decade considered one of the genre's artistic and cultural high points—the otherwise stable soundtracks of westerns suddenly allowed for a significant variation. This chapter focuses on that prominent but neglected period in the musical history of the western, when sung title songs became a prominent feature of the genre. While the western had previously and typically employed instrumental theme songs, the new practice of including title songs with evocative lyrics immediately established itself as a common element of the genre, functioning in effect as an invented tradition without obvious precedent.[2]

Before focusing exclusively on the western title song, however, it should be emphasized that this variation within the genre took place within a larger but rarely considered shift in the overall construction of Hollywood soundtracks and credit sequences. Among other changes, credit sequences became more detailed, and more unique in their design, abandoning the standard house styles associated with particular studios rather than film genres in previous decades. Most significantly, previously brief credit sequences were extended, so that they could now accommodate the typical two to three minute duration of popular songs. The critical neglect of credit sequences featuring title songs is especially curious since such songs, especially when employing attention-grabbing vocals and meaningful lyrics, often present themselves as a prominent, even obtrusive element in the experience of a film, in marked contrast to the commonly noted goal of the unobtrusive, "inaudible" Hollywood film score to ease a spectator into the emotional mood of a film. Rather, when considered at all, the vocalized title song is often summarily dismissed; for instance, Mervyn Cooke declares "The least creative application of popular music common in 1960s soundtracks was the showcasing of main-title songs and interpolated songs performed by commercially viable artists."[3] Notably, the moment most often identified with initiating this ongoing lack of creativity, establishing the persistent reign of the semi-autonomous title song in Hollywood cinema, involves the success of a cowboy song in a western, although the subsequent practice has relied most often upon the rise of rock and roll as the dominant form of American popular music. Echoing other historians of film music, Russell Lack cites Elmer Bernstein's damning claim that "the death of the classical film-music score began in 1952 with an innocuous pop song that was used in the title sequence of the classic Gary Cooper Western *High Noon*."[4]

Moreover, the practice unleashed by *High Noon* has typically been viewed as a blatantly commercial effect, affirming the increased interdependence of the film and music industries as corporate partners but not necessarily as artistic collaborators. Jeff Smith thus emphasizes that "as important as *High Noon* was for the techniques of film scoring, it was perhaps more important to the business of film music marketing."[5] Smith notes that the song, by composer Dimitri Tiomkin and lyricist Ned Washington, was aggressively marketed through the common practice of releasing multiple versions (in this case six) of the same song. (While Neil Lerner also recognizes that the song "played no small part in transforming how the industry planned, produced, and marketed their soundtracks," he also argues that *High Noon*'s "film score meaningfully subverts a number of the established Hollywood conventions for musical accompaniment."[6]) Performed in the film by the unseen veteran singing cowboy star Tex Ritter, the title song to *High Noon*—most often identified by its first line as "Do Not Forsake Me, Oh My Darlin'" but simply named "High Noon" in the film's credits—became even more popular in a version recorded by Italian American singer Frankie Laine (born Francesco Paolo LoVecchio), whose subsequent career would be dominated by his title songs for film and television westerns. Cooke, also citing the "aggressive pre-release exposure of the *High Noon* song by United Artists, who intended it to be a popular hit from the outset," summarizes the industrial impact of the new strategy:

> Songs carrying titles identical to those of the films to which they were attached were at the same time beginning to exploit the attractive proposition that the films would inevitably be mentioned every time the songs were broadcast; not surprisingly, producers were quick to seize on a

phenomenon that neatly combined the generation of additional royalties with free airtime advertising.[7]

Although the film and popular music industries had already been intertwined for decades, historians imply that the success of *High Noon* and especially of its title song fully established a new model and level of cross-media promotion and revenue.

There is certainly evidence to support such claims. Advertising for major westerns began to regularly promote their title songs as a major attraction. Posters for *Wichita* (1955), seeking to mine the renewed popularity of *High Noon*'s original vocalist, induced audiences to "Hear TEX RITTER sing the title song," while posters for *The Maverick Queen* (1956) promised "Joni James sings 'The Maverick Queen' by Ned Washington and Victor Young," drawing upon Washington's new status as Hollywood's top western song lyricist. Increasingly informative credit sequences also prominently identified title songs and singers in addition to composers, and advertised for recording companies: in typical fashion, a title card for *3:10 to Yuma* (1957) credits the composer, George Duning, and conductor, Morris Stoloff, of the film's score while also identifying the title song that audiences were currently listening to as written by, once again, Ned Washington and George Duning, and sung by Frankie Laine, "a Columbia Recording Artist."

In some cases, western title songs allowed the film's stars an additional outlet for their talents: acting singer Dean Martin provided the title song for *Five Card Stud* (1968), as did singing actor Robert Mitchum for *Young Billy Young* (1969); late entries in the cycle. Earlier, the casting of Elvis Presley in his first film motivated the addition of four songs and a title change from *The Reno Brothers* to *Love Me Tender* (1956), already the title of Presley's million-selling single, based on the Civil War ballad "Aura Lee," released two months earlier. Even Presley's later desire to play his only non-singing role in the western *Charro!* (1969) seemed to require at least a western-style title song, by Billy Strange and Mac Davis, from the singer.

If the cross-promotional function of title songs to drive the sales of film soundtrack albums is undeniable, blatant commercialism alone might not fully explain the other purposes such songs can play in westerns, or entirely account for their arrival at a historical moment. In one of the few critical considerations of the function of title songs and credit sequences in Hollywood cinema, Will Straw acknowledges the commercial drive behind the practice of using pop songs to start a film, but also considers how "self-contained theme songs" as well as the design elements of credit sequences participate in an overlooked "history of filmic ornamentation."[8] Straw thus encourages an investigation of the western title song that might consider its formal or cultural functions in addition to more obvious commercial aims, as I hope my consideration of one of the genre's most celebrated examples will soon illustrate. Given its pervasive impact, it might simply be pedantic to point out that *High Noon* is often wrongly identified as the *first* western and even the first Hollywood movie to employ a sung title song: at least one western precedent can be found in *Man in the Saddle* (1951), which includes a title song—touted as one of the film's attractions in its trailer—performed by rising country music star Tennessee Ernie (who soon added Ford to his name).[9] But *High Noon*'s popularity and influence, reinforced by Oscars for a rarely celebrated genre, rather than its primacy, fully justifies its identification as a watershed in the history of western film soundtracks. Phillip Drummond effectively summarizes the innovation of the film's song and score:

> *High Noon*'s musical originality lies . . . in its overall departure from Hollywood conventions in three main ways. First, the film does not commence and conclude on a full-orchestral *fortissimo*, but *pianissimo*, with a ballad-singer accompanied only by guitar, accordion and drums. Second, the single theme-tune becomes part of the dramatic underscore, anticipating Tiomkin's Greek chorus-like ballad for Sturges' *Gunfight at the OK Corral* (1957). The score is virtually monothematic, the tune acting as the source of virtually every bar of the orchestral incidental music. Third, the role of the symphony orchestra changes, with the burden of expression being taken away from the strings. The violins are dispensed with altogether, and the lower strings which remain (violas, celli and double basses) are totally subordinate to a wind, brass, and piano-dominated sonority. The result is a darker, starker, de-glamourized quality of tone-colour, one that accords perfectly with the nature of the scenario.[10]

While *High Noon's* success probably motivated the use of title songs in a wide range of films, it immediately altered the construction and marketing of westerns, whether low-budget independent films or the prominent studio productions by the genre's most celebrated directors.

For instance, early in his illuminating book on John Ford's masterpiece, now celebrated as perhaps the greatest Hollywood western, Edward Buscombe directs our attention to "the first word of *The Searchers*. It's a question. 'Ethan?'"[11] But Buscombe soon recalls that, "Strictly speaking, 'Ethan?' is not the first word uttered in *The Searchers*, nor the first question. Over the credits we hear the opening stanza and chorus of a song written by Stan Jones and sung by Sons of the Pioneers, a singing group Ford had earlier used on screen in *Rio Grande*."[12] Buscombe's strict correction not only retrieves the film's suggestive title song for any analysis of the film, but his seemingly casual identification of *two* "first" words "*in The Searchers*" suggests the curious way in which a title song may function, not only in this classic western but also in other examples of the genre and perhaps in other types of films.[13]

Strictly speaking, the title song is heard in the film, but does not take place in the story, or diegesis, that contains other performed songs. Like the more typical non-diegetic score, the title song is neither produced nor heard by any of the narrative's characters, and so is only performed for us, the viewing and listening audience, even though, in the manner of classical Hollywood cinema, we are not otherwise explicitly acknowledged or directly addressed by the film.

As Will Straw perceptively notes, credit sequences as a whole, including music, "presuppose a direct, pragmatic communication with the audience frequently at odds with notions of the self-contained diegetic fiction."[14] Although the title song in *The Searchers* is presumably linked to the story (it first asks the questions the narrative will continue to pose), its formal function is to precede or even exceed the story that unfolds within the film, clearly marked at its outer edges by on-screen credits as well as the off-screen song: we know the story is beginning when the song fades away a few minutes after the film has begun, and we know that the story is ending when the song rises again on the soundtrack to anticipate the actual end of the film which follows a few seconds later. Although the title song is clearly part of the film, it's not fully part of the story, and thus seems relevant to the theatrical context of the cinema hall and the film's exhibition, functioning somewhat like the lowering of the lights and the drawing open of a curtain, both components of the ritual of presentation rooted in earlier theatrical practice rather than specific to the medium of film. The title song serves as a formal announcement or opening gesture to the subsequent narrating of a story rather than a part of the story itself, much like the on-screen credits it accompanies, which themselves offer sparse visual information, even though they are distinctly generic. As Buscombe recognizes, the film's credits are "in the familiar Playbill typeface favoured by Ford for most of his sound Westerns, set against the backdrop of an adobe wall."[15] But by initiating the presentation of the film through a series of sung questions soon picked up by the film's first line of inquisitive dialogue (as well as a score that will rely upon the music of the song), the hermeneutic lure of the song's lyrics does begin the story in some sense, raising questions that will drive the narrative and, in this case at least, remain open when the song, still asking questions rather than providing answers, is reprised to conclude the film.

The title song to *The Searchers* is therefore simultaneously in the film and outside the story, heard only at the far edges of a narrative that famously begins with a door opening and ends with a door closing, and which is centered around a character whose ambivalent status as an insider and outsider to a community is constantly explored. As a formal rather than narrative device, the song not only announces some of the story's themes, but also allegorizes the questions around (actual and symbolic) frontiers and liminal spaces central to this film and perhaps to the larger western genre. (In a somewhat similar vein, Lerner demonstrates in precise detail how the title song for *High Noon* "works to blur the boundaries between the diegetic and nondiegetic," supporting his more historical claim that the film can be considered a "subversive text in the way it knowingly violated the accepted paradigm of a carefully contained diegetic and nondiegetic sound world."[16]) Straw suggests we "explore analogies between the credit sequence and the architectural entrance," noting that both are "intended to be the crossing of a ceremonial threshold."[17] Drawing suggestively on the literary critic Gerard Genette's emphasis on the functions of paratextual features, such as prefaces, dedications, title pages and other elements that fall outside most considerations of a "text," Straw considers how credit sequences, including theme or title songs, "respond, in innovative ways, to the question of how we enter a film," a concern typically focused on narrative engagement alone.[18] Critics have often emphasized the poignancy of the door that closes on Ethan Edwards (John Wayne), excluding him from family and community at the end of the film. But he is also additionally "shut out" by the arrival of the song and the appearance of "The End," paratextual elements like the same words on a final page, and the closed back cover of a book, that reassert our literal isolation from him as well. The song removes us from the narrative and returns us to the theater where only we are allowed to hear the film, as it were, comment on the character's exclusion from our world as well as from the lives of his fellow characters.

If *The Searchers* seems especially invested in allegorizing its content through its form, title songs in westerns seem to reinforce similar concerns as a generic ritual. As Drummond efficiently suggests by noting key examples composed by Dimitri Tiomkin, a western's title song can serve as a chorus in the tradition inherited from ancient Greek theater, and the fact that many such songs actually feature a group or chorus of singers, or a chorus backing a lead vocalist, supports this curious inheritance, another violation of the realist style of most Hollywood films. Title songs, in other words, emphasize the films they introduce as narration, or lyric, rather than as narrative, or drama. (The subordination of the chorus in the history of theater is in effect the triumph of story over discourse, or of realism over artifice.) In the Greek theater, the chorus was also often used to express what characters could not. Buscombe notes that the questions posed by the song in *The Searchers*—"What makes a man to wander, What makes a man to roam?"—may remain more ambiguous than the superficially similar but more straightforward questions frequently posed by the film's characters: "perhaps the question is more generally addressed, to us all."[19]

Drummond also recognizes that, for the 1950s adult western, this social function is both psychologized and gendered: the unspoken is not so much a secret, a fact simply unknown to a tragic character, but is his repressed, unconscious desire. Within the genre of the western, this silence is of course typically associated with the masculine traits of the taciturn, stoic cowboy. When spoken by the main character, or spoken about him, a title song functions as a displacement of the silent cowboy's thoughts and emotions: one cannot imagine John Wayne's Ethan Edwards voicing out loud the questions the title song of *The Searchers* ponders ("That'll be the day," to quote the character's key line). Nor can Gary Cooper's Will Kane bring himself to beseech his new bride in the emotionally vulnerable words *High Noon*'s title song articulates for him. As Drummond notes, a number of western title songs articulate the desire for romance that the male characters and values of the genre otherwise keep in check, such that the musical emphasis provided by title songs, as much as any plot element, literally brings the Hollywood western and romantic melodrama (recalling the *melos*, or music, at the heart of the term) together.

I would like to emphasize another significant function of the title song in westerns, already suggested by Straw's architectural analogy as well as the opening and closing doors of *The Searchers*. Often placed on the edges of the film, often literally at its borders, a title song may figure the border or frontier that the popular western genre transformed from a spatial to a symbolic trope. Title songs often take place on or across the borders between on- and off-screen space, which renders the presumably less flexible border between diegetic and non-diegetic space permeable. In a genre often defined by literal as well as figurative and metaphorical borders, with the historical frontier being invoked to signify the frontier between civilization and savagery—following the foundational texts of Fredrick Jackson Turner and Henry Nash Smith on the symbolic significance of the frontier in American culture—the edges of the film itself can play an important role. Like the Greek chorus, which marked a play's beginning and end by its own arrival and departure from the location of the stage (transitions moreover reinforced by shifts to sound or silence), the title song itself occupies a curious, liminal space in relation to the cinematic drama that it surrounds. It can be inside and outside of the main text or narrative, such that (as Nietzsche famously argued) the chorus is both in the play and outside of it, aligned with or mediating the actors as well as the audience. If landscapes, so crucial to the visual experience of the western, invite us to enter the historical and geographical space of the narrative, title songs acknowledge the formal function of conveying the cultural object of the western—the text itself rather than the fantasy within—to us as viewers and listeners. Unlike the diegetic folk songs that had appeared in Hollywood westerns previously, western title songs do not pretend to offer the actual sound of the historical West, but perform the sound of the western as a crafted work of popular art and commercial entertainment.

While most title songs are heard during title sequences, in westerns the location of title songs quickly became a matter of some variety and suggestive uncertainty, with songs often escaping the borders of credit sequences alone. In rather perfunctory examples such as the almost meaningless title song for the moody *The Lonely Man* (1957), performed by Tennessee Ernie Ford, the song has been tailored to extend no longer than the credit sequence. But other examples modified this strict containment, including simultaneous examples such as *Gun Glory* (1957), which includes an unusually allegorical and religious song, "The Ninety and Nine," sung by Burl Ives, which extends well beyond the credits into the opening sequence of the film, an extension into the narrative that never transforms into diegetic sound. While most western title songs were held tightly within the borders of credit sequences, quite a few others spill outside of these confines, exceeding their clear status as paratexts by bleeding into the text. Many examples, unlike *High Noon* (with nine uses, including at its edges) or the more symmetrical *The Searchers*, offer no reprise of their title song at the film's conclusion, whereas the highly unusual *Johnny Guitar* (1954) confirms its oddness by only introducing its very brief title song, sung by Peggy Lee (in the voice, it seems, of Joan Crawford's character Vienna), as the film concludes. *Tulsa* (1949) does not at first appear to have a title song: the film actually begins with a lecture on the city's history directly addressed to the audience by actor Chill Wills. Soon thereafter, however, the actor, now clearly playing a character in the film, performs the title song diegetically in a short scene rather awkwardly embedded within the narrative. As already noted, in some cases such as *High Noon* and *Gunfight at the O.K. Corral* (1957), title songs weave their way through a film. Another notable example is *Rancho Notorious* (1952), which employs its ominous, recurrent ballad of "hate, murder, and revenge" as a prominent motif, echoing through repetition the wheel of fate embodied in the film's symbolic roulette wheel.

Indeed, *Gunfight at the O.K. Corral*, which Drummond directly associates with the function of a Greek chorus, may be a typical example insofar as it functions generically but also demonstrates some of the persistent oddity of western theme songs when considered in specific films. Written by Tiomkin and Washington, and sung by Frankie Laine, the title song introduces the film, running just past the opening sequence overlaid with credits, and is briefly reprised to signal the film's conclusion. In a very brief period, these had become established, generic uses. Since the film, like many town-taming westerns, begins and ends with a main character (Wyatt Earp, played by Burt Lancaster) arriving and departing on horseback, the music provides a familiar and even somewhat redundant formal entrance and exit for the film. The song is also redundant insofar as it twice matches a lyric about "killers laying side by side" with an obvious visual support, a shot that pauses on the Boot Hill cemetery on the edge of town, itself a literal divide between the town and frontier, as well as life and death. What makes the song simultaneously generic yet also somewhat odd is the narrative content provided by its lyrics. The song (like the title of the film which it shares) more or less announces the major event, although quite brief in this rendition, that concludes the film. While many other films dramatize this historical and even mythic event, most do not announce it in their titles. Whereas the haunting questions of the title song for *The Searchers* remain unanswered when its song is reprised at the end, "Gunfight at the O.K. Corral" makes sitting through the film, at least for the satisfaction of narrative resolution, rather unnecessary. This might seem unusual for a Hollywood film, which typically poses an enigma—what will happen?—motivating a carefully, enjoyably delayed response. But as a western, a genre film, its producers could assume not only that its conclusion would come as no surprise, but also that aficionados would already know the specific story being told here, already told in many previous films. The song, in other words, seems designed to serve the western genre rather than whatever variation might be found in the plot of this particular western, affirming the repetitive experience of the overall genre through the condensed model of a specific song and its reprise. The song is also a bit odd insofar as its speaker, although hard to identify by name, seems to be one of the characters directly involved in the conflict being summarized, rather than an omniscient observer common to other title songs: once again, the song renders the film simultaneously generic and specific, providing the perspective of a participant in one of the genre's iconic events without granting that figure any specificity. (The song seems to be addressed to an equally undefined woman, again reinforcing the genre's easily neglected but in fact persistent inclusion of romance within its otherwise masculine, action-driven plots.)

In films with such songs, which more or less summarize their plots and even at times give away endings, the songs reinforce the status of the films as not only repetitive works within a genre, frequently recounting familiar tales yet again, but also mythologize the stories and figures associated with the genre: they are now the stuff of legend, recounted in ballads, with repetition as much a ritual function as a commercial imperative. Although the characters in a film such as *Gunfight at the O.K. Corral* are introduced to us, and the story of the event the film names unfolds chronologically as if it takes place in the present, the retrospective song—from the beginning—insists that this is already a well-known story, frequently recounted in song as well as cinema. When we meet characters such as Wyatt Earp or Doc Holliday in the film, we are really meeting them again, indulging in the pleasures of repetition that both genre films and popular myths or legends offer, a pleasure of course provided by popular songs themselves, typically structured by patterns of musical and verbal repetition, and typically consumed through repeated listening.

Generic expectations thus explain what can otherwise seem an extreme obviousness or explicitness in many western title songs: *Wichita*'s title song (by Hans Salter with lyrics by Ned Washington) is performed non-diegetically by Tex Ritter, whose unusually specific, upbeat summary of the film's plot ("No one fooled with the Marshal of Wichita," we learn, "and today it's a very nice town!") undercuts narrative suspense. "He had a gal and he courted and married her" effectively removes any audience's speculation about the film's romantic subplot. A late example, *The War Wagon* (1967) also features an explicit song with a lead vocal by Ed Ames: "Look at those horses, what are they dragging, heavily guarded, what is that wagon?" a male chorus wonders. "Those men are fighting for a wagon full of gold!" Ames bluntly clarifies, efficiently summarizing the film's basic action. Other examples are more playful: *Canyon Passage* (1946), which does not employ a title song per se, includes the prominent songwriter, performer and sometimes actor Hogey Carmichal as a minstrel-like character who wanders through and provides a running, sung commentary on the actions of the plot. This technique is also employed in Samuel Fuller's famously baroque *Forty Guns* (1957), in which the singer Jidge Carroll, playing a minor character, appears on-screen singing the ostensible title song "High Ridin' Woman" (by Harold Adamson and Harry Sukman). But this on-screen performance follows a conventional, orchestral rendition of the song without lyrics to accompany the credit sequence (which itself follows a brief, unusual prologue that withholds music altogether). Playfully, the diegetic song's initial location is uncertain: we hear a ballad about Barbara Stanwyck's character Jessica Drummond, "a high-ridin' woman with a whip," softly sung as Carroll, far from the camera, carries two buckets of water in a long shot, and so it's not immediately clear whether or not he is the source of the vocals, which are accompanied by a quietly strummed guitar. A series of shots of the western town leaves the actor behind, but the song continues at its steady volume until a closer shot of Carroll confirms that he is the diegetic source of the song. As he enters the public bathhouse of bathing cowboys to empty his buckets, he passes a guitarist, who confirms that even the soft music we have heard has a source within the film. Soon a conversation about the "high ridin' woman" by the main characters (covered in suds in their baths) will lead the singer to confirm that she is the subject of the ballad he has written and was just singing. In effect, the title song of *Forty Guns* slides from its initial non-diegetic location into the diegesis of the film, where it becomes a topic of discussion by characters pondering the function of such ballads in the construction of western legends.

Forty Guns thus takes advantage of the new convention of the western title song in order to play its own formal games along the borders of the film. A final, briefly interrupted reprise of the song also, again, slowly reveals itself to be diegetic, although the song, at first performed only with a guitar, returns to its origins when it blends into the non-diegetic orchestral score. While less formally audacious, the earlier Barbara Stanwyck western, *The Maverick Queen*, featured its prominent title song (by Ned Washington and Victor Young) sung by Joni James (who receives a prominent credit). Her pretty voice, invoking romance, is immediately replaced by an authoritative male voice-over, supplying the historical background for the story ("The little town of Stillwater, towards the end of the last century") that the song did not: "There was something about her since she was sixteen, that attracted the men to the Maverick Queen," the song vaguely asserts. While westerns featuring a prominent female star such as Stanwyck might be expected to challenge the genre's usual, presumed masculine emphasis, even the presence of a female vocalist does not dislodge conventional distinctions. Sharply distinguishing between the sound of a male speaker and female singer, *The Maverick Queen*'s soundtrack isolates the voicing of the emotions of the narrative from its historical narration.

As noted earlier, critics have generally identified the rise of the title song in Hollywood with increased industrial and commercial ties between the film and popular music industries after World War Two, but there may be other less obviously commercial reasons for the seemingly sudden practice occurring at a relatively precise historical moment. Kathryn Kalinak, explaining the preference for American folk songs in A westerns of the 1930s and 1940s, argues that the avoidance of more immediately popular material, then commonly identified as country-and-western music, was based upon a class divide. The commercial (and often brand new rather than traditional) cowboy songs that dominated B westerns featuring singing cowboys were nowhere to be heard in most major studio westerns, since the studios apparently did not consider the rural white working class—the presumed audience for B westerns and hillbilly music—a significant market. As Kalinak carefully summarizes, the attraction of American composers of art music such as Roy Harris and Aaron Copland as well as a growing field of professional folklorists and musicologists to the rich body of folk music established a cultural legitimacy and historical authenticity that Hollywood filmmakers drew upon when producing prestige westerns.[20] This plausibly explains the absence of what would have been variously identified as cowboy or hillbilly or country-and-western songs in major westerns between the late 1920s and early 1950s, when such songs were confined to the hundreds of B westerns produced in the same period. But by the early 1950s, perhaps influenced by the steady rise of rock and roll as America's dominant commercial music (leading to the generational divide that redefined mainstream, popular music as "youth music"), certain forms of country-and-western music, retrieved from earlier decades, were significantly repositioned as folk music. As a number of music historians have demonstrated, the 1950s were crucial for redefining country music as authentic American music: as country music broadened its commercial appeal through the development of a slick Nashville Sound, its earlier varieties, once clearly promoted as commercial, were successfully reconfigured as authentic roots music.[21]

To cite a prominent example, the collector and experimental filmmaker Harry Smith's influential six-disc Anthology of American Folk Music, released by Folkways Records in 1952, offered an eccentric selection of eighty-four songs, complied from 78 rpm records originally released between 1927 and 1932. While containing an eclectic mix of blues, jazz, and country songs, the collection also included two notable cowboy songs, including "Bandit Cole Younger" (1930) by Edward L. Crain and, most curiously, early cowboy movie star Ken Maynard's "The Lone Star Trail" (1930), a once explicitly commercial recording for an early western movie now represented as an example of earlier American folk music. In the same period, Folkways released The Cowboy: His Songs, Ballads, and Brag Talk (1957) and The Library of Congress released a number of recordings of cowboy songs, often by the era's most influential folk music performers, including Woody Guthrie, Cisco Houston (whose album Cowboy Ballads was released in 1952), and Pete Seeger (who released Frontier Ballads in 1954), among others. This work followed the pioneering work of the folklorist John A. Lomax, who compiled and published his groundbreaking collection Cowboy Songs in 1910. Songs of the Cattle Trail and Cow Camp followed in 1919 and a number of later editions enlarged and revised the earlier work, which has remained a key source of "authentic" western music for later historians as well as performers. Subsequently, working with his son Alan, the two made extensive field recordings for the Archive of the American Folk Song of the Library of Congress: among the many recordings derived from this project, Cowboy Songs, Ballads, and Cattle Calls from Texas was released as part of the larger series Folk Music of the United States (1952). The singing cowboy, who had emerged as a commercial, popular entertainer only a few decades earlier, was therefore reinvented as an icon of authentic American folk music traditions.

While a great deal of the music recovered by archivists and ethnomusicologists was true folk music, preserved from oral and non-commercial traditions, a good deal of the music released in this period (such as Smith's anthology) was originally produced as popular music, a status denied by its folk revival, which asserted the authenticity of forms of music that it directly opposed to blatantly commercial music. Cowboy songs—even those newly composed for movies— could thus derive some of this authenticity by affiliation with a style of music (and singing) and with a subject matter increasingly seen as old-timey, redolent of the earlier era it nostalgically invoked, even if it did not in fact derive from that historical period. Sound effects such as horses' hooves (or percussion meant to simulate the clip-clop of horseshoes), cracking bullwhips, or pistol shots also attempted to "preserve" the sounds of the Old West in new (often stereo) recordings. While some western title songs rely on soaring, orchestral backing, many, including *High Noon*'s title song, are relatively sparse arrangements, emphasizing what were increasingly presumed to be authentic western instruments such as guitars and harmonicas and thus reminiscent of the other types of songs then being recovered and recontextualized.

While, as noted earlier, a few critics have cited examples of westerns with title songs that precede *High Noon*, the search for an actual first example seems less worthwhile than identifying another broad precursor to the western title song: the cowboy songs central to the earlier B western, especially its most popular variant, the singing cowboy film. The notion that the film and music industries evolved toward greater interdependence in the 1950s relies upon an ignorance or repression of the already dynamic relation between these industries in earlier decades, including the 1930s when the B western became a major new form—along with sheet music, recordings, and radio—of dissem-inating the music of singing cowboys such as Gene Autry.[22] Autry's films, as the few critics to attend to them have demonstrated, were relentlessly self-reflexive despite their seemingly naïve plots. Autry's status as a contemporary recording and radio star—most of his films are set in the present rather than the historical past—is persistently emphasized (and often parodied), and virtually all of his films showcase a series of songs, including title songs for almost every film.[23] Indeed, the titles of Autry's films and his catalog of hit records overlap almost completely, so that the songs typically advertise the films, and vice versa. Almost twenty years before *High Noon* influenced A westerns, B westerns solidified the notion of the western employing a title song rather than an unsung theme song, although most of Autry's films present their title songs along with very brief credit sequences without his singing, thus creating anticipation for the fully realized or performed rendition of the song, usually soon to follow in films that ran just over an hour. *Back in the Saddle* (1941) is a typical example, one of Autry's seven films released that year, featuring the hit song co-written by Autry and Ray Whitley that immediately became the star's signature tune (usually rendered as "Back in the Saddle Again"), which he eventually selected as the title of his 1976 autobiography. The song, already popular with Autry's fans when the film was released, is heard without vocals as the short credit sequence appears, as it had already been a few months earlier in *Melody Ranch* (1940). For most of Autry's fans, the song thus engendered both recognition and anticipation, unlike a new song being heard for the first time, which may or may not have an immediate impact. In other words, this song, about getting back in the saddle *again*, was most likely being enjoyed again by the 1941 film's initial audience, participating once more in the pleasurable repetition crucial to the consumption of pop music as well as to an extremely conventional genre such as the B western. The opening of the film offers a montage sequence of rodeo events at Madison Square Garden, and a shift to the backstage dressing room immediately leads—first by the off-screen sound of his voice and band—to Autry performing the title song, apparently for his own amusement, although a radio reporter soon rushes over to hold a microphone up to Autry in order to broadcast the tune. (One of the persistent dilemmas in Autry's films is his arriving at the location of a live radio broadcast in the nick of time.) As in this case, although almost all of Autry's many films share their titles with songs featured in them, the very brief credit sequences in B westerns usually wait for the title song to function as the first sequence. While, as noted, "Back in the Saddle" accompanies the credits of *Melody Ranch* (already the title of Autry's radio program), a performance of the title song functions as the film's first sequence. In typically playful style, it appears to be sung outdoors at night around a campfire until the location is revealed, via a tracking shot that first shows a microphone and then the edge of a stage, to take place within a radio station. Again, the surprising expansion from a limited, misleading view is matched by fairly elaborate sonic games that allow songs to weave playfully between the soundtrack, radio airwaves, on-screen playing of recordings, and the narrative space of the stories.

By the late 1950s and early 1960s, following the decline of the B western format, the western title song moved across another border to play a key role in television westerns, along with singing cowboy stars such as Gene Autry and Roy Rogers, who were among the new medium's most popular performers. In addition to ongoing commercial viability as recordings, television title songs enjoyed the benefit of weekly repetition, and in many cases have remained more familiar to audiences than their cinematic precursors. In some cases the musical contributors to the new television westerns were familiar Hollywood talent: Dimitri Tiomkin and Ned Washington wrote "Rawhide," sung with manly vigor by Frankie Laine, for the CBS television program (1959–66) that featured rising star Clint Eastwood. The innovative hour-long Warner Bros. series *Cheyenne* (ABC, 1955–63) relied on a booming all-male chorus for its title song, while *The Life and Legend of Wyatt Earp* (ABC, 1955–61) featured a quieter, frequently humming barbershop quartet. "The Ballad of Paladin" was the popular closing title song for *Have Gun Will Travel* (CBS, 1957–63), sung by (the actually named) Johnny Western, who had written the song with series star Richard Boone and Sam Rolfe. The title song for *Branded* (NBC, 1965–66), like some earlier films, conveniently summarized the background story motivating the series every week. A number of instrumental western television theme songs were also additionally popular when released as recordings with lyrics, often sung by series stars such as *Bonanza*'s (NBC, 1959–73) Lorne Greene in 1963, following hit recordings by others, including Johnny Cash in 1962.

However, as the once mighty stream of film westerns diminished to a trickle, more traditional theme songs once again became the norm for the genre, although semi-autonomous title songs dominated many other popular films, which fully embraced rock and roll (too obviously anachronistic for use in conventional westerns) and compilation scores which ironically resembled in structure if not style the collections of folk songs that characterized classic models such as John Ford's *Stagecoach* (1939) and *My Darling Clementine* (1946). Other American westerns tentatively followed the experimental lead employing unconventional instruments initiated by Ennio Morricone's distinctive scores for Sergio Leone's Italian spaghetti westerns in the 1960s. Within a decade of their first prominent and immediately widespread use, however, western title songs became ripe for parody in comic westerns such as *Cat Ballou* (1965), which includes singers Nat "King" Cole and Stubby Kaye as a pair of troubadours who wander through the film singing the tongue-in-cheek "The Ballad of Cat Ballou." By another decade, when Mel Brooks released his wildly successful western parody *Blazing Saddles* (1974), the genre itself was almost dormant, and Brooks's inclusion of a prominent title song, featuring his own music and lyrics, with vocals by the iconic—but undeniably dated—Frankie Laine, was less an established tradition than one of the hoary clichés the film sent up. In other words, the relatively recent innovation had become, within a mere two decades, a tired and outdated device, itself a summary reminder of the work of genre more broadly as a mechanism for rapidly incorporating and eliminating originality. Western songs, once too lowbrow and blatantly commercial to be included in major studio westerns, and then briefly available as affirmations of historical authenticity, simply become too corny and old-fashioned for revisionist Vietnam-era and later westerns. Such films, despite their residual genre trappings, sought a form of grim realism—for instance, through explicit representations of violence and the acknowledgment of foundational racism—that might be undercut by the ornate, stylized artificiality of a generic title song. At the moment when the genre of the western itself no longer spoke, as it had for previous decades, to a mass audience, the briefly viable conceit of a shared public voice, in the form of a cowboy chorus, could also no longer be sustained.[24]

Notes

I wish to thank Kathryn Kalinak for her consistent encouragement, keen critical eye (and ear), and editorial patience.

1   Adorno and Eisler are unsurprisingly critical of genre and musical conventions: "Mass production of motion pictures has led to the elaboration of typical situations, ever-recurring emotional crises, and standardized methods of arousing suspense. They correspond to cliché effects in music." However, they allow "Pictures that frankly follow an established pattern, such as 'western' or gangster or horror pictures, often are in a certain way superior to pretentious grade-A films. What is objectionable is the standardized character of pictures that claim to be unique; or, conversely, the individual disguise of the standardized pattern. This is

exactly what happens in music." See Theodor Adorno and Hanns Eisler, *Composing for the Films* (New York: Oxford University Press, 1947; repr. New York: Continuum, 2007), 9–10.

2 While "theme song" and "title song" are often used interchangeably, I will maintain an admittedly loose distinction between the two, with "theme songs" including instrumental examples, and "title songs" limited to songs with sung lyrics, or vocals. In this sense, most Hollywood feature films employ theme songs, whereas title songs are a more recent and less pervasive historical practice, although they undoubtedly have earlier examples as well.

3 Mervyn Cooke, *A History of Film Music* (Cambridge: Cambridge University Press, 2008), 405.

4 Russell Lack, *Twenty Four Frames Under: A Buried History of Film Music* (London: Quartet Books, 1997), 207. Lack does not cite a source for this comment from Bernstein, but Neil Lerner does. See Neil Lerner, "'Look at the big hand move along': Clocks, Containment, and Music in *High Noon*," *South Atlantic Quarterly* 104, 1 (Winter 2005), 169. Lerner cites Elmer Bernstein "Whatever Happened to Great Movie Music?" *High Fidelity* 22, 7 (July 1972), 58.

5 Jeff Smith, *The Sounds of Commerce: Marketing Popular Film Music* (New York: Columbia University Press, 1998), 59.

6 Lerner, 153.

7 Cooke, 121.

8 Will Straw, "Ornament, Entrance and the Theme Song," in *Cinesonic: The World of Sound in Film*, ed. Philip Brophy (North Ryde, Australia: Australian Film Television & Radio School, 1999), 213–28.

9 I will not presume to locate the "first" example of the practice, but Rudy Behlmer, in addition to *Man in the Saddle*, cites *A Walk in the Sun* (1945) and *Smoky* (1946) as precursors of what he terms "singing ballads" employed in title sequences. Rudy Behlmer, *America's Favorite Movies: Behind the Scenes* (New York: Frederick Ungar, 1982), 285–86.

10 Phillip Drummond, *High Noon* (London: British Film Institute, 1997), 62–63.

11 Edward Buscombe, *The Searchers* (London: British Film Institute, 2000), 7, 12. While frequently noted in the large body of criticism on the film, the song receives its most extensive treatment in Kathryn Kalinak, *How the West was Sung: Music in the Westerns of John Ford* (Berkeley: University of California Press, 2007), 158–80.

12 Buscombe, 12.

13 In fact, the song sometimes identified as "The Searchers" is a curious example, since the title of the song (and film) is *not* used in the lyrics, although the words "search" and "searching" do appear in the original lyrics (only a small portion of which are heard in the film). Many accounts of the film and song assume that its title is "What Makes a Man to Wander?," the first line heard in the film but not, again, the first line of the original, full lyrics, which are provided in Buscombe, 70.

14 Straw, 220.

15 Buscombe, 13.

16 Lerner, 161, 169.

17 Straw, 218–19.

18 Straw 215–16.

19 Buscombe, 12–13.

20 Kalinak, 52–53.

21 For accounts of the historical development of authenticity in commercial country music, see Richard A. Peterson, *Creating Country Music: Fabricating Authenticity* (Chicago: University of Chicago Press, 1997) and Joli Jensen, *The Nashville Sound: Authenticity, Commercialization, and Country Music* (Nashville: The Country Music Foundation Press and Vanderbilt University Press, 1998). Both Peterson and Jensen follow Bill C. Malone's seminal *Country Music U.S.A.* (Austin:

University of Texas Press, revised edition, 1985) in emphasizing the importance of the displacement in the 1930s of the negative image of country musicians as rural Southern hillbillies for the more positive image of the singing western cowboy.

22 For a comprehensive overview of the phenomenon of the singing cowboy, see Douglas B. Green, *Singing in the Saddle: The History of the Singing Cowboy* (Nashville: The Country Music Foundation Press and Vanderbilt University Press, 2002).

23 For one of the few critical assessments of Autry and the singing cowboy B western, see Peter Stanfield, *Horse Opera: The Strange History of the 1930s Singing Cowboy* (Urbana: University of Illinois Press, 2002).

24 There are possible exceptions to this general conclusion, of course: Bob Dylan's score for Sam Peckinpah's *Pat Garrett & Billy the Kid* (1973) features a few songs with vocals by Dylan (who appears but does not sing in the film) that serve as distanced commentary on the film. Robert Altman's *McCabe and Mrs. Miller* (1971) prominently incorporates three older songs by Leonard Cohen that also function, despite their reappropriation, as commentary. Many contemporary westerns also, like most contemporary films, include songs with vocals during their lengthy end credits (which thus go unheard by most audiences).

Chapter 2

"A Cowboy Has to Sing"
John Ford, Walt Disney, and Sons of the Pioneers

Ross Care

In *About John Ford*, Lindsay Anderson comments of *Wagon Master* (1950):

> Absence of plot does not mean lack of incident or character: *Wagonmaster* is acted by a number of Ford's most likable players, and there are a succession of encounters, cheerful, sinister or strange, as the Mormon pilgrims push on to their promised land. But once again, it is the feeling which gives importance to the action; and the feeling for these pioneers, for their courage and good faith, is all admiration and love.[1]

Anderson also notes that "a full and tuneful musical score contributes to the lyricism of style."[2] In his Ford biography, *Pappy*, Dan Ford devotes only one paragraph to *Wagon Master*, but calls it "one of the most purely lyrical films John ever made" and compares it to *The Quiet Man* (1952), which he deems "almost a musical."[3] The seldom cited songs of Stan Jones, and the musical uniqueness of Richard Hageman (Ford's only slightly better known musical director/composer in the 1940s and early 1950s), should be given their due for memorably crystallizing the compassionate poignancy and complex grandeur of this most American of directors. Both musicians contribute mightily to what remains one of Ford's most moving and compassionate works. It is important, however, to point out that the innovative use of music in Ford's *Wagon Master* was preceded by the work of another American icon whose integration of music with story telling and imagery was also a key element of his work, Walt Disney. The *Wagon Master* musical mode is surprisingly similar to that of the "Pecos Bill" episode in the Disney musical anthology feature *Melody Time* (1948). Since both films prominently feature performances by Sons of the Pioneers perhaps we should not be surprised. Nonetheless, the musical similarity between Disney and Ford remains largely unexplored in the literature of film music[4] and has much to tell us about the evolution of the western film score at a key moment in its development.

Ford and Music

When John Ford directed his silent epic, *The Iron Horse* (1924), it was already his forty-ninth film and fortieth western. In this formative era, some true-life western characters such as Buffalo Bill Cody, and even veteran soldiers and Indians who had actually participated in the last of the Indian wars, performed before the silent cameras. But Ford would eventually produce a series of films which evoked the Old West with such acute resonance and spiritual intensity, and with such meticulously designed period authenticity, that his West ultimately surpassed even the western verisimilitude captured on film during the early days of American cinema.

Music quickly became a key element in Ford's films, delineating both the physical and the emotional terrain of his films. Indeed music proved integral to westerns in general wherein soaring and often poignant orchestral sonorities, many influenced by the ballet scores of Aaron Copland, became an anticipated adjunct to the visual imagery of the wide open spaces.[5] Copland, ironically a gay urbane Jewish concert composer from Brooklyn, would exuberantly capture this mythic aspect of the American West in his ballet scores for *Billy the Kid* (1938) and *Rodeo* (1942) which feature such masculine icons as the outlaw and the rancher. Later he also created an essential and much emulated western film score for Republic Pictures' adaptation of John Steinbeck's *The Red Pony* (1947). Erno Rapée, who created a popular standard with his "Diane" theme from *Seventh Heaven* (1927), scored Ford's *The Iron Horse*, and later co-scored Ford's *Four Sons* (1928) with S. L. Rothafel. But it was with *Stagecoach* (1939) that Ford established the enduring relationship that definitively set the musical tone for his most distinctive westerns of the late 1940s and early 1950s. Richard Hageman was a Dutch-born concert composer who seemed to understand, somewhat surprisingly, Ford's taste in music, and was a key part of the musical team including Louis Gruenberg, W. Franke Harling, John Leipold, and Leo Shuken, who collaborated on the *Stagecoach* score.

Hageman's work in Hollywood commenced with *If I Were King* (1938), and included work on nearly fifty ensuing feature films, among them *The Shanghai Gesture* (1941), *Angel and the Badman* (1947), and *Mourning Becomes Electra* (1947). From 1941 to 1946 he scored over twenty-five B pictures, mostly uncredited, and mostly for poverty row studios. Hageman also acted in nearly a dozen films, not least opposite Elizabeth Taylor in MGM's musical melodrama *Rhapsody* (1954). He also made an uncredited appearance as a saloon pianist in Ford's *3 Godfathers* (1948). And when Ford formed his production company, Argosy Pictures, in 1946, Hageman provided scoring for most of its releases. Hageman died in Beverly Hills in March 1966; his most prestigious and remembered Hollywood work remains his scores, both rousing and elegiac, for John Ford.

It's a unique collaboration that, to a certain degree (and like the films themselves) is a throwback to the very wellsprings of Hollywood filmmaking and scoring. Ford began his career in silents at Universal, an era in which the live musical accompaniments for most films were a pastiche of familiar tunes and classical excerpts. Ford never lost this early penchant for simple music and tunes. For example, "The Girl I Left Behind Me" and "I'll Take You Home Again Kathleen," Irish songs that became a part of the American western heritage, thread their way and overlap in the classic works of the late 1940s and early 1950s. Throughout his career Ford continued to utilize familiar Euro/American folk tunes. Even a major studio release such as Fox's *The Grapes of Wrath* (1940), scored by Alfred Newman, integrates the folk tune "Red River Valley" as a major musical motif. When Alex North departed from this pattern for Ford's troubled *Cheyenne Autumn* (1964), providing one of the most craggy scores ever devised for a western, Ford allegedly hated it! Indeed, the jagged, symphonic assault of North's writing turns the Ford mood inside out. Unfortunately for Ford, his encrusted preference for audience-friendly folk melodies harked back to an era of film scoring that composers such as North, Elmer Bernstein, and other 1950s newcomers were quickly rendering obsolete.

Even apart from the layering of sentimental folk melodies, Hageman's original cues and descriptive/transitional passages epitomize the by now classic retro western sound: harmonically simple programmatic music for modest orchestral forces, replete with what are now considered western clichés. Easy to parody today, the style nonetheless blends effectively with Ford's vision of a willfully mythic, ferociously onerous American past. Especially exemplary are Hageman's amicable cues accompanying scenes of travel, such as those heard in the opening stagecoach ride across Monument Valley in *Fort Apache* (1948), a cue which aurally paints a quaint but unmistakable picture of a stagecoach and horses on their unthreatened way through vast open spaces. Curiously, the majesty of Ford's familiar locations is seldom evoked in the music for *Fort Apache* (as opposed to the score of *She Wore A Yellow Ribbon* (1949) say, where Hageman is much more expansive in his treatment of landscape), as if Hageman's charge was to foreground the human emotional landscape, rather than the spectacular terrestrial lunarscape through which Ford's pilgrims pass.

Most any of Hageman's Indian cues are in a similar classic 1930s/1940s style, and even Victor Young trucked out the primitive clichés for the Indian attack in *Rio Grande* (1950), a stereotypical Indian sound composed of short minor or pentatonic mode motifs and tom-tom-like ostinati.[6] A fine example of a solution to the post-1950 problem of Indian music (which would of course persist in westerns of any vintage) is Jerry Goldsmith's score for the remake of *Stagecoach* (1966) in which the composer comes up with some remarkably fresh variations on the ominous musical evocation of Native Americans who were continued to be viewed as the enemy, the threatening Other to the imperiled and generally heroic Anglo protagonists in traditional Hollywood westerns.

John Ford, Stan Jones, and Sons of the Pioneers

Wagon Master might be called the director's musical. Lindsay Anderson cites the film as Ford's "most purely lyrical; and perhaps also the most original."[7]

Although technically not part of Ford's cavalry trilogy of *Fort Apache*, *She Wore A Yellow Ribbon*, and *Rio Grande*, *Wagon Master* is very much of a piece with this famous triptych. In fact, the film is built around two secondary characters from *Rio Grande*—Travis (Ben Johnson) and Sandy (Harry Carey, Jr.)—who, as *Wagon Master* commences, are civilian horse traders just off a successful roundup, who take on the leadership of a Mormon wagon train on a perilous journey to California. The leisurely paced film places more emphasis on mood and atmosphere than plot, but is very strong on warmth and humor, and contains some of Ford's most picturesque character studies, not to mention one of the most varied and appealing musical scores of any of his films.

Musically, *Wagon Master* is closely related to *Rio Grande*, produced in the same year with much of the same talent. However, the key musical figure for *Wagon Master* remains Hageman, while *Rio Grande* uses Victor Young. The difference here can probably be traced to the differing studio affiliation of each film: *Wagon Master* being an Argosy/RKO production, while *Rio Grande* was released by Republic, a small studio at which Young, a key Paramount composer and musical director, sometimes moonlighted.[8] However, a songwriter worked on both *Wagon Master* and *Rio Grande:* a multi-talented jack-of-all-trades, Stan Jones, who composed one of the major country-and-western hits of the late 1940s, "(Ghost) Riders in the Sky." A National Park Ranger with an MA in Zoology, Jones first met Ford and his company during the filming of *3 Godfathers* in Death Valley while Jones was serving as a guide for the company location scouts. But it was not until late 1949, and after Jones had written "(Ghost) Riders in the Sky," that Carey and George O'Brien met again with Jones and reintroduced his music to Ford, who then signed the songwriter for *Rio Grande* and *Wagon Master*. In the meantime "Riders" had become a major hit[9] and Jones had appeared in two Gene Autry films including *Riders in the Sky* (1949), which featured his hit song. Jones would not only provide songs for *Rio Grande* and *Wagon Master*, but also eventually write a title tune for Ford's *The Searchers* (1956). Jones was a prolific songwriter who produced various other songs integrated into sundry westerns. In an interesting convergence, Jones would later work for Disney.[10]

In *How the West Was Sung: Music in the Westerns of John Ford*, Kathryn Kalinak describes that 1949 meeting of Ford and Jones:

> Jones was a friend of actor George O'Brien, with whom Ford had recently reconciled after years of icy relations. It was O'Brien who brought Jones to Ford's office at RKO to sing. Harry Carey, Jr., who was present, said Jones's performance, accompanied only by his guitar, "made the hair stand up on the back of my neck. I thought the walls were going to tumble down when he got to the end." Then Jones sang "Rollin' Dust," and three other new songs for *Wagon Master*: "You've got a hell of a start with that 'Rollin' Dust' thing. Make the others in the same vein. You know, western as hell. About a wagon train." At that first meeting, Jones called Ford's attention to Sons of the Pioneers. Initially, the score was going to be performed exclusively,

both vocally and instrumentally, by Sons of the Pioneers, but at some point, Ford decided to augment their vocals and use RKO studio musicians for the instrumentals.[11]

Sons of the Pioneers were a durable, extremely popular group and by the mid-1930s were established as an enduing presence in American country-and-western music. When, as the Pioneer Trio, the western balladeers performed on radio, the announcer spontaneously changed their name to Sons of the Pioneers because he felt they all looked too young to be actual pioneers. Sons of the Pioneers' personnel evolved over the next several decades, but initially the core group included Hugh and Karl Farr, Tim Spencer, Bob Noland, and Len (Leonard) Slye. Slye changed his name to Roy Rogers in memory of Will Rogers, one of the first people to recognize the potential of the Sons, just prior to his tragic death in a plane crash in 1935. Slye soon went his own way and would become the "King of the Cowboys."

As the identity and style of the group developed, recordings introduced the Sons to national audiences. Their music gained in popularity and the Sons, like Rogers, made the transition into films. Their feature breakthrough was in Paramount's *Rhythm on the Range* (1936) where the Sons shared the screen with Bing Crosby, and introduced with him the Johnny Mercer classic, "I'm An Old Cowhand." The Sons appeared on screen with both Gene Autry and Roy Rogers. Television marked the beginning of the end for the B westerns that were Autry's and Rogers's forte. Although they continued to record and make personal appearances, the Sons likewise faded out cinematically, their on-screen work relegated to affectingly nostalgic stints for Disney, where they can be heard in the "Pecos Bill" segment of the animated feature *Melody Time* and in several Disney television episodes in the 1950s, and for Ford, where they can be heard in *Rio Grande* (where they appear on screen as cavalry musicians) and in *Wagon Master*.

Wagon Master

Jones wrote only three songs for *Rio Grande*, and they are mostly performed as source music on screen as part of what was essentially a song score, that is, a score comprising a series of songs that function as the score. However, even before *Rio Grande*, Jones composed four ingratiating numbers for *Wagon Master*: "Song of the Wagonmaster," "Wagons West," "Rollin' Dust," and "Chuckwalla Swing."[12] Jones's four songs seldom veer beyond the tonic, subdominant, dominant (I, IV, V) progressions of the typical folk song, spiced only with (as in the case of "Rollin' Dust") an occasional minor seventh chord. Indeed Jones's songs each seem as authentically period as Ford's meticulously rendered visuals. Only the sudden insertion of pungent chords from a distant key lends a slightly contemporary edge to "Chuckwalla Swing," but even these are in keeping with the modal roots of much American folk music. Text-wise the songs bear an even closer resemblance to folk music: "Oh, the white-tops are a rollin', rollin', the big wheels keep on turnin'. And when I reach the promised land for my gal I will be yearnin'." Jones was a disarmingly artless contemporary troubadour and it's easy to see why Ford was drawn to his music which effortlessly blends with and enhances the emotional tone of *Wagon Master*, while still providing a fresh, appealing twentieth-century sound. Jones's background as a ranger also occasionally pops up in his lyrics. The "chuckwalla" (of "Chuckwalla Stomp") is a rather fattish lizard—*sauromalus obesus*—found in the Mojave/Sonoran deserts of the West.

In *Wagon Master* the songs of Stan Jones are crucial to the overall score, and serve to vividly reflect and accentuate the film's shifting moods and emotions. Several of these songs are so fluidly integrated into the film's overall narrative that it could be argued that they function as exposition, Jones's melodies (sometimes orchestrated by Hageman to fuse with the Sons' simple and haunting western plaintiveness) effectively enhancing the overall tempi of the film's narrative thrust.[13] *Wagon Master* is completely underscored during its first five minutes, a combined prologue/credit/introductory sequence which employs visuals, music, and minimal dialogue to neatly establish key characters and the plot's tension. A one minute prologue fades in on a "Wanted" poster for the five Cleggs, a notorious family gang of father (oddly dubbed "Uncle Shiloh") and four apparently inbred sons, whose lethal villainy is tersely introduced with a robbery that climaxes in the elder Cleggs's cold-blooded murder of a young clerk. Hageman here first sounds the heavier, more serious musical tone that throughout the film connotes the coyly smarmy, yet ruthless, evil of the Cleggs. The prologue segues into the main title, set to a three-part music cue in which a short instrumental interlude forms a bridge between two Stan Jones songs, "Wagons West" and "Song of the Wagonmaster." Both songs are performed by Sons of the Pioneers, the second vocal showcasing the group's distinctive solos, while the interlude sustains the modest force of their instrumental back-up with a short, quietly heroic cue for minimal strings and guitar. Visually, the credit sequence cross-cuts between the outlaws and the Mormons, whose fates will dramatically intersect in the course of the saga.

The story proper opens with a short dialogue scene introducing Travis and Sandy as they ride into town to sell their horses, accompanied by Jones's "Chuckwalla Swing" in a jaunty arrangement which aptly suggests the humorous camaraderie of the two young horse traders. Without a break, the score shifts to a classic western street musical setting, mostly for piano player, as Travis and Sandy bring the horses into town, fading out as the marshal questions the two to make sure they are not desperadoes. This street sequence, played on the edge of the corral in which Travis has penned the "gentle horses," features two of Ford's most wonderful scenes: Travis selling the trick horse to the marshal (a humorous incident which will, however, bear narrative consequence later in the film), and that in which three Mormons, including the hot-tempered Elder Wiggs (Ward Bond), approach the cowboys about guiding the Mormon train to its destination, an offer that Travis initially turns down. The next music cue is a brief Mormon hymn tune "Come, Come Ye

Saints," sung to the source music of accordion and fiddle as the Mormons prepare to leave town. As Sister Ledyard (Jane Darwell) blows her raucous bullhorn, the music segues into a plucky instrumental version of Jones's "Wagons West" as the cowboys sit on a fence watching the wagons depart.

Sandy picks up the opening vocal phrase of "Song of the Wagonmaster"— "I left my gal in old Virginny"—and Travis responds with "fell in 'hind the wagon train," giving the distinct impression that they are about to launch into a musical number. Instead the song telegraphs narrative information, signaling their spontaneous decision to serve as guides for the train, with an instrumental version of the "Chuckwalla Swing" heard as they ride off to join it. "Chuckwalla" leads without pause into an extended instrumental/vocal cue based on a full-blooded version of "Wagons West." Perhaps the most stirringly coalesced visual/musical sequence in the film, the arrangement accompanies Ford's pristine imagery of rolling wagons and trekking pioneers.

At the conclusion of the number Travis, Sandy, and the Elder ride ahead, and, led by the sounds of Miss Denver (Joanne Dru) wearily strumming a guitar, discover the stranded medicine show wagon. After the troupers are reluctantly accepted into the train, a comic version of the "Chuckwalla Swing" from the troupe's fife and drum with another atonal horn blast from Sister Ledyard leads into contrastingly subdued traveling music, as if the wagon train's energy and momentum were gradually wearing down. A haunting long shot of the train crossing iconic western terrain (actually shot in Moab, Utah, sometimes referred to as Little Monument Valley) is accompanied only by a ghostly version of "Wagons West" sung by a cappella male voices as night falls.

After the subsequent morning scene, which includes a fight between Sandy and a young Mormon man and further Mormon interaction with the worldly newcomers and the first hint of a flowering romance between Travis and Denver, another extended musical number ensues. The three-part cue here further etches the weariness overtaking the travelers on their long trek toward the river, a subdued version of "Wagons West" imparting an air of quiet exhaustion. As Travis gallantly presents Denver with a new pair of walking shoes, the score melds to a gentle, old-fashioned waltz tune with hints of "Red River Valley," further suggesting their growing attraction. Both sections are scored for little more than flute, fiddle, and guitar, and lead directly into yet another music/image sequence of the wagon train moving through a windblown desert landscape to Jones's plaintive "Rollin' Dust" performed in a softly emotional arrangement with the Sons' distinctive vocal obbligato.

The arrival at the river cues *Wagon Master*'s supreme musical set piece, Jones's infectious dance tune "Chuckwalla Swing." A spontaneous, populist counterpart to the stirring but rigidly formal military dance sequence in *Fort Apache*, "Swing" follows fast on a brief, introductory hoe-down. The catchy, energetic tune is first played by the combined Mormon and medicine show instrumentalists, then sung and square-danced by members of the train. Although filmed like a traditional musical number, the scene never exceeds the bounds of a plausibly impromptu amateur performance. Ford, of course, characteristically interweaves several thematic and emotional strands at the same time. The hoe-down furthers the budding relationship between Travis and Denver, the ongoing rivalry between Sandy and the feisty Mormon with whom he earlier picked a fight over pretty Sister Prudence (Kathleen O'Malley), and the gently humorous dignity of the Elder and his buxom female medicine show counterpart. Above all, the sequence exhibits the positive solidarity now shared by the wildly eclectic group, "Mormons, show folk, and horse traders" as one of the townsmen disparagingly comments at the gambling table of the town saloon, just before Travis decides to guide the train.

One of the most exhilarating dramatic/musical sequences in all of Ford's work, the joyous mood is broken by the sudden, insidiously quiet materialization of the outlawed Cleggs, who inexorably attach themselves to the train. As a result, rather than concluding with a high-spirited musical flourish, the scene simply winds down as Hageman's scoring counterpoints the mood of impending threat with a curiously elegiac cue for minimal strings and humming male voices.

Ford navigates the initially tentative encounter between the settlers and the gang, the music is vaguely melancholic, with alternating close-ups of the smarmy gang members and the wholesome, stoic (if now apprehensive) faces of the wagon train's men. At one point Uncle Shiloh (Charles Kemper) remarks of one of the sons, "He ain't quite right," a dire understatement given the near-drooling menace of his "boys." A second cue for solo male voice and guitar in a similarly mournful mood also underscores the Cleggs scene.

Further variations on Jones's songs, and one curiously unemotional cue from Hageman are heard, as next morning the wagon train, now including the Cleggs, continues its journey. The ensuing peaceful encounter with the Navajos is scored with naturalistic Native American music: regular, subdued percussion for the dance in which the Mormons join; a more violent outburst of percussion under the scene in which a tribal woman hysterically reports being abused by one of the Clegg boys. The use here of at least superficially authentic-sounding Native American sounds (i.e., semi-atonal music without the keen subjective impact of the Jones/Hageman scoring) aurally accentuates the train's sudden encounter with the ethnic Other, a contrast emphasized by the almost startlingly sober shots of the gaunt face of the pioneer woman watching, with something close to terror, the otherwise gently comic scenes of the oldest Mormon pioneer and Sister Ledyard in the line of shuffling Indian dancers. Even the opening scene, in which the Navajos seemingly pursue Travis back to the train, eschews the stereotypical Indian music often found in Ford's other films.

After the evening at the Navajo camp (which concludes with the wheel-whipping of the guilty Clegg boy to appease the tribe), the train continues the next morning to a brief banjo version of Stephen Foster's "Oh! Susanna." When the medicine show wagon reaches the point of departure on its own, Travis comments to Sandy that he's "going courting." The touching scene in which he haltingly suggests marriage to Denver is underscored with one of the film's more conventionally sentimental cues, although in characteristic fashion, Hageman never violates the structural and instrumental limits set throughout in the score's consistent minimalist approach. Travis's romantic proposal concludes with a disturbed Denver smoking a cigarette in the back of her wagon. The show folk, however, are soon brought back to the train by the Cleggs to insure no report on the outlaws' whereabouts.

Wagon Master's narrative thrust reaches a dramatic climax with a final showdown with the Cleggs. The consistent use of Jones's melodies, particularly the journey motif of "Wagons West," gives the film the overall structure of a musical rondo, as the same melodies regularly recur to emphasize the train's sequential forward movement, reflecting with musical variations the pioneers' alternately heroic and laborious progress. Following the violent denouement, Ford highlights two hymn tunes in a brief coda, "At the River" and "Come, Come Ye Saints," a Mormon hymn that the pioneers sing as they first view the promised land of California. The film's final musical moments belong to Jones, however: a brief, celebratory reprise of the "Chuckwalla Swing," and a parting medley of songs as couples pair off and the film closes with a colt cantering ahead of one of the wagons into the new land.

The score for Wagon Master exists in an interesting space in terms of the western film score. Certainly other westerns of the period used songs, but such songs were usually either interludes in terms of the film's narrative progression or relegated to the background score, and in either case not used to further the narrative but to claim authenticity and establish mood and atmosphere. In Wagon Master, songs no longer recede into the background the way they do in earlier westerns, including Ford westerns such as Stagecoach. Songs in Wagon Master come to the forefront. Once Ford committed to Sons of the Pioneers and wanted to showcase their talent, he had new priorities, necessitating a score with a more self-conscious use of song. Sometimes the songs perform the traditional function of authenticity and atmosphere as in "Chuckwalla Swing." But sometimes something different is going on as in when the lyrics comment on the narrative or even move it forward as in "Wagons West," a use of music that was different from Ford's past practice. Ford, however, was not the first major filmmaker to use Sons of the Pioneers in a top-of-the-line studio product—Disney was. Ford and Disney shared more than a popular country-and-western singing group, however. Disney's Melody Time also exhibits a self-conscious use of song to showcase its stars, Roy Rogers and Sons of the Pioneers, and employs a musical mode that diverged from conventional western scoring practices.

Sons of the Pioneers and "Blue Shadows on the Trail"

Melody Time is a kind of pop music Fantasia (1940), with two major episodes founded on various bits of folklore and Americana, and presented as a concert of eight musical sequences. Most, but not all, of the episodes are based on original songs written for the film and performed by various pop artists of the period, ranging from the Andrews Sisters' "Little Toot" to Ethel Smith's florid Hammond organ stylings in the psychedelic "Blame It On The Samba" sequence. The climactic "Pecos Bill" sequence is a musical spin on the western tall tale, featuring Roy Rogers and Sons of the Pioneers, its hyperbolic Americana idiom is an ideal pretext for the medium of Disney animation. Disney's performers were drawn from popular recording artists of the mid-1940s. Sons of the Pioneers had just completed a series of films with Roy Rogers so their pairing was a natural.

Also, one of the group's most popular numbers was "Tumbling Tumbleweeds," one of several popular standards written for the Pioneers by key member Bob Noland. Writing about the group's status in the 1970s, Bill O'Neal and Fred Goodwin note: "The Pioneers name still was magic, and so were the group's signature songs, 'Tumbling Tumbleweeds' and 'Cool Water'. When the Pioneers performed 'Tumbling Tumbleweeds' the opening note seemed to charge the air."[14] This was certainly just as true in the 1940s. Disney was no doubt aware of the number's popularity though he was apparently unwilling to license (and pay for) the use of Noland's song. Instead "Blue Shadows on the Trail," an original Disney tune, was written for *Melody Time*. But the opening "Pecos" sequence, which tracks a pair of tumbleweeds across a nocturnal desertscape, could just as easily have had the Bob Noland song as musical backup.

The Pioneers would later work again for Disney, providing music for *The Saga of Windwagon Smith* (1959), *The Swamp Fox* (1960), *Sancho the Homing Steer* and *Legend of Lobo* (1961). These were among the group's last film efforts, but, as O'Neal and Goodwin comment "counting early cartoons and shorts, the Sons had amassed ninety-nine movie credits by the early 1960s."[15] The authors note: "Lensed in splendid Technicolor, with lots of humor and with Roy and the Pioneers in excellent voice, *Melody Time* is one of the most charming and entertaining features the Pioneers ever filmed."[16]

Melody Time features some of Disney's most adventurous and surreal animation and color styling of the late 1940s. Bill's outlandish heroics and the bizarre situations of the tale itself, such as the explosive bouncing bustle finale, inspired some of Disney's wildest and most liberating animation since the early Mickey Mouse shorts. The attention to quality on every level and to meticulous technical detail emphatically points the way to the renaissance of feature animation that commenced with *Cinderella* (1950). More importantly for our purposes here, "Pecos Bill" provided an alternative musical mode to the conventional western score, one related to Disney's long established patterns for the incorporation of song into the narrative, a musical mode that used song as exposition.

Musically "Pecos Bill" enfolds by fusing song and rhythmic, rhymed (and drolly colloquial) voice-over narration with instrumental accompaniment. As in the later *Wagon Master*, in "Pecos" much of the music is performed by Sons of the Pioneers, often accompanied by colorful orchestral backgrounds. They appear as backup to cowboy star/narrator/singer Roy Rogers, who shares the story telling and vocals with the Pioneers ensemble, and their distinctive vocal harmonies are heard in the haunting "Blue Shadows on the Trail" opening and in the folk-like "Pecos Bill" (where they even yodel).[17] Rogers and the Sons, Disney child stars Bobby Driscoll and Luana Patton, both from Disney's then-recent *Song of the South* (1946), plus Trigger (who contributes a blubbery horse-laugh to set-up Bobby's chagrined reaction at Roy's mention of Sluefoot Sue) all interact with cozy, chuck wagon bonhomie in introducing Pecos Bill's fanciful legend in a live-action prologue to Bill's animated story. The intro-duction to the campfire prologue is one of the most lyrically beautiful openings since *Bambi* (1942): an extended animated lateral tracking shot through a softly stylized, sometimes multiplane nocturnal desert, following the paths of a graceful pair of tumbling tumbleweeds that intersect with various desert creatures on their way to look in on a long shot of the live-action campfire and actors set in a painted starlit western landscape.

Disney's "Pecos Bill" is also a droll and fairly explicit parody of the classic western male bonding mythos, beloved of westerns ranging from *Red River* (1948) to *Butch Cassidy and the Sundance Kid* (1969) and beyond. In this instance, the inseparable buddies are Bill and his horse, Widowmaker, an intense and long-standing bromance which is suddenly disrupted by the appearance of the seductive Sluefoot Sue. The misogyny that peppers the "Pecos Bill" episode is unabashedly sounded by Bobby Driscoll in the live-action prelude when, at Roy's mention of Sue's appearance in the tale, Bobby acidly comments: "Aw shucks, a woman in the story!" a terse but obviously heartfelt comment that naïvely divulges the unspoken subtext behind many of Hollywood's male-bonding films (and not only westerns) of that and later eras.

"Blue Shadows on the Trail" bookends the "Pecos Bill" sequence, with the folk-like song "Pecos Bill." "Blue Shadows on the Trail" functions typically, establishing atmosphere with its lyrics visually embodied in the animation. "Pecos Bill" operates in a different way. The number commences with Bill's firing directly into the camera (and thus at the audience), shattering the on-screen image, a tongue-in-cheek echo of a "shot" in what is considered to be the first American western, Edwin Porter's *The Great Train Robbery* (1903). At one point Bill ropes the ensuing frame and drags it on screen, a variation on the alienation effect used in the "El Gaucho Goofy" episode in *Saludos Amigos* (1942). Individual episodes contain stunning and sometimes surprisingly eroticized imagery, no doubt a contribution of animator Ward Kimball who manages to sneak some outrageously sexual gags into the (mostly) benign Disney *oeuvre*: Bill's courtship of Sue atop of a phallic mesa whose climax has Bill's guns shooting off by themselves when Sue finally takes the initiative and grabs the diffident Bill for a passionate fade-out kiss; Bill's first reaction to seeing her where he becomes manically mesmerized by her appearance and also both feminized (playing a harp and gracefully strewing flower petals, in a ballet-like dream sequence) and ridiculous (ending up barking like a dog); and the conclusion of the animated story in which a pile of Bill's clothing is seen after he has apparently wandered off into the desert nude (and reunited) with Widowmaker, his horse.[18]

Throughout, we hear the song "Pecos Bill," a series of verses with a rousing and catchy chorus: "So, yip-pee-i-ay i-ay, yip-pee-i-oh/Fer the toughest critter West of the Alamo." The song not only accompanies the series of wildly staged and fantastically colored tall tale anecdotes that constitute Bill's legendary exploits (digging the Rio Grande, bringing rain from "Californy," etc.), it narrates it. Vocal music provides the exposition with lyrics telling the story that we see enacted somewhat generically in the images. It is the song here, and not the images, that drives the telling of Bill's legendary exploits.

The background instrumental score by Paul Smith,[19] develops the songs into orchestral underscoring that proves crucial to the dramatic flow. A fine example of Smith's compositional skills being put to narrative purpose occurs about a third of the way into the story, in the episode of young Bill's first meeting with his loyal, beloved horse. The Pioneers lugubriously describe the lost pony's desert wanderings, their vocals accompanied by a spiraling string tremolo figure that aurally suggests the slow, circling buzzards in the visuals. Smith makes visceral the flying predators' inevitable attack with characteristic use of brass. The sequence as a whole is beautifully done, from both the standpoint of Smith's dramatic underscoring and the animation, the latter commencing with an atmospheric long shot of the slowly circling buzzards that moves to medium shots of the attack, in which the birds (surprisingly, and as if in anticipation of Hitchcock and Bakshi) are shown actually drawing blood from the beleaguered pony's back as they swoop down. The shrewd deployment of cinematic and musical rhythms fuel both the attack sequence and the ensuing scenes in which visual and musical momentum gradually, but steadily, escalates in a brief episode in which the young Bill and his pony irresistibly bond and cement their life-long attachment with a quick but affectionate kiss. A brief series of shots depicts the two characters growing up together (indeed almost manically interacting) and the filial intensity inexorably builds until the adult Bill lets out with a raucous "Yaaaaa-Hoooo" (drolly echoed by the also grown-up Widowmaker) and fires into the screen, literally shattering the image and releasing the homoerotic momentum generated by Bill and his buddy's burgeoning bromance, just as Rogers and the Pioneers give expression to that release of energy in a spirited down-home version of the "Pecos Bill" song.

The western, crystallized in memory by the likes of John Ford, Anthony Mann, Budd Boetticher, Henry Hathaway, Delmer Daves, and Walt Disney partook of myriad cultural and musical influences from abroad and from America's own past to mythologize the West. The very plurality of these influences testifies to a willed, nostalgic, mid-twentieth-century allegiance to both America's imagined past and its presumed glorious future. Ford's feature, *Wagon Master*, and indeed the entire "Pecos Bill" segment of Disney's *Melody Time* absorb these influences to become exhilarating tours de force of music, imagery, and narrative, including vividly human characterizations and their emotional resonance, fusing to produce visceral sensations of momentum, tension, and liberating release. The stirring celebration of powerful American imagery in both of these films may appear quite different initially but their musical scores operate in much the same way with song at the forefront, driving the narrative, and beckoning audiences to pay more conscious attention. Although Ford and Disney are not usually paired in studies of the western, in studies of the western film score this pairing cannot be overlooked.

Notes

1 Lindsay Anderson, *About John Ford* (New York: McGraw-Hill, 1981), 128.
2 Anderson, 127.
3 Dan Ford, *Pappy: The Life of John Ford* (Englewood Cliffs, NJ: Prentice-Hall, 1979), 231, 245.
4 To the best of my knowledge, none of the scholarship on Ford, including Kathryn Kalinak's definitive study of Ford westerns and music, *How the West Was Sung: Music in the Westerns of John Ford* (Berkeley: University of California Press, 2007), or the scholarship on Disney, including my own, mention this connection between Ford and Disney.
5 For a thorough-going analysis of how Copland translated wide open spaces into music, see Neil Lerner, "Copland's Music of Wide Open Spaces: Surveying the Pastoral Trope in Hollywood," *The Musical Quarterly* 85, 3 (2001), 477–515.
6 For more on the musical stereotypes that developed in Hollywood for the representation of Indians, see Michael Pisani, "'I'm an Indian, too': Creating Native American Identities in Nineteenth- and Early Twentieth-Century Music" in *The Exotic in Western Music*, ed. Jonathan Bellman (Boston: Northeastern University Press, 1998), 218–57, and Claudia Gorbman, "Scoring the Indian: Music in the Liberal Western" in *Western Music and Its Others: Difference, Representation, and Appropriation in Music*, ed. Georgina Born and David Hesmondhalgh (Berkeley: University of California Press, 2000), 234–53; rev. and rpt. as "Drums Along the L.A. River: Scoring the Indian" in *Westerns: Films Through History*, ed. Janet Walker (New York: Routledge, 2001), 177–95.
7 Anderson, 127.
8 Young would also score Ford's *The Quiet Man* (1952) and *The Sun Shines Bright* (1953), both released by Republic, and the last films produced by Argosy.
9 "(Ghost) Riders in the Sky," a colorful ballad about damned cowboys condemned to drive the "devil's herd across these endless skies," became an instant hit. Big-band singer Vaughan Monroe's recording became a best seller, and the song was eventually covered by everyone from Peggy Lee to Morton Gould, who transcribed it into a vivid orchestral tone poem. Jones's arrival in the American hall of pop music fame was further certified by Spike Jones's version of "Riders," done in a hilariously incongruous Brooklyn/Jewish accent! Eventually Sons of the Pioneers recorded it as well.
10 Jones produced the lyrics, music, and narration featured on the album *Songs of the National Parks* (1958) and contributed one song to the collective score of the live-action feature *Westward Ho The Wagons!* (1956) as well as tunes featured in *Spin and Marty* (1955–57), the Western television serial spun off from *Mickey Mouse Club*. For *Spin and Marty* Jones wrote, among other tunes, "The Triple R Song" which was featured prominently throughout the series.
11 Kalinak, 113. It's interesting to note that Kalinak also mentions that the Sons originally passed on Jones's "Riders in the Sky."
12 Although no soundtrack was ever issued from *Wagon Master*, all four songs were published by Alamo Music in 1950. The sheet music cover design makes the film

look quite epic, and cites Ben Johnson being "remembered as Sergeant Tyree in *She Wore A Yellow Ribbon.*" In 1993 Varese Sarabande Records issued a complete soundtrack from *Rio Grande* on CD. However, no soundtrack was ever released from *Wagon Master.*

13   Three RKO staff arrangers also worked on the score: Leonid Raab, Gilbert Grau, and L. D. Gordon.

14   Bill O. Neal and Fred Goodwin, *The Sons of the Pioneers* (Austin, Texas: Eakin Press, 2001), 201.

15   Ibid., 187.

16   Ibid., 138.

17   Both "Blue Shadows on the Trail," a wistful ballad, and the rousing "Pecos Bill," the sequence title song, were written by lyricist Johnny Lange and composer Eliot Daniel. (Sons of the Pioneers recorded "Pecos Bill" in 1961.) Daniel was under contract at Disney as a composer/conductor and had composed several songs for Disney including the popular "That's What Uncle Remus Says" from *Song of the South,* and served as one of the two music directors for *Melody Time.* Lange had worked in B films and westerns and co-wrote the Frankie Laine hit, "Mule Train." Paul Smith composed the background instrumental score and Ken Darby handled the vocal direction for the film.

18   Although this curious shot can still be seen on DVD, in a nod to current PC standards a verse of the "Pecos Bill" song (at the droll, if not perfectly rhymed lyrics "As that cyclone bucked and flitted, Pecos rolled a smoke and lit it") has been excised from the number.

19   After a long apprenticeship scoring shorts and secondary episodes in early studio features, Smith (who joined Disney in the 1930s) came into his own in the 1950s as the studio moved in live-action production. He scored most of Disney's *True Life Adventures* short documentaries, including atmospheric evocations of the natural American West for the feature-length *True Life Adventures, The Living Desert* (1953) and *The Vanishing Prairie* (1954). He also scored the epic *20,000 Leagues Under the Sea* (1954) and a variety of other 1950s Disney live-action features.

Chapter 3

Reinventing the Western Film Score

Jerome Moross and *The Big Country*

Mariana Whitmer

Buoyed by the wave of popularity for his score to *The Big Country* (1958), Jerome Moross claimed that he invented the archetypal western theme. In an interview from 1978, he boasted, "This is the way to do a western now; the way I did it in *[The] Big Country* . . . a western with American rhythms, American tunes and a boldness and brashness about it."[1] For a composer who, in 1958, had limited experience with scoring films, and had only scored one other western, to make such a pronouncement was brashness itself. The western film score absorbed a variety of sources and influences as it evolved in the decades after the introduction of sound, including American folk and popular songs of the nineteenth century, American concert hall music, and the well-known musical clichés that accompanied silent films. While Copland's role in the formation of an American sound is significant in the development of the western film score,[2] Moross can certainly take credit for introducing a fresh new approach in *The Big Country*, and in a style that is appreciated and imitated to this day.

That Moross did so may also be partially due to Copland, who was the first choice of composer for this film (more on this later), as well as Moross's colleague and friend. By virtue of living in the same city as Copland, Moross was similarly influenced by the musical life around him. Not only did their experiences with other contemporary composers shape their compositional styles, but also the music heard at clubs and concert halls in New York City. It was this interaction with the Copland milieu that influenced Moross's approach to film music in general and his western scores in particular.

Moross's relationship with Copland dates from 1931. "When I first met Copland," Moross reminisced, "I was 18 and Copland was about 32 and he was already an established composer."[3] Copland appreciated Moross's compositional talent and included him in the Young Composers' Group. Within the group, Moross allied himself with Bernard Herrmann whom he had met in high school. Together they impressed the group, as Oscar Levant (another member of the group) described, as "two remarkably unpleasant young men."[4] Herrmann's antagonistic and aggressive behavior is legendary, and their association may have led to Moross being similarly labeled.

In his 1926 article "America's Young Men of Promise," Copland assessed the current crop of young composers born in the US, classifying them either as revolutionaries, "free-lances," students of Ernst Bloch, or students of Nadia Boulanger. Since this original list of seventeen included those "whose ages lie between twenty-three and thirty-three," at thirteen Moross would have been too young.[5] However, Copland did include Moross in his follow-up article in 1936, "America's Young Men—Ten Years Later," listing him among "the most gifted men" of the younger generation along with Samuel Barber. Notably, Copland added, "Moross is probably the most talented of these men. He writes music that has a quality of sheer physicalness, music 'without a mind,' as it were. It is regrettable that we cannot yet point to any finished, extended work. What he seems to lack is a sense of artistic discipline and integrity, which his talent needs for development."[6]

Moross benefited from his friendship with Copland and their paths crossed more than once during the course of their lives. Copland recommended Moross to Ruth Page, who commissioned Moross to compose three ballets: *An American Pattern* (1936), *Frankie and Johnny* (1938), and *The Last Judgment* (1953). Moross was always appreciative of Copland's assistance: "He told Ruth Page she should hire me to do ballets. . . . He was always doing things for us."[7] When CBS and Alan Lomax commissioned a radio program for children (*American School of the Air: Folk Music of America*), Moross was invited to participate alongside Copland and others. Moross's contribution, called *Ramble on a Hobo Tune*, was based on the folk song "Midnight Special" and eventually became the Third Movement of his First Symphony.

Moross went to Hollywood in 1936, in advance of Copland, originally with the touring production of Gershwin's *Porgy and Bess*. Initially supporting himself and his family by playing piano, it was Copland's score for *Our Town* (1940) that gave Moross his first big break when he was hired to help orchestrate. By 1942 Moross had a steady position as an orchestrator for Warner Bros., but no composing jobs. The two composers continued to meet socially when in Hollywood at the same time[8] and their periodic correspondence provides some insight into their involvement with film music. Copland wrote to Moross in October 1942 concerning obtaining scoring commissions, "If you have any good advice as to who might turn me up a job out your way I wish you'd let me have it. Abe [Abe Meyer, Copland's agent at MCA] had been stringing me along for quite a while, and I was about ready to make a change."[9] When Copland returned to Hollywood to score *The North Star* (1943), Moross was asked to arrange that score as well.

Copland also commiserated with Moross about the difficulties of composing, "like you, I began a Symphony—so we can weep on each other's shoulders together. It's tough going even without having to sandwich in movie music." In a postscript Copland added, "If you hear of any outstanding picture assignment that's available for the spring—let me know."[10] On November 16, 1942 Moross responded, offering the names of potential agents to replace Abe Meyer (who had recently joined the armed services) adding "If you have anything in mind and I can help you in any way please let me know."[11] Although Copland had just completed the successful *Appalachian Spring* (1944), he may have been considering a return to Hollywood for the financial rewards, as well as the broad-based exposure of his music that film scores offered. It is likely that Copland did not need Moross's help in acquiring film score jobs, and he may have been only half-serious. Indeed, Copland turned down Wyler's invitation to score *The Best Years of Our Lives* (1946), citing too much involvement with the Third Symphony. Instead Moross assisted Hugo Friedhofer with his admittedly Copland-inspired score.[12] Moross dipped into film music only when necessary to support his other work and, again like Copland, called it quits after completing a limited number of films.

The relationship between the two composers was friendly, but not animated, probably due to the difference in ages, and with Copland often in the role of mentor. Moross summed up his feelings about Copland in a later interview: "A man of warmth and dignity who had a genuine interest in seeing American music grow so he welcomed all of us and nurtured us."[13] Ultimately, that relationship came to bear fruit in the score for *The Big Country*, which combines Moross's individual style with the prevalent sentiment of infusing Americanism into modern music. It was his participation in the Young Composers' Group and the Group's cooperative interest in establishing an American music that gave Moross the confidence to score this film his own way.

Searching for the American Composer

When William Wyler set about conceiving the film *The Big Country*, he was particularly inspired by the newest cinematic technology to make the film larger than life. While the wide screen of Technirama would capture the vast landscapes, Technicolor would enrich the color and make it vividly realistic. Wyler sought to make everything big, not just big scenery, but also big stars. To match this, Wyler needed a big score, with dramatic music, by a composer with a big name. His first choice was Aaron Copland, whose reputation as a western composer was well established, primarily as a result of his ballets *Billy the Kid* (1938) and *Rodeo* (1942), as well as his more recent film score for *The Red Pony* (1947), amongst others.

For Wyler the music was all about establishing atmosphere. Five years earlier Wyler had sought out a European composer for *Roman Holiday* (1953) to make the film sound Italian, or at least European. As Colin Roust explains:

> In a film that is set within the debates over the establishment of the European Community, Wyler and his production team placed value on having a European composer. While it was initially considered ideal to hire an Italian, ultimately they felt that a Frenchman could adequately compose music with an "Italian flavor."[14]

For *The Big Country* Wyler sought a composer who could provide American flavor, and Copland would be ideal.

Wyler had worked with Copland on recent and previous films. He began *The North Star* with Copland, but the relationship was cut short by the war;

after Wyler enlisted, Lewis Milestone completed the film. Copland had successfully worked with Milestone on *Of Mice and Men* (1939) and would also work on his other western, *The Red Pony*. Wyler was a big fan of Copland's, having previously approached Copland to work on another American film, *The Best Years of Our Lives*.[15] His Oscar-winning score for Wyler's *The Heiress* (1949) was not as gratifying to Copland as previous scores had been and, due in part to artistic differences with Wyler, he stopped composing for films for several years.

The production team for *The Big Country* contacted Copland in June 1957, just before shooting started. Copland seemed interested, and responded: "On the assumption that the movie script will soon be available, I am hoping that you will be able to send me it so that I may have a better idea of how much music will be needed and where it may best go. As soon as I am able to judge the overall requirements of the film, I shall be in touch with you again."[16] But by the time shooting started, in July, Copland had changed his mind, citing a full schedule coupled with a desire not to repeat himself or become typecast as a western composer. In a letter dated July 27, 1957, Copland wrote:

> I have been giving a good deal of thought to my own possible role as composer for *The Big Country*. Its Western locale and characters present me with a purely personal problem: that of repeating myself. In the past I composed two ballets (*Rodeo* and *Billy the Kid*) and two film scores (*Of Mice and Men* and *The Red Pony*) with similar backgrounds. Since I have composed nothing for films since *The Heiress* I am particularly anxious to make a return to Hollywood after so long a time in some new capacity, and not again as a composer of western locale. I'm very much afraid that I have exhausted that vein as far as I am concerned.[17]

Several other well-known Hollywood composers were considered for *The Big Country*; indeed, a long list was compiled and many were contacted. Most of the names are familiar and their names appear (suggesting they were considered and perhaps even contacted) in the following order: Hugo Friedhofer, Miklos Rozsa, Alfred Newman, Andre Previn, David Raksin, Franz Waxman, Dimitri Tiomkin, Bernard Herrmann, and Elmer Bernstein.[18] Jerome Moross was close to the bottom of the list but before Gerald Fried and George Antheil. Moross's selection was likely due to the strong endorsement by Samuel Goldwyn, Jr. who had worked with Moross on his previous western, *The Proud Rebel* (1958).

Wyler got his big score, yet he never liked it. Almost as soon as shooting was over, and well before Moross began composing, Wyler left for Rome to begin shooting *Ben Hur* (1959). Prior to his departure, however, Wyler urged Moross to travel with him and work on the score overseas. The union problems that were plaguing the Hollywood studios were also making conditions favorable for recording in European venues. Moross was not against the idea at first, but as time went on he became more and more opposed to it. Eventually he was allowed to stay in Hollywood to compose. "It now begins to look as if they will allow me to do the picture here. At least Mr. Wyler has unbent enough to think it might be better."[19]

One reason for his increasing resistance to the idea is that it was becoming evident to Moross that he and Wyler were in complete disagreement over the score. "Yesterday Wyler made me see *The Bridge on the River Kwai* [1957]," Moross wrote to his wife. "It absolutely puzzled me. If that is the kind of score he wants he should have hired Benny Herrmann or someone who writes like that. But it is the opposite aesthetic to my style and I don't intend to even try. I am writing this in my way and that is that."[20] While he was in Rome, Wyler hardly acknowledged Moross's work, except to complain.[21] Despite the enthusiastic approval of the production manager and others, Wyler's criticism was scathing.

Composing a Different Western Soundscape

To our contemporary sensibilities, the film and its soundtrack are not extraordinary, but to the audience watching *The Big Country* for the first time in 1958, it was probably electrifying[22] in its unconventional conception. The music begins almost a full two seconds before the first visual appears, a stagecoach pulled by six horses at full gallop. The initial shots focus on the horses until the first cadential point, when the focus shifts to the wide open plains, putting the stagecoach in perspective. Moross draws the audience immediately into the action with the sound of full strings, reiterating a motive as consistent and captivating as the turning wheel on the stagecoach. It is this opening that alerts us to a different kind of western film score. At a time when film scores were moving away from the full symphonic orchestra, and more toward smaller ensembles and popular song tracks, Moross thrilled audiences with a big symphonic score to accompany this impressive film. Moross utilized the resources of the entire orchestra, with varied thematic materials that underscore the emotions and intensify the drama.

By the late 1950s, opening a western film score with a song was the standard practice, particularly since the tremendous success of Tiomkin's "Do Not Forsake Me, Oh My Darlin'" in *High Noon* (1952). The result was more westerns featuring scores derived from quasi-folk song idioms. As Moross reflected, "[Western film composers] would even do like Tiomkin [did] in *High Noon* . . . [and] write a Russian folk song . . . This became a prototype score. It's been imitated to death."[23] Moross felt that this approach was "all wrong" and later stated that he had been determined not to "do it in the typical fashion" that was so popular at the time.[24]

In his ballet and theatrical works, Moross was accustomed to composing music to accompany live gestures that expressed emotions, and this dramatic style informed his film scores. Moross viewed the stage action from a broader perspective, taking in the overall narrative and emotional content of a scene, rather than each individual gesture. Transferring this approach to the motion picture screen, he avoided composing music that was determined by the action on the screen, and unlike many western film composers, refused to use the music to mimic or respond to what was happening on the screen. As Moross explained,

> I like to get the sense of the scene that I'm going to compose for, and write a piece of music that will fit the scene, but I don't want to follow the character's every movement. The sense of the whole scene I think, is more important . . . music can give the scene a sense of form and of unity.[25]

This approach to scoring films, and especially westerns, was unconventional, if not radical. By aurally describing and accompanying the film's most important locations and the emotional content, rather than its action, Moross's score does what Copland thought a good score should do: establish atmosphere.

Although he was not Aaron Copland, Moross was the next best thing. Moross's score departs significantly from previous western film scores, with original melodies and rhythms that reflect the influence of Copland and the Young Composers' Group. Moross's score incorporates some of those characteristics that Copland used to communicate the pastoral trope, as suggested by Neil Lerner, including sparse textures, preference for the perfect fourth (melodically and harmonically), simplistic melodies, and the use of pedal points or ostinati.[26] Moross differentiates his composition by placing more emphasis on triadic melodic material, formal structures, and syncopated rhythms in his score for The Big Country. As Christopher Palmer observed, Moross endeavored "independently of his friend Copland . . . to develop an authentically American nationalist idiom which was not exclusively jazz-oriented but drew nourishment from a great variety of American folk and popular music cultures."[27]

Ultimately, Moross's score successfully accomplishes much of what Copland felt was the function of film music. It should describe the atmosphere of time and place, reveal the "unspoken thoughts" of a character, provide "neutral background filler," build continuity (particularly through the film's editorial seams), and heighten as well as mold the drama.[28] After an overview of the film and its score, I will focus on three particular scenes that exemplify Moross's style as it modernized the western film score, fulfilling Copland's objectives and enhancing the narrative.

Synopsis

The Big Country is the story of an Eastern dude, Jim McKay (Gregory Peck), a sailor and son of a ship owner, who travels west to marry Pat Terrill (Carroll Baker), a girl he met while she was visiting acquaintances in Baltimore. Almost as soon as he arrives, McKay becomes aware of the long-standing dispute over water rights between the Terrills and the Hannasseys, a less affluent and lower-class family. After McKay is subjected to a hazing by Buck Hannassey (Chuck Connors), tensions escalate when Pat's father, Major Terrill (Charles Bickford), and his foreman, Steve Leech (Charleton Heston), organize a raid on the

Hannassey ranch in retaliation. McKay refuses to be involved in any violence and while initially unresponsive to Pat's need for him to prove his courage, he eventually succumbs to the challenges of Leech and fights him. As the relationship with Pat falls apart, McKay develops a friendship with the local schoolteacher, Julie Maragon (Jean Simmons). When she is kidnapped by the Hannasseys, and suffers an attempted rape at the hands of Buck, McKay goes to her rescue. In the unavoidable duel with Buck Hannassey, it is the pacifist who proves to be the better man, as Buck cowers in fear. The film concludes with the death of Buck Hannassey, as well as both patriarchs, Major Terrill and Rufus Hannassey (Burl Ives). Behind the end credits we see McKay and Julie literally riding into the sunset.

To demonstrate how Moross's music modernized the western film score and met Copland's criteria, I will analyze the cues from three scenes that are par- ticularly pivotal to the narrative: "The Raid," "The Death of Buck Hannassey," and "The Fight." "The Raid" and "The Death of Buck Hannassey"[29] frame the film to establish the pacifist theme and then bring it to a conclusion. During the raid scene, we observe the first indication that McKay is not going to participate in the violent lifestyle of the West, and Pat's negative reaction signals the beginning of the end of their relationship. At the other end of the spectrum, the death of Buck, which is foreshadowed in the earlier scene, "The Attempted Rape," resolves the conflict in the film, establishing that the pacifist is the better man. The music for these two notable scenes is related in a manner that highlights the emotional dissonance, and also features related melodic elements that are heard throughout the film. The third cue, "The Fight," accompanies the fight between McKay and Leech. The scene is pivotal in that it succeeds in altering Leech's hostile attitude and leaves him questioning his participation in the violence against the Hannasseys. This scene is not only a narrative turning point, but also a cinematic triumph and a stunning musical moment as Moross accompanies the action with subtle melodic material that builds and molds the drama.

The Raid

We are first introduced to the serious animosity between the Terrills and the Hannasseys at the beginning of the film with McKay's arrival. However, it is not until the next morning, in the breakfast scene and the subsequent scene on the porch (the cue for this scene is titled "The Raid, Part One"), that the extent of this feud is made evident. Notable in these two scenes is how quickly the audience is clued in to the participation of McKay's fiancée in this feud. The music plays a key role in alerting us to this fact and subsequently establishing our expectation for the end of her engagement with McKay, a relationship we now know is doomed.

Prior to Terrill's men riding out to seek vengeance on the Hannasseys, there is a lengthy scene in the dining room where McKay is having breakfast with the Major, eventually joined by Pat and then Leech. It is during this scene that Leech reveals to McKay that the Major is leading a posse of men to punish the Hannasseys for the hazing they gave McKay the previous day. It is at this time that the seriousness of the feud between the two families is revealed. The music that Moross composed to accompany this scene (orchestrated but not recorded or used in the film) has its own thematic material, yet it previews the longer cue that accompanies the subsequent scenes on two levels. The most obvious connection is the introduction of the syncopated rhythms and reiterated seventh chords that will accompany the first part of the raid. (Figure 3.1). The syncopated seventh chords establish an ostinato that continues through the breakfast scene and then after a pause resumes in the scene on the porch (Raid, Part One). Moross frequently uses ostinati throughout *The Big Country*, a compositional trait that he shares with Copland.[30]

Less apparent is the association between the descending/ascending major second (D–C–D) in the melody of the breakfast scene and the descending minor second (F–E) in the following scene (see Figure 3.3). This minor second, heard coinciding with a close-up of Pat's angry face, signals her extreme displeasure with her fiancé. The introduction of these two musical elements in anticipation of the raid lends weight to the emotional content of the breakfast scene, as the seriousness of the feud is revealed.

One of the most significant features of Moross's score is the rhythm, particularly in scenes such as these where emotions are intense and action results. Most of Moross's rhythms in the score are syncopated and it is in the formulation of rhythms where his distinctly American style is most notable: not only in the syncopated rhythms evident through the raid scenes and those with action, but also in cues such as "Cattle at the River" (Figure 3.2), which

Figure 3.1   Accompaniment from "The Breakfast Scene." All examples are transcribed from the original sketches, Jerome Moross Papers, Rare Book & Manuscript Library, Columbia University. © 1958 (Renewed) CHAPPELL & CO., INC. All Rights Administered by STATE ONE MUSIC AMERICA. All Rights Reserved. Used by Permission.

Figure 3.2 "Cattle at the River" © 1958 (Renewed) CHAPPELL & CO., INC. All Rights Administered by STATE ONE MUSIC AMERICA. All Rights Reserved. Used by Permission.

was cut from the film. In this cue, in particular, the rhythm is reminiscent of something Moross may have assimilated from Gottschalk, having previously arranged "Le Banjo" for four hands. In the main title theme we hear echoes of Moross's "Biguine" (1935), an early example of his rhythmic exuberance and enthusiasm for dance rhythms. It is as if Moross could not wait to showcase the syncopated rhythms characteristic of the popular music idioms he used as the basis for his dramatic music. This is what sets it apart from other western scores and influenced future scores.

From production documents, including scripts, memos, and continuity lists, we know that in the rough cut that Moross viewed in early February, 1958, the first part of the raid scene did not include any shots of Pat. Once Pat retreats into the house, leaving McKay alone on the porch, we do not see her until much later in the film. An early version of the script (dated August, 1957) describes McKay's somber attitude, "Unsmiling, troubled, he watches the Major and Leech as they go. . . . McKay continues to stare after them, his expression that of a man who does not believe what he sees."[31] The shot then dissolves to the Terrill men riding, returns to McKay, and then shifts to the main street of San Rafael.[32]

At some point after Moross finished the composition of the cue, and after it was orchestrated, the scene was revised to include three new cutaway shots of Pat: changing her clothes in the bedroom, riding her horse quickly across the horizon, and finally dismounting and sitting under a tree. These intervening shots tangibly communicate her anger and frustration at McKay's perceived cowardice in not participating in the raid. Moross revised the music based on the new visual content to integrate Pat emotionally into the scene.

The original cue (Table 3.1) begins much like the final version, with the descending minor second, alternating with the syncopated accompaniment (Figure 3.3). As the shot shifts to McKay standing on the porch (as suggested by the scripts), the cue continues with the main title theme stated in the English horn, strings, and woodwinds. (Figure 3.4) Moross's revision of the cue accompanies this more complex series of shots, which develops the scene (Table 3.2). Moross included a new motive that is associated with Pat. It is a fast and furious repetitive melodic figure, which reflects her frustration and anger (Figure 3.5). Accompanying this melody is a relentless bass line that

Table 3.1 Raid Scene, Part One (Original Version)

Visual Cue	Measure Numbers	Musical Cue
Close-up shot of Pat, cutaway to McKay watching Terrill and his men ride away, expanding to include door closing as Pat leaves.	[Part 1] mm.1–16	"Deliberate" Descending minor second with syncopated accompaniment (in $\frac{3}{4}$).
McKay walks across the porch as he watches the Major and his men ride away.	mm.17–27	"Slow" Main title theme (in $\frac{4}{4}$).
[McKay]	mm.28–35	Secondary theme.
[McKay]	mm.36–39	"Meno Mosso" main theme returns.

reiterates the first portion of the syncopated rhythmic motive that characterizes the breakfast and this scene. Once the cue was completed Moross was required to go back and remove four measures of Pat's music, most likely due to an edit in the scene.

This new music, which solely underscores Pat's cutaway scenes, continues in collaboration with the main title theme that accompanies McKay. Moross

Figure 3.4 "The Raid," original version © 1958 (Renewed) CHAPPELL & CO., INC. All Rights Administered by STATE ONE MUSIC AMERICA. All Rights Reserved. Used by Permission.

Figure 3.5 "The Raid" Part One revised © 1958 (Renewed) CHAPPELL & CO., INC. All Rights Administered by STATE ONE MUSIC AMERICA. All Rights Reserved. Used by Permission.

adjusts these statements to match the new emotional climate rendered by Pat's music. The result is that Pat's aggression colors the music of the raiding party as it rides away, even while we hear the main title theme when viewing the situation from McKay's perspective. Whereas Moross originally conceived this theme as slower and altered a few notes, the revision warranted additional adjustments. Moross initially expands the theme from four measures to six by including an inversion in a higher tessitura (Figure 3.6, last two measures). This inversion changes the theme, infusing a heightened sense of tension especially

Table 3.2 Raid Scene, Part One (Final Version)

Visual Cue	Measure Numbers	Musical Cue
Close-up shot of Pat, cutaway to McKay watching Terrill and his men ride away, expanding to include door closing as Pat leaves.	Part 1: mm.1–16	"Deliberate" (in $\frac{3}{4}$) Descending minor second with syncopated accompaniment.
McKay walks across the porch as he watches the Major and his men ride away.	mm.17–22	"Slow" Main title theme accompanied by tremolo chords (in $\frac{4}{4}$).
Interior shot of Pat pulling clothes out of her closet and angrily kicking off her shoes.	mm.23–30	Pat's angry music, includes rhythm of raid accompaniment in the bass.
Shot of McKay on the porch, watching the Terrill men riding away in the distance.	mm.31–36	Main title accompanied by angry music and raid accompaniment.
Long shot of Pat walking out of the house, getting on her horse.	mm.37–43	Angry music with chords.
Cut to McKay standing on the porch still looking out, although the men are long gone.	mm.44–47	Main title with angry music; no inversion.
Long shot of Pat riding across the horizon.	mm.48–56	Angry music with chords; change in rhythm.
Pat gets off her horse and sits under a tree.	mm.57–64	Chords only.

Figure 3.6 "The Raid" Part One © 1958 (Renewed) CHAPPELL & CO., INC.
All Rights Administered by STATE ONE MUSIC AMERICA. All
Rights Reserved. Used by Permission.

highlighted by the extended phrase structure. As the scene continues, Moross continues to vary the main theme, but leaving out the inversion and adding a note at the end.

The final version of this cue establishes a clear contrast between McKay's personality and the Terrill's, especially demonstrated by their differing actions. While McKay stands on the porch watching what is happening around him, the Terrill's are all action: Pat gets dressed and goes riding while the Major and his men go after the Hannasseys. This is the first indication that McKay's character and temperament is significantly different from his fiancée, clearly foreshadowing the inevitable breakup. The changes in the music reflect their differing personalities and priorities. The result adheres to Copland's suggestion that the music express the unspoken thoughts of the characters, as it communicates the unequivocal difference between the couple.

Moross reprises Pat's angry music several times in the film, evoking Pat's unhappiness with McKay and her own situation. For instance, it returns in "McKay is Missing" (Figure 3.7), which accompanied the scene where Leech kisses Pat. The motive enters haltingly at first, and then gains momentum as the tension in the scene builds. This cue was cut from the film, possibly due to other editorial changes.[33] In "Night at Ladder Ranch" we hear the first interval (descending major third) briefly as Pat storms upstairs after McKay tells her he is moving into town so they can re-think their engagement. It returns a third time in a similar fashion in "Pat's Mistake," the cue that is played when Pat finds out that McKay has purchased Big Muddy for her as a wedding gift. Unfortunately, that portion of the cue was also cut from the final release of the film. Instead the editors replaced it with a slow, minor motive that reflects Pat's disappointment, but not her anger.

Figure 3.7 "McKay is Missing" © 1958 (Renewed) CHAPPELL & CO., INC. All Rights Administered by STATE ONE MUSIC AMERICA. All Rights Reserved. Used by Permission.

The Death of Buck Hannassey

Moross musically differentiates the Hannasseys and the Terrills early in the film, during the hazing scene. The dissonant chromatic line stated in the brass indicates a tense situation, but it is short-lived and neither McKay nor the music takes it seriously. The subsequent cues associated with the Hannasseys are similarly dissonant and harsh, particularly those in the latter half of the film, when the Hannasseys kidnap Julie Maragon. Generally, this group of cues features syncopated seventh chords supporting a series of reiterated descending/ascending seconds, as well as the ascending chromatic line from the hazing scene at the beginning. The music that accompanies the attempted rape (which occurs while Julie is held captive) features completely new music that is even more dissonant. The ascending chromatic material from the hazing returns in the scene where McKay and Buck duel, representing the antagonism between the two men. In this instance the tempo is slowed and the original melodic line is fragmented and repeated as the tension mounts. All of the music associated with these scenes feature strident orchestration, chromatic melodic motion, and dissonance; a sharp contrast from the consonant melodies associated with the more affluent and refined characters, the Terrills and Julie Maragon.

In addition to musically differentiating the two sets of protagonists, Moross often reiterates specific melodic materials, not as themes representing specific characters, but rather to recall previous action and the subtext associated with it. While Moross doesn't assign specific themes to specific characters, he does recall music associated with particular narrative aspects of the film. For instance, the music of the hazing is recalled as the Terrills capture the Hannasseys prior to beating them up in the barn. Similarly, the music of the raid is heard during the final ambush in Blanco Canyon, recalling the general antagonism between the two families. This recycling of musical material is evident throughout the score, but with particular significance during the death of Buck.

The death of Buck Hannassey, with its poignant and stirring music, brings to the forefront the tragedy of the violence that permeates this film. That his father shoots Buck makes the scene particularly significant. The cue for the death of Buck consists of music heard previously in different contexts although most of it is re-cast in keeping with the tragic nature of the scene (Table 3.3). By recycling this music, Moross establishes continuity in the narrative as he refers back to previous scenes and comments on this tragedy through the changes he makes in the music.

The cue starts with an altered version of the music that was to accompany the scene with the deceptively wild horse, Old Thunder.[34] Instead of D major, we hear it in C-sharp minor, in a slower tempo, played by the trumpets as a dirge (in the earlier cue it was played by the strings). Moross also changes the rhythm from $\frac{6}{8}$ to $\frac{4}{4}$, which emphasizes the dirge-like quality (compare Figures 3.8 and 3.9). The Old Thunder theme recalls how McKay faced that challenge and subdued the horse. In this case, he has subdued, or rather embarrassed, Buck.

Table 3.3 The Death of Buck Hannassey

Visual Cue	Measure Numbers	Musical Cue
McKay throws down his gun. Rufus jumps from the wagon and approaches Buck, then spits on him.	mm.1–9	"Old Thunder" recast in minor mode, played by the brass. (Figure 3.9)
Buck comes out from under the wagon, wrestles the gun away from a bystander. Rufus shoots him, and Buck falls into the water trough.	mm.10–18	Motive from "The Attempted Rape" (Figure 3.10)
Buck drops his gun in the water, Rufus gradually approaches, Buck moves toward Rufus on his knees. Rufus says "I told you. . ."	mm.19–26	Sustained chords. (Figure 3.11) Ends with G.P. [This is where it stops in the film.]
Buck utters a final, "Pa" and dies. Rufus holds him, while McKay, Julie, and Ramone get on their horses and ride away.	mm.27–42	Pat's angry music, stated slowly and fragmented. (Figure 3.12)

Figure 3.8 "Old Thunder" © 1958 (Renewed) CHAPPELL & CO., INC. All Rights Administered by STATE ONE MUSIC AMERICA. All Rights Reserved. Used by Permission.

As Buck struggles for the gun, the reprise of the music from the attempted rape reminds the audience of his violent nature as it was demonstrated in that scene. It also recalls the tussle with his father. When this music was heard previously, his father told him, "Someday I may have to kill you." Here that comment comes to mind unbidden when we hear the same music. This particular melodic material, which is unique to the attempted rape and Buck's death, features a three-chord motive (Figure 3.10). The chords repeat, as they had during the attempted rape, with a final statement rhythmically augmented at the end of this section, heard as Buck collapses.

It is in this ten-measure phrase (Figure 3.10) and the subsequent phrase (Figure 3.11) where we experience the stylistic influence of Charles Ives's music on Moross. Only fifteen years old when he first encountered Ives through Henry Cowell, Moross often spoke of how he championed his works, specifically the

Figure 3.9 "The Death of Buck Hannassey" © 1958 (Renewed) CHAPPELL & CO., INC. All Rights Administered by STATE ONE MUSIC AMERICA. All Rights Reserved. Used by Permission.

Figure 3.10 Motive from "The Attempted Rape" as heard in "The Death of Buck Hannassey" © 1958 (Renewed) CHAPPELL & CO., INC. All Rights Administered by STATE ONE MUSIC AMERICA. All Rights Reserved. Used by Permission.

114 Songs, to Copland, and others. Moross also recalled that he gave the first performance of Ives on the radio and that he spent considerable time studying the piano sonatas as well as the songs. The ambiguous tonal center communicated by the reiterated triads in the first four measures of Figure 3.10 and the sustained seventh chords in Figure 3.11 are reminiscent of Ives's style. The music that accompanies Rufus and Buck as they approach each other is even harsher and amplifies the horror and anguish that Rufus feels when he realizes what he has done (Figure 3.11).

Figure 3.11 "The Death of Buck Hannassey" © 1958 (Renewed) CHAPPELL & CO., INC. All Rights Administered by STATE ONE MUSIC AMERICA. All Rights Reserved. Used by Permission.

As Rufus holds the dead Buck, the music continues with a funereal dirge (Figure 3.12). Starting with a gong (rarely heard in this score) and building in intensity, it is a recasting of Pat's "angry" music from the raid scene (Figure 3.5). The melodic line is stated slowly and accompanied by a reiterated motive in the brass that heightens the tragic atmosphere.

This thematic material was also included in the cue "Pat's Mistake" (referenced earlier and shown in Figure 3.13) when Julie tells Pat that McKay has bought Big Muddy for her as a wedding gift. Although the melodic motive in this instance is essentially the same as "Pat's Mistake," it is re-orchestrated to fit the tragic setting and altered by the rhythm in the accompaniment, which gives the scene a sense of finality. The music composed by Moross for this part of the scene contains all of the emotions: the horror, the relief, the tragedy, and the eventuality of this moment.

That Moross would link Pat's motive with Buck's death invites speculation. The intent may have been to link the two important characters with one narrative theme: Pat's and Buck's relationships with their fathers. Both these characters seek parental approval by participating in the pursuit to obtain Big Muddy, and by their actions both encourage the feud between the two families. Eventually neither succeeds, and although Pat does not die, she does not reappear after her breakup with McKay. The subtle manner in which Moross brings out this narrative connection speaks to his concern for molding the drama through the music, another of Copland's objectives.

The section of Moross's cue that features Pat's music was cut in the final release of the film. In the film the music fades away when Rufus says "I told you! I told you I'd do it. I told you, but you wouldn't believe me, damn your soul," and there is silence as McKay, Julie, and Ramone get on their horses and ride away. The editors may have wanted to ensure that this line be heard and also

Figure 3.12 "The Death of Buck Hannassey" © 1958 (Renewed) CHAPPELL
& CO., INC. All Rights Administered by STATE ONE MUSIC
AMERICA. All Rights Reserved. Used by Permission.

Figure 3.12 Continued

Figure 3.13 "Pat's Mistake" © 1958 (Renewed) CHAPPELL & CO., INC. All Rights Administered by STATE ONE MUSIC AMERICA. All Rights Reserved. Used by Permission.

provide a solemn silence. However, the sketch includes a pause ("G.P." grosse pause), so that the music could resume after Rufus's statement (and after Buck has breathed his last).

Significantly, this same musical material was also cut from Pat's scene (discussed previously). That the editors would remove both of these instances of tragic music suggests that they did not like the overall affect the music conveyed. Perhaps it was too loud or considered distracting. Moross admitted to being present at the dubbing of *The Big Country*, so he would have been aware of these editorial changes. He later defended the role of the editors, however, stating that they knew what they were doing, so he would not argue with them if they cut his music. He had faith in their expertise and felt that they edited the film with the best intentions, independent of their egos.

The Fight

Earlier in the film Pat's angry music is heard as a transition from the scene where she and McKay argue, to the fight between McKay and Leech. It features only the opening descending major third, but it is enough to aurally reinforce Pat's unhappiness. It also sets up the emotional stage for the upcoming scuffle.

McKay refuses to fight during the entire film, no matter how much he is antagonized by Leech. However, after the argument with Pat, in the middle of the night, he knocks on Leech's door, wakes him up and challenges him to a fight where no one will see them; not Leech's preference, since he craves witnesses. Filmed in the middle of a large open field in the dark (perhaps just prior to dawn or just after sunset, judging by the faint light that illuminates the horizon), the scene was conceived so that nature overpowers the men, dwarfing them and their insignificant violent interactions. As Wyler later commented, "The fight between Gregory Peck and Charlton Heston, I thought was much more meaningful precisely because we staged it on a huge plain. . . . This composition emphasized the futility of two men throwing fists at one another in this vast open country."[35]

Moross complements Wyler's cinematic intention through the placement of the cue, as well as its content. He enhances the psychological weight of this scene by withholding the music until the very last part of the scene, where it enters very quietly and subtly. This is very unlike fight music from previous westerns, which typically tends to be loud and dissonant. This cue almost anticipates the style of Ennio Morricone (as exemplified in the spaghetti westerns) with its subtle and sparse texture. From the time that Leech and McKay walk out onto the field until the music starts is over three minutes. Moross's decision to begin the music well into the scene was probably guided by a desire not to overwhelm the scene, or the scenery, with music. It keeps the scene realistic, keeping the music out of most of the scene so we could hear them breathing and gasping for air, as well as the punches.

The music sneaks in, almost unheard, and it is also incredibly simple: a descending melodic line in the low strings and low brass, based on a syncopated rhythmic pattern. The melody outlines two descending fourths: F to C, and B to F-sharp (Figure 3.14). This gesture is expanded harmonically as the fight continues, with the juxtaposition of the chords F major and B major (Figure 3.15). Significantly a tritone apart, the interval may be a reference to the "diabolus in music" as a representation of the discord between McKay and Leech; no two men could be further apart ideologically.

When the fighting ends (as McKay queries, "Tell me Leech, what have we proved?"), Moross recalls the hymn-like chords from the previous scene ("Night at Ladder Ranch") when McKay makes up his mind to confront Leech alone, with no onlookers (Figure 3.16). While the previous phrase consisted of only two major chords, in this passage the harmonic progression is expanded, notably encompassing all major chords, primarily centered in F major. The six short phrases (two measures each) may be analyzed thus:

a)   VI–V–I–II
b)   VI–V–I–II–VI–I
c)   II–I–IV–V
d)   II–I–IV–V–II–IV.

Table 3.4 The Fight[36]

Timing	Visual Cue	Measure Number	Musical Cue
1:33:42	Long shot of McKay and Leech walking onto field.	The first minute consists of the two men walking out into the middle of the prairie, and then circling one another, not throwing a punch until almost a full minute later (at 1:34:28).	No music
1:33:56	Medium shot of McKay and Leech, followed by medium shots of the two men fighting; each shot averages 10 seconds.		
1:35:17	Change in perspective, so the house is behind them.		
1:35:25	Dissolve to a different perspective, with the open fields behind them. The dissolve gives the impression that a certain amount of time has passed.		
1:36:53	Leech slowly stands and says "Come on."	mm.1–31	Figures 3.14 and 3.15
1:38:10	Finished fighting, and stand up.	mm.32–44	Figure 3.16 (from "Night at Ladder Ranch" and "Night in Blanco Canyon")
1:38:47	Dissolve to house.	mm.44–52	Variant of main title. Cut in the film release to four measures.
1:39:02	Dissolve to next morning and McKay being driven out of the ranch.	mm.53–56	Phrase from "Courtin' Time"
1:39:06	Dissolve to Leech and Terrill men sitting under trees.	mm.57–65	Figure 3.14
1:39:34	"They're getting near the river, Steve."		Music stops

The same progression in B-flat:

e) II–I–IV–V–I–IV
f) V–IV–VII–I–IV–II (V in F), then resolves on F.

Figure 3.14 "The Fight" © 1958 (Renewed) CHAPPELL & CO., INC. All Rights Administered by STATE ONE MUSIC AMERICA. All Rights Reserved. Used by Permission.

Figure 3.15 "The Fight" © 1958 (Renewed) CHAPPELL & CO., INC. All Rights Administered by STATE ONE MUSIC AMERICA. All Rights Reserved. Used by Permission.

Thus, Moross connects the two scenes, much as he had previously connected the breakfast scene with the raid, both musically and psychologically. Ending the scene with the same musical material that preceded the fight enhances the sense of dramatic closure and illustrates Moross's viewpoint that "music can give the scene a sense of form and of unity."[37] The closure of the narrative (Leech finally gets the fight he has been asking for) is reflected in the music. Significantly, in the previous cue, "Night at Ladder Ranch," Moross ends the phrase on the C major chord and avoids the sense of closure provided by the F major chord, finally present in this second hearing.

The fight music (Figure 3.14) is recapitulated as the scene changes to the next morning and we see a bruised Leech sitting under a tree with the other Terrill men. It is also heard briefly at the beginning of the scene that portrays Major Terrill ready to ride into Blanco Canyon for the final showdown. Leech initially rebels, refusing to enter into the canyon to avoid potential bloodshed, emulating some of the strength and courage he has observed in McKay.

It is recalled once again in the final scene, as "The Stalking" when Rufus Hannassey and Major Terrill shoot each other. However, Moross changes the music so the motive increases in intensity and dynamics as the men approach each other and the tension builds. The face off between the Major and Rufus parallels the confrontation between McKay and Leech, except this time with a more tragic conclusion.

Figure 3.16 "The Fight" © 1958 (Renewed) CHAPPELL & CO., INC. All Rights Administered by STATE ONE MUSIC AMERICA. All Rights Reserved. Used by Permission.

Conclusion

These cues exemplify how Moross composed music not for individual character representation, but more for atmosphere and situation, while expressing the unspoken emotions. These are standards that Copland set as well in his film scores, and may have passed along to Moross while they worked together in Hollywood. Moross's interactions with Copland's Young Composers' Group also influenced his compositional style, particularly their shared search for establishing an American sound that could differentiate their music from the predominant European approach.

While taking the western film score in a different direction, Moross's music draws the audience into the story, engaging their attention with vibrant orchestration and lucid formal structures not previously seen realized so completely in the western genre. He felt strongly that a solid musical structure could enhance the dramatic action, which is why many of his film scores are able to stand alone, without the visual, and his soundtracks continue to sell.

Moross was often asked about this score, since it is probably the best known of his compositions. With great humility, he usually responded that he did it in his own style, "Style is something so deep in you that it exists in what you write without your really thinking about it and it varies and alters according to the needs of the moment."[38] Nothing about this composition was artificial or imitation. As Moross explained, "I was surrounded all my life by American music and American folk music . . . I found myself writing themes that used the intervals and the rhythms . . . that I was surrounded by. They became part of me, they're part of my style, I don't have to think about it, it's there."[39] Moross concluded, "my own style is American, unconsciously American, I just write that way."[40]

Notes

1 Jerome Moross, interview by Andy Trudeau, tape recording. Although the identity of the interviewer is not acknowledged on the recording, the content is the same as that identified by Charles Turner as an interview dated September 1975. See Charles Turner, "Jerome Moross: An Introduction and Annotated Worklist," *Notes*, 61, 3 (2005), 659–727. This statement is reiterated in various ways in several interviews Moross granted later in his life. I am indebted to William Rosar for graciously sharing these recordings with me.

2 For an analysis of Copland's development of a pastoral mode which would become influential on composers of western film scores, see Neil Lerner, "Copland's Music of Wide Open Spaces: Surveying the Pastoral Trope in Hollywood" *The Musical Quarterly* 85, 3 (2001), 477–515.

3 Jerome Moross, interview by Craig Reardon, tape recording. Identified by Turner (in *Notes*, op. cit.) as dating from April 16, 1979.

4 Quoted in Howard Pollack, *Aaron Copland: The Life and Work of an Uncommon Man* (New York: Henry Holt, 1999), 186.

5 Aaron Copland, *Copland on Music* (Garden City, NY: Doubleday 1960), 159.

6 Ibid., 161.

7 Jerome Moross, interview by Craig Reardon.

8 Pollack, 188. Moross and Copland both maintained primary residences in New York City and only stayed in Hollywood while working on film scores.

9 Aaron Copland to Jerome Moross, October 12, 1942, Jerome Moross Papers, Rare Book & Manuscript Library, Columbia University.

10 Aaron Copland to Jerome Moross, November 7, 1944, Jerome Moross Papers.

11 Jerome Moross to Aaron Copland, November 16, 1942, Jerome Moross Papers.

12 "I am happy to admit that Copland has been an influence on my work, especially with the score for *Best Years*. . . . His influence helped me weed out the run-of-the-mill schmaltz and aim to do more straightforward and simple, even folklike scoring." Friedhofer quoted in Fred Karlin, *Listening to Movies: The Film Lover's Guide to Film Music* (New York: Schirmer Books, 1994), 273.

13 Jerome Moross, interview by Craig Reardon.

14 Colin Roust, "The Continental: Georges Auric and Hollywood," paper presented at the annual meeting of the Society for American Music, Denver, March 2009, 5.

15 Pollack, 428.

16 Aaron Copland to Tom Andre (*The Big Country* Production Manager) June 14, 1957, Gregory Peck Papers, Margaret Herrick Library, Academy of Motion Picture Arts and Sciences.

17 Aaron Copland to Tom Andre, July 27, 1957, Gregory Peck Papers.

18 Gregory Peck Papers. This is only a partial listing of the composers considered.

19 Jerome Moross to his wife, undated, Jerome Moross Papers.

20 Jerome Moross to his wife, undated, Jerome Moross Papers.

21 In one interview Moross describes how Wyler sent a disparaging telegram criticizing the main title cue, which almost caused the composer to quit.

22 Christopher Palmer very aptly used this word to describe the first few measures of the main title theme in *The Composer in Hollywood* (London: Marion Boyars Publishers, 1990), 314.

23 For evidence that substantiates Moross's observation, see Ildar Khannanov, "*High Noon*: Dimitri Tiomkin's Oscar-Winning Ballad and its Russian Sources," *Journal of Film Music*, 2, 2–4 (2009), 225.

24 Jerome Moross interview by Mike Snell, February 4, 1978. Transcript located in the Jerome Moross Papers.

25 Jerome Moross interview by John Caps, August 31, 1971. Tape recording.

26 Lerner, op. cit.

27 Palmer, 312.

28 Aaron Copland, *What to Listen for in Music* (New York: McGraw-Hill, 1957), 154–155.

29 The cue titles (always in quotation marks) are those given by Moross on the original sketches and scores.

30 As William Rosar notes in his excellent commentary to the laserdisc release of the film (*The Big Country*, 166 min., Image Entertainment, 1996, laserdisc), every cue (but one) is built on an ostinato. Lerner refers to a "dronelike pedal" in "The Wood at Night" cue in Copland's score for *Of Mice and Men* (Lerner, 491).

31 Final screenplay, dated August 14, 1957 by Robert Wilder. William Wyler Papers, Performing Arts Special Collections, University of California, Los Angeles. An additional copy of this screenplay is also in the Gregory Peck Papers.

32 The initial version may not have included the trip to the Hannassey ranch and the music was used to accompany the ride to San Rafael. Donald Hamilton's original short story, the basis of the screenplay, does not include the trashing of the Hannassey homestead and the original rough cut may have followed that story line. Despite Gregory Peck's strong suggestion that the shots of Pat be cut from the film, Wyler's decision to leave them in points to their importance in the development of the plot.

33 The cue is several measures too long for this scene, suggesting that something may have been cut at the beginning of the scene. The music capably reflects the mounting tension, the kiss, and Pat's frustration at the end.

34 Moross's original cue is included in the soundtrack, however, in the film it was replaced with canned music.

35 Quoted in Gabriel Miller, ed. *William Wyler Interviews* (Jackson, MS: University Press of Mississippi, 2009), 74. Wyler directed other scenes similarly, so that the environment looms large over the actions of men. All of the shots that constitute the two forays into Blanco Canyon, for example, are viewed from above, making the men look especially small and insignificant.

36 Timings taken from *The Big Country*, prod. and dir. William Wyler, 166 min., United Artists 1958, DVD.

37 Jerome Moross interview by John Caps.
38 Ibid.
39 Ibid.
40 Jerome Moross, interview by Andy Trudeau.

Chapter 4

Silencing the Truth

Music and Identity
in *The Unforgiven*

Ben Winters

> For Huston . . . confronting and remaining faithful to truth is at the center of heroism.
>
> (Lesley Brill)[1]

> Some of my pictures I don't care for, but *The Unforgiven* is the only one I actually dislike.
>
> (John Huston)[2]

The Unforgiven (1960, not to be confused with Clint Eastwood's 1992 Oscar-winner, *Unforgiven*) is a film seldom encountered in studies of the western. Starring Burt Lancaster and Audrey Hepburn, and based on an Alan LeMay novel about an Indian girl raised by white Texans, its similarity to that other more celebrated LeMay adaptation, *The Searchers* (1956), has ensured that it remains the poor cousin of a film almost universally acknowledged as one of the great examples of the genre. Where *The Searchers* concentrated on a pair of white men searching for a girl kidnapped by the Comanches, *The Unforgiven* suggests a captivity tale in reverse, and in so doing emphasizes the racism of white settlers. Thus, in the context of the growing civil rights movement, Christopher Sharrett has suggested that the film offers "a remarkably pointed attack on the racism of frontier America, and by extension of bourgeois white society."[3]

Rachel (Audrey Hepburn) is a foundling raised by Will and Matthilde Zachary (Lilian Gish) in 1870s frontier Texas, and the adopted sister of three brothers, Cash (Audie Murphy), Andy (Doug McClure), and Ben (Burt Lancaster). Now long after the murder of Will Zachary by Kiowa Indians, it is a period of peace, and Ben and his brothers are part of a lucrative cattle business with their neighbor, Zeb Rawlins (Charles Bickford), employing the likes of Indian horse-tamer Johnny Portugal (John Saxon). The peace is shattered, however, when Abe Kelsey (Joseph Wiseman) appears, sowing discontent between the two families by claiming that Rachel is Kiowa born. While some aspects of his tale appear suspicious, it soon transpires that he speaks the truth. Rachel's real Kiowa brother, Lost Bird, comes to claim back his sister, and although abandoned by Rawlins and a confused Cash, Ben and Andy defend their adopted sister in a climactic shoot-out. Matthilde is killed, Cash returns at the crucial hour, and Rachel shoots Lost Bird to finally reject her Indian identity. The film ends (ostensibly) with the promise of Rachel's marriage to her adoptive brother, Ben. The film hinges, then, on Rachel's identity and the casual racism of a community fearful of Kiowa reprisals, a racism that in its suspicion of any Indian blood (such as the character of Johnny Portugal) is similar to Ethan's in *The Searchers*. Yet, while *The Searchers* is primarily concerned with one character grappling with his own racism, *The Unforgiven* depends on the idea of a community's reaction to a hidden threat.[4] As a result, Rachel's safety relies on the keeping of a secret, and the efforts of others to expose the truth.

As director John Huston's quotation above reveals, he was dissatisfied with the final film, feeling that the producers' attempts to artificially emphasize the action scenes undermined his vision of a racially complex drama.[5] This adds to the notoriety of a troubled production in which Audrey Hepburn fractured a vertebra falling off her horse and co-star Audie Murphy nearly drowned.[6] As Edward Buscombe points out, seemingly agreeing with Huston, the film's treatment of the Kiowas does appear to undo much of the complex racial discourse that is suggested by the community's reaction to the truth:

> the film is not nearly so liberal as it thinks it is. Though it condemns the racism of the whites, the Indians are not an alternative culture but a totally alien "other". Hepburn may in a moment of anger assert her Indian identity by smearing paint on her face, but there's never any real doubt she will choose to stay with her adopted family.[7]

But while the film's apparent soft-pedaling of contemporary racial issues might partly account for the lack of scholarly attention among film studies scholars, such socio-political concerns have not always affected the reception of a film's score. Yet *The Unforgiven* is also rarely singled out amongst score composer Dimitri Tiomkin's impressive list of films, and is certainly not ranked alongside his music for the Westerns *Red River* (1948) or *Duel in the Sun* (1946) by the composer's biographer, Christopher Palmer.[8] We have, then, a film that the director seemed to disown, and that is largely ignored in studies of the film's composer. This presents us with an intriguing prospect: could the two facts possibly be linked? Might we even trace part of Huston's dislike to the way in which the film engages with its music?

Music can be said to play an important role in articulating the conflict surrounding Rachel's identity in *The Unforgiven*. Although there are also commercial pressures on Tiomkin at play here that deserve exploration, and which required Rachel's theme to form the basis of a hit song, I will look within the film to explain the music. In other words, I see the music's content shaped not by a narrator figure commentating on the story from a position of omniscience, but by the motivations and actions of the characters within the narrative.[9] And while we might imagine music to be on the side of truth, it actually deceives more than it enlightens, especially when shaped by Rachel's adoptive mother, Matthilde.[10] After examining the film's repeated references to truth and lies, then, I shall explore the way in which Rachel's conflicted identity is whitewashed by her musical theme. It is this that I contend may be partly to blame for Huston's dislike of the film. Of related interest is the way in which Matthilde engages with an on-screen piano (a plot detail curiously absent from LeMay's novel). In diegetic performances of two Mozart fantasias, and a rendition of "Turkey in the Straw," Matthilde reveals her role as chief conspirator in manipulating the film's music, and silencing the truth.

Huston and the Truth

Truth and lies inform much of the dialogue in *The Unforgiven*. Characters are constantly invoking the truth, whether in casual throwaway phrases ("truth be told," "tell the truth, I don't recall," "It's true. I kissed her!"), or in more meaningful statements: "You tell Zeb we don't see eye to eye. And that's the truth" (Ben to Cash); "You run from the truth" (Abe Kelsey to Ben); "I am the sword of God—the fire and the vengeance, whereby the wrong shall be righted and the truth be told" (Kelsey to Rachel). Similarly, the veracity of Rachel's identity is at the core of the film, and the need to establish the truth of her parentage is of importance not for the character herself but also for her family, who must defend her from the fears and racism of the wider community. The link Lesley Brill observes in Huston's films between heroism and truth, then, is certainly germane to *The Unforgiven*; however, the syllogism that assumes Huston's heroes tell the truth is not necessarily the case in this instance. Some of the characters, such as Abe Kelsey or Zeb Rawlins, are at once the guardians or seekers of truth, and the enemy; others, notably Matthilde or Cash, are our notional heroes, yet try to deny the truth out of maternal or fraternal love. Moreover, few of the characters' motives are unproblematic. Zeb Rawlins wants an explanation for the death of his son, seemingly killed by the Kiowas for his romantic attachment to Rachel; but his wife, Hagar Rawlins (June Walker), is also motivated by an intense racial hatred. Abe Kelsey wants revenge for his kidnapped son, for whose safe return Will Zachary refused to swap Rachel; Matthilde's actions in taking in Rachel as a foundling, and keeping her identity a secret, are complicated by her grief at her own baby's death. Although our hero Ben Zachary challenges the stories offered him by both Kelsey and Matthilde, he does not so much confront the truth of Rachel's identity as run from it, threatening to fight all those who even question him. Rachel's identity has long been built on a lie, and Ben merely replaces it at the end of the film with another falsehood: that Rachel's conflicting roles of sister and Kiowa foundling can be successfully erased through their marriage. As Armando José Prats points out, this ending evades the issue of Rachel's race: Ben abrogates it, erasing her racial identity for the sake of possessing her sexually—a romantic pairing that Arthur M. Eckstein argues is motivated by the need to fulfill the thrill of two psychosociological taboos: that of miscegenation and incest.[11] In Rachel, we end up with someone who is neither white nor Kiowa, but American, and whose racial identity for Ben becomes secondary to her status as an object for sexual exchange. For Prats (and, one suspects, for Huston), this results in a film that, in offering a resolution based on the romantic attraction between hero and heroine, deflects the complex racial problems it raises, and suggests a country all too keen to forget its past.[12] Although supposedly the hero of the film, then, Ben is at once both as duplicitous and as truthful as any of the film's many antagonists.

Rachel, on the other hand, is kept largely in the dark about matters, and seemingly has no control over her destiny. Her confusion is even more acute in LeMay's novel, since her adoption (never mind her race) is itself a surprise to her. Moreover, it falls to Georgia Rawlins to tell her that she is not a Zachary.[13] Matthilde initially refuses to confirm the fact, preferring to remain silent, but when specifically asked by Rachel she is less than honest:

> [Matthilde] was tempted to invent an elaborate story, giving Rachel an inspiring family history and a romantic orphaning. She would have done it, too, had she not known perfectly well that she would be tripped up by it, soon or late. She compromised by telling part of the truth . . . it came out a whole lot more lie than truth, before she wiggled out of it, perhaps because so little truth was known.[14]

On several occasions Matthilde has the opportunity to reveal the whole truth, but crucially the novel never settles Rachel's identity conclusively: Matthilde dies in the battle, and Ben burns the Kiowa parchment that contains the definitive answer. The community rallies round, and Rachel is idolized. In the film version, however, we witness the Zacharys reading the parchment, and are left in no doubt that Rachel is who Kelsey says she is. The film finishes with the surviving Zacharys alone.

Rachel's identity (as daughter/sister, as lost Kiowa child, as sexualized exotic Indian) is not something we learn about, then, primarily through her agency in the narrative, since it is imposed on her by the pronouncements and actions of the other characters. Nor are we given much insight into the turmoil of her position, and the agony she suffers in shooting her real brother, Lost Bird, is glossed over surprisingly quickly.[15] Only in one sequence do we witness her distress, when she confronts her true identity in the mirror (the scene to which Buscombe refers). Yet, even that is carried out mostly behind closed doors: she emerges with her hair in plaits and a streak of war paint across her forehead, ready to go back to her people. Although Buscombe claims that the decision to remain with her white family is her choice, it is a choice imposed on her, since Rachel's only viable option is marriage to Ben. The alternatives are an embracing of a Kiowa identity of which she is almost fully ignorant, or a life as a Wichita prostitute. Her anguish about the truth of her identity seems real enough ("when Mama told the truth this morning I wanted to die"), but she is soothed by Ben, who intones softly: "Little Injun. Little redhide Injun." His words are accompanied by her musical theme, which seems to erase her identity as threatening racial other, and replace it with the kind of sanitized and eroticized fantasy of the exotic that Prats suggests. It is this musical white-washing of her character—carried out by Ben but instigated by Matthilde—that may partly explain Huston's dislike of the film.

Rachel's Theme

Following the first audible moments of the film, the howling of the wind—which brings to mind the description in the early pages of the novel that "mostly it just blew, hard and monotonously, hour after hour, day in and day out, until silence became unrememberable"[16]—we hear Rachel's theme in the underscore. Full of reverberation, and recorded in Rome by the Santa Cecilia Orchestra, the music suggests the wide open spaces of the American West; yet, Rachel's theme sounds curiously familiar, and distinctively European. Tiomkin had spent time in Berlin in the early 1920s and had written a number of popular songs, many of which resurfaced in later films, including two for *The Guns of Navarone* (1961) that sound like they could almost have been written by Kurt Weill. In this light, Rachel's theme sounds rather like a pastiche of the "Moritat von Mackie Messer" ("Mack the Knife") from Weill's *Die Dreigroschenoper* (*The Threepenny Opera*). Both feature similar repetitive melodic and rhythmic contours, and share certain interval classes (such as the falling seventh). Rachel's theme is detailed in Figure 4.1 in the version most comparable to Weill's song (there are several rhythmic variants). Since Weill's stage work was not produced in Berlin until 1928, the connection is presumably accidental, but in any case the tune proved amenable to being turned into a sentimental popular song, with a lyric by Ned Washington entitled "The Need for Love":

> The Need for Love is a need fundamental
> The human heart has to know someone cares
> The need for love that is tender and gentle
> Is more important than worldly affairs
> And to the ones who are still unforgiven
> Love is a food and they need every crumb
> A thing that's treasured
> That can't be measured
> By any scale or rule of thumb
> Sometimes, hearts are driven
> Into their own little shell
> All the unforgiven and those who have loved too well
> My need for you will continue
> As long as there is a star, or a sky up above
> There is no force in the world that's as strong as
> The need for love
> The need for love
> The need for love

Figure 4.1 Rachel's Theme

Figure 4.2 "The Need for Love"

Following the success that United Artists had enjoyed with Tiomkin's "Do Not Forsake Me, Oh My Darlin'" from *High Noon* (1952), the studio appears to have encouraged this kind of title song to gain added revenues for a film. As Jeff Smith reveals, the Tex Ritter version of "Do Not Forsake Me" was followed by versions by Frankie Laine, Billy Keith, Lita Rose, Bill Hayes, and Fred Waring, and United Artists used the song as part of its promotional campaign abroad. Similarly, Tiomkin's song "The Green Leaves of Summer" from *The Alamo* (1960) was recorded in seventeen different versions within a year of the film's release. Clearly, as Smith notes, Tiomkin was the "undisputed master" of this technique, and "The Need for Love" can be seen as another example of the practice (see Figure 4.2).[17]

It seems probable, then, that Rachel's theme was not intended to accurately reflect her character's changing self-awareness, but rather was conceived as advertising for the Tiomkin/Washington song with which it shares its tune. As it happens, though, "The Need for Love" seems to have had relatively limited success: a version by the McGuire Sisters peaked at number 41 in the week of May 6 to May 13 1960 in KRLA's top 40, though a Don Costa instrumental version went as high as number 10 in the week of June 24 to July 1 and reached number 7 in KFWB's charts in the same week.[18] The fact that the famous Ella Fitzgerald version of "Mack the Knife" had also been in the charts in late April was, perhaps, coincidental—although the possibility remains that the song's popularity influenced Tiomkin's choice of a similar-sounding theme.

Leaving aside its ubiquity for the purpose of selling records, however, Rachel's theme within the text of the film is unsettling. What rankles, and what may have contributed to Huston's dislike of the final film, is that Rachel's theme remains essentially unchanged from beginning to end. It does not grow with her newfound self-knowledge, and therefore adds to the impression that her identity is essentially constructed, and imposed on her, by others. That her theme should be unchanged at the end of the film might suggest simultaneously that her journey of racial discovery has been whitewashed in favor of this rather bland and inoffensive melody,[19] and (more disturbingly even) that Ben's view of his adopted sister as a sexual object has always been thus. In short, Rachel's theme does not confront or remain faithful to the truth of her identity in the manner that she, herself, attempts. She is thus essentially powerless to control her own music.

Rachel's theme, in fact, is surely created by Matthilde's idealized view of her adopted daughter. As the novel relates, when asked to tell the truth, Matthilde informs Rachel that she was a white baby: "Matthilde stated it as a simple fact, because that was what it was to her, and always been; for she had wanted it to be that way."[20] In the film—when faced with the Kiowa chronicle that documents Rachel's birth and capture, and forced to tell her story of the baby's origins—Matthilde induces a version of Rachel's theme in the underscore, rather like an unreliable Wagnerian narrator using music to help persuade others of her position. Although she grudgingly admits that Rachel is Kiowa, it is clear she has always regarded her as white. Indeed, Matthilde's tendency to whitewash questions of race may also reflect the cultural consciousness of the late 1950s in its increasingly conflicted attitude toward race relations. We therefore hear Rachel's theme as the audible force of Matthilde's conviction; Rachel is white because the music says so, and it is a conviction that survives Matthilde's death to resurface at the film's end. For all the truth that Abe Kelsey brings, the survival of Rachel's theme represents the survival of Matthilde's lies, and the unwillingness of the Zacharys to deal with the truth.

Such is Matthilde's power over the music that it shapes the underscore even when she is not present. When Lost Bird asks for the return of his sister, for example, Ben refuses, restating the lie of Rachel's identity ("the woman in my house is white"). The confrontation also extends to the score, however, over which Ben and Lost Bird apparently vie for control. Ben invokes Rachel's theme as a musical display of resistance and refusal to accept the truth—his view of Rachel still shaped by his mother's lies. Lost Bird's own theme, however, is stereotypically Indian, according to those codes identified by Claudia Gorbman, and consists of falling thirds, the first note of which is strongly accented.[21] As such, it too might be believably heard as the product of the Kiowa-fearing Matthilde, although she is not present in the scene. Similarly, when Rachel, grappling with the truth of her identity, smears a line of war paint across her forehead, it is Matthilde's auditory view of Indians we hear in the score (complete with stereotypical tom-toms and parallel fourths)—see Figure 4.3. Rachel is hearing her own identity through the prejudices of her mother, and is scared as much by the otherness she *hears* as by that which she *sees*.

Matthilde's musical power over the underscore is likewise reflected in her actual abilities as a performer. The Kiowas' own diegetic flute music, to which (as Ben informs us) they ascribe magical properties that will make them bullet-proof, prompts Matthilde to respond with some sorcery of her own: in a climactic scene, she plays Mozart's *Fantasia in C minor* K. 475 on the piano that Ben had brought back from Wichita. It has its desired effect, and the flutes fall silent. When the Kiowas attack in the next scene, it is the piano they destroy first, lancing it with their spears, in a display of cultural confusion (see

Figure 4.3 Rachel confronts her identity

Figure 4.4). Indeed, the piano's role in the film functions as a symbol for white society. For Rachel, significantly, it is a wondrous thing, and when Ben brings it back from Wichita at the start of the film, her unfamiliarity with it as a cultural object is such that she tentatively twangs its strings, prompting Matthilde to exclaim: "Why, you're playing the wrong end, daughter!" This adds to our suspicions that Rachel is not the white girl her family claim her to be: after all, she also rides her horse bareback, and has to be cajoled into accepting her duties inside the domestic space of the soddy.[22] These somewhat clumsy signs of her racial otherness are concentrated symbolically in the piano, and Rachel's cultural confusion about its role and function anticipates that of her Kiowa brethren.

The piano's presence in the story and its use to ward off the Kiowas is entirely the invention of screenwriter Ben Maddow. There is no mention of it in LeMay's novel, but it may well have been inspired by this passage after Matthilde's death: "Now the drums built up to one more climax, and did not start again. They left a silence that rang in the ears. Andy said wonderingly, 'why it's just as if Mamma has gone out there, and stopped them some way.'"[23] Matthilde's musicality in the film, then, is the sign of the supernatural sorcery ascribed to her in the novel. While others around her can engage with the musical vernacular (Georgia and Hagar Rawlins sing "Down in the Valley," and Andy plays the jaw harp), she is the only one with the supernatural powers necessary to tame the high-culture piano.[24] When Matthilde sits down to intone another piece of Mozart (the *Fantasia in D minor* K. 397), the passing Hagar Rawlins exclaims that it "sounds like angels."

Commenting on the piece played to ward off the Kiowas, Edward Buscombe makes an interesting error: he mistakes the *C minor Fantasia* for Beethoven's *"Moonlight" Sonata*. Perhaps the image of Matthilde playing outside at night resonated more with his romanticized view of Beethoven, or the nocturnal associations of the sonata.[25] Nevertheless, the mistake is a telling one. For there is something unusual in Matthilde's playing of both these Mozart fantasias—namely, the tempo. The short K. 397 extract she chooses is from the D-major

Figure 4.4 The piano after the Kiowa attack

Allegretto section that ends the fantasia (see Figure 4.5). Matthilde, however, plays it with deep reverence at a snail's pace. That in itself would not be so unusual (she is, after all, merely demonstrating the instrument). When asked to play to ward off the Kiowas, however, her performance of a much larger section of the C *minor Fantasia* (see Figure 4.6) is equally unusual: rather than too slow, she performs the opening at nearly double the usual speed. It is fortunate she stops when she does: the demisemiquavers of the next bars would be challenging at that tempo, to say the least. That there is something that does not quite ring true in her performances is surely significant given her repeated attempts to mislead. It is all the more ironic, then, that the third piece of music she performs, in an attempt to diffuse an earlier moment of tension, should reveal truths she is attempting to hide.

The Truth behind "Turkey in the Straw"

When the Rawlins family come to visit and mention is made of "the old man" that Georgia had seen (Abe Kelsey), Cash asks his mother whether she has received a visit. Matthilde lies outright: "Nobody, Cash. Nobody at all." When reminded by Rachel of the man with the sabre, she quickly brushes it off, and jumps up to play "Turkey in the Straw" on the new piano, leading to some rather unmusical clapping, and general merriment. Her choice of music is telling, however. "Turkey in the Straw" is what Kathryn Kalinak calls a "sanitized version" of the minstrel song "Zip Coon."[26] Zip Coon was one of two stage characters that became popular in the minstrel shows of the 1820s and 1830s. Unlike his Southern plantation cousin, Jim Crow—played straight as a buffoon for laughs—Zip Coon was a boastful urban and stylish blackface character, who appeared in fancy clothes (see Figure 4.7). Although Kalinak has argued that, in spite of its ridiculing function, minstrelsy was a complicated phenomenon that offered contradictory responses to representations of race (and even included anti-slavery images),[27] the joke, such as it was, centered

Figure 4.5 Mozart *Fantasia in D minor* K. 397 bars 55–62

Figure 4.6 Mozart *Fantasia in C minor* K. 475 bars 1–17

around the fact that Zip Coon was trying to be something he was not. While his dandified appearance adheres to the norms of polite white society, his song gives him away. As sung by George Washington Dixon, the words of the song "Zip Coon" include:

> O its old Suky blue skin, she is in lub with me
> I went the udder arter noon to take a dish ob tea;
> What do you tink now, Suky hab for supper,
> Why chicken foot an posum heel, widout any butter.
> O ole Zip Coon he is larned skolar,
> O ole Zip Coon he is larned skolar,
> O ole Zip Coon he is larned skolar,
> Sings posum up a gum tree an coony in a holler.[28]

The exaggerated dialect is part of the ridicule. Zip Coon is not what he seems to be, and the black man underneath (the Jim Crow inside) threatens to overturn his disguise. Minstrelsy reached the peak of its popularity in precisely the post-Civil War period in which *The Unforgiven* is set, and Matthilde's playing of "Turkey in the Straw" (as it would be known by a 1960s audience) might well have been a rendition of "Zip Coon." As such, it reveals the truth of Rachel's identity. She is Zip Coon, the racial other pretending to be white. Even as Matthilde lies about the presence of Abe Kelsey to deny the truth of Rachel's identity, her guard slips in her choice of dance tune. It is the one moment in the film where Matthilde's music tells the truth (albeit through the medium of a racially troubling song).

Nor is Matthilde the only character powerful enough to manipulate the music. Abe Kelsey, represented musically by recurring contrapuntally treated snatches of "Battle Hymn of the Republic," not only brings the truth with him—no matter how suspicious we are of his motives—but also can silence Matthilde's lies in the underscore. Indeed, his theme in referencing the lyrics of "Battle Hymn of the Republic" (with its repeated refrain of "His truth is marching on") is doubly appropriate: it not only identifies him as a Union soldier,[29] but also buttresses his claims to be the bearer of truth.[30] In his initial encounter with Rachel, her theme is nowhere to be heard, as Kelsey silences her false musical representation just as surely as he questions Matthilde's lies. Captured by Ben, and facing death with a rope around his neck as a horse thief, Kelsey embarks on a narrative account, the parallel of Matthilde's revelatory scene later in the film. When Zeb Rawlins demands of Kelsey—"Rachel Zachary. I want to know about Rachel Zachary!"—the score is notably silent. Kelsey replies melodramatically, "Redhide whelp as ever was. True. It's true." He narrates the circumstances of Rachel's origins to musical silence, and yet we still doubt the truth of his statements. Perhaps because, as Brill points out, characters in Huston's films that utter the truth often border on the inarticulate when they attempt it, we are suspicious of his oratory skill.[31] A Wotan-like wanderer (Georgia Rawlins has noticed that he only has one eye) and poten-

Figure 4.7 Zip Coon

tially as equally unreliable a narrator, Kelsey is challenged in turn by Ben's account of Rachel's parentage (that she was found in a settler's wagon wrapped in a Boston blanket). As an audience we are unsure whom to believe. Only Matthilde knows the truth, and she ensures that Kelsey will not live to tell any more. Wresting control of the music and with the underscore re-entering as her ally, she strikes the horse, causing it to bolt and leaving Kelsey hanging. Free of his truth, the underscore is full of *Dies Irae* menace as Matthilde announces wild-eyed with relish "I hanged him! I hanged him! Abe Kelsey won't go on to destroy no-one else with his lies."[32] With Kelsey's death, there is no one else to challenge (musically) Matthilde's control, and despite the truth emerging, the falseness of Rachel's musical identity lives on.

Endings

We have, then, two explanations for *The Unforgiven*'s music. Looking at the film as a historical text, released in the midst of a trend for turning prominent film tunes into hit songs, Rachel's theme doubles effectively as "the theme from *The Unforgiven*." It is very much the product of Dimtri Tiomkin, the master of the theme-tune film score, and every iteration can be seen as enforcing its presence in the minds of an audience, who might then be expected to go out and purchase the McGuire Sisters' version, the Don Costa instrumental interpretation, or even the sheet music. Thus, the ending of the film—in which Cash and Andy join Ben and Rachel outside the burnt-out remains of their home in quiet contemplation of the geese flying high in the sky—triggers a final statement of it, leaving the audience with the catchy tune uppermost in their minds. If, however, we approach the music for *The Unforgiven* not as a docu-ment of a film scoring technique or as the product of a composer, but as a part of a cinematic text to be interpreted, we find alternative explanations for Rachel's music and its treatment. Then it is the consequence of a mother's idealized and whitewashed view of her daughter, a theme that seems to delib-erately mislead with regards to the truth of Rachel's racial identity, and to continually restate it when all others around her are questioning it. While this may sound suspiciously like the rather old musicological habit of reinforcing notions of a work's immanent meaning, cut off from socio-historical contexts, it is an interpretation grounded in the film's *fictional* contexts. In other words, we can look for possible explanations for the ubiquity of Rachel's theme within the diegesis.

In this context, then, the film's end scene might be more ambiguous than the score initially seems to suggest. Huston and Prats may have interpreted its conclusion, wherein Rachel's theme rings out triumphantly accompanied by celebratory wedding bells, as an indication that the filmmakers are sanctioning the abrogation of her racial identity and her union with Ben, but other explanations are possible. This may be a last desperate attempt by Ben, for example, to persuade Rachel to accept a future identity she is no longer able to countenance. There are certainly suggestions leading up to this final moment in which Rachel realizes the impossibility of her position and is ready to challenge the various identities imposed on her. The last few minutes of the film are devoid of dialogue, and meaning is provided entirely through gesture and music. Thus, Rachel shoots Lost Bird in evident anguish, and although Ben looks at her with pride, her shame does not allow her to return fully his gaze. Instead, her conflicted feelings are heard in a sorrowful melody not performed since the opening titles: her first act of musical independence, perhaps, and one that suggests a newfound unwillingness to see her (musical) identity constructed by others. Cash returns, and his anguish at Matthilde's death echoes directly with Rachel's sorrowful melody: it is music to mourn a family member with (a mother or a brother), and Cash in empathizing with Rachel's grief through shared music perhaps emerges as Huston's real hero. Rather like Ethan in *The Searchers*, he has faced the truth of his sister's identity, and has conquered his racism (albeit perhaps only temporarily). Tellingly, it is his arm Rachel takes as he and Andy join her and Ben outside, with Cash standing between the supposedly still engaged couple—see Figure 4.8.[33] The prospective wedding between Rachel and Ben now feels in doubt in the light of Lost Bird's death, and they avoid each other's gaze. As the four look up to the geese flying overhead, the emergence of Rachel's theme in the music might thus be read as Ben's final attempt to abrogate her racial identity, to persuade her that she is essentially the same person she was at the beginning of the film (although in giving into his quasi-incestuous desires, Ben simultaneously needs to persuade himself that she was always different: perhaps he now hears in her the prominent falling third also heard in Lost Bird's music). Rachel's theme swells on the soundtrack, its reverberations telling in the emptiness of the acoustic. The music, with its peal of wedding bells, rings false.

Huston's dislike of the film is, of course, unlikely to be solely the result of Tiomkin's score, but its emphasis on a musical theme that might be suitable for commercial release and whose return at the film's close seems to suggest an uncomplicated happy ending could be attributable to the same outside pressures to which Huston himself points.[34] If we allow the characters to influence the music, and read the ubiquity and unchanging nature of Rachel's theme as evidence of their motivations, we are faced with a more complex and ambivalent film that might indeed be closer to Huston's original vision—one that chimes with the larger themes of the narrative: of truth, and its subversion, and the construction of identity. Although it leaves us with a far less positive view of the ostensible hero, Ben Zachary, Tiomkin's score arguably adds layers of subtlety to the narrative while simultaneously providing what the producers needed: a catchy theme song to swell the coffers.

Figure 4.8 The final group shot of the film's main protagonists

Notes

1   Lesley Brill, *John Huston's Filmmaking* (Cambridge: Cambridge University Press, 1997), 85.
2   John Huston, *An Open Book* (London: Columbus Books, 1988), 284.
3   Christopher Sharrett, "1960: Movies and Intimations of Disaster and Hope" in *American Cinema of the 1960s: Themes and Variations*, ed. Barry Keith Grant (New Brunswick: Rutgers University Press, 2008), 24.
4   This is perhaps an idea that chimed problematically with producer Harold Hecht, who himself had been a Communist and had named names to the House Un-American Activities Committee. See Kate Buford, *Burt Lancaster: An American Life* (London: Aurum Press, 2005), 130–31.
5   Huston, 283.
6   Ibid.
7   Edward Buscombe, "The Unforgiven," in *The BFI Companion to the Western*, ed. Edward Buscombe (London: BFI, 1993), 307.
8   Christopher Palmer, *Dimitri Tiomkin: A Portrait* (London: T E Books, 1984).
9   For more explanation of this approach to music in film, see my article "The Nondiegetic Fallacy: Film, Music, and Narrative Space," *Music & Letters* 91, 2 (May 2010), 224–44.
10 Carolyn Abbate has written of our assumptions that music (in opera, at least) generally tells us the truth, though she herself problematises this view in her examination of later Wagnerian Music Drama. See her *Unsung Voices: Opera and Musical Narrative in the Nineteenth Century* (Princeton: Princeton University Press, 1991).
11 Eckstein notes that the film was shot only three years after the Production Code had given up its strong opposition to the depiction of miscegenation. See Arthur M. Eckstein, "Incest and Miscegenation in *The Searchers* (1956) and *The Unforgiven* (1959)" in *The Searchers: Essays and Reflections on John Ford's Classic Western*, ed. Arthur M. Eckstein and Peter Lehman (Detroit: Wayne State University Press, 2004), 211. The suggestion of incest is, however, far more overt in the film version of *The Unforgiven* than in LeMay's novel.
12 Armando José Prats, *Invisible Natives: Myth & Identity in the American Western* (Ithaca: Cornell University Press, 2002), 109–18.
13 In contrast, Rachel in the film knows she is not a Zachary by blood.
14 Alan LeMay, *The Unforgiven* (London: Collins, 1958), 92.
15 This is entirely the invention of the screenwriter; in the novel, it is Cash who shoots Lost Bird.
16 LeMay, 8.
17 Jeff Smith, *The Sounds of Commerce: Marketing Popular Film Music* (New York: Columbia University Press, 1998), 59.
18 See the lists compiled by Bill Danning on http://www.oldiesloon.com/ca/la.htm (accessed July 2, 2010).
19 The outward similarity of Rachel's theme to the "Moritat von Mackie Messer" is ironic indeed: the shocking text of the original song and its intended alienation effect, delivered through an expressionless performance, is essentially lost in the popular romanticized versions of "Mack the Knife" by Ella Fitzgerald, Bobby Darin, and Louis Armstrong. In that sense, the allusion to Weill's song and the song's potential to alter its identity are strangely appropriate to Rachel's character. See Lawrence Kramer, *Musical Meaning: Toward a Critical History* (Berkeley: University of California Press, 2002), 216–27.
20 LeMay, 180.
21 Claudia Gorbman, "Scoring the Indian: Music in the Liberal Western" in *Western Music and its Others*, ed. Georgina Born and Desmond Hesmondhalgh (Berkeley: University of California Press, 2000), 235.

22 Bareback riding is often a sign of Indian-ness in Hollywood Westerns. In *The Searchers*, for example, the part-Indian character Martin Pauley (Jeffrey Hunter) makes his entrance by jumping off a horse he has been riding bareback. A soddy, or sod house is, as the name suggests, a dwelling that uses prairie grass to construct its walls.

23 LeMay, 230.

24 Ironically, this connects her with the Indian horse-tamer, Johnny Portugal.

25 See Kramer, 29–50.

26 Kathryn Kalinak, "How the West was Sung" in *Westerns: Films through History*, ed. Janet Walker (London: Routledge, 2001), 151–76.

27 Kalinak, 159.

28 Richard Crawford, *America's Musical Life: A History* (New York: Norton, 2001), 201.

29 His uniform is so old and dusty that his identity is somewhat in doubt, visually.

30 The anti-slavery message of "John Brown's Body" (the song this camp-meeting hymn tune was associated with before Julia Ward Howe's words were attached) ensures that Abe carries a moral authority that belies his own racism. See Annie J. Randall, "A Censorship of Forgetting: Origins and Origin Myths of 'Battle Hymn of the Republic'" in *Music, Power, and Politics*, ed. Annie J. Randall (London: Routledge, 2005), 5–24.

31 Brill, 86.

32 We might also note that the *Dies Irae* was a favorite of Tiomkin's (as it had been of his compatriot, Rachmaninov), and was used in the scores for *I Confess* (1953) and *Red Light* (1949). See Palmer, 98.

33 Andy seems to hold his arm in homage to Ethan Edwards in the last scene of *The Searchers*, a gesture that was in itself John Wayne's act of homage to the actor Harry Carey. See Buscombe, *The Searchers* (London: BFI publishing, 2000), 65.

34 As Smith notes, United Artists' David Picker regularly met with films' independent producers prior to shooting to discuss the score's commercial potential. See his *The Sounds of Commerce*, 62.

Chapter 5

A Tale of Two Cowgirls

Songs, Western Novelty Acts, and 1950s Hollywood

Caryl Flinn

In the early 1950s, western icons Annie Oakley and Calamity Jane made it to the Hollywood silver screen. Although audiences had encountered these characters in films before—notably, Barbara Stanwyck as Annie Oakley in 1935—now the cowgirls sang, and sang big: each was backed by a multi-million dollar budget. After its failed start with Judy Garland in the title role, MGM selected Betty Hutton to depict Annie Oakley in *Annie Get Your Gun* (1950), adapted from Irving Berlin's 1946 stage hit. Then, in response to *Annie's* success, Warner Bros. released *Calamity Jane* (1953), an original musical with Doris Day; Broadway and movie baritone Howard Keel co-starred in both. Both of these movies did very well; *Annie Get Your Gun* was MGM's largest grossing picture to date and took home the Oscar for Best Score. *Calamity Jane* was nominated for three Oscars, winning Best Original Song with Sammy Fain and Paul Francis Webster's "Secret Love," sung by Day. Released as a single in 1954, "Secret Love" topped the Billboard and Cash Box charts; the film's original soundtrack made it to number 2.[1]

Calamity Jane and Annie Oakley, of course, were historical figures whose ripened tales were at the ready for the entertainment industry—indeed, the two sharpshooters were showbiz veterans during their own lives, women who had had stories, songs, and plays written about them, and both toured in *Buffalo Bill's Wild West and Congress of Rough Riders of the World*. The gendered exceptionalism of these two shooters with masculinized skills accrued added value when their stories were re-enacted through song—first on stage and then on-screen in their big-budget incarnations. Not only were two blond girls doing the work of tough frontier men, but they were also doing so in a glitzy, song-and-dance West that had shed the romanticizing verisimilitude of the western in favor of the lavish artifice of A studio musicals. Suddenly, the subdued seriousness and intense masculinities of the West seemed at risk or, at the least, sent up. Although the 1950s featured other gender-bending westerns, notably, *Johnny Guitar* (1954), these two films jousted with conventions with a play-fulness that other westerns of the time kept under wraps, at least narratively, if not always at the level of film form and style.

It is easy to call *Annie*, and especially *Calamity*, quirky, straddling as they do conflicting verisimilitudinous demands of two different genres and the gender demands of the same. Yet the weird meshings of the films' girl gunslingers and gender impersonation are not as off the grid as they might appear, nor pose the kind of ideological dislocation often assumed to accompany what Eric Savoy calls, in his analysis of *Calamity*, its "gay and lesbian incipience."[2] For during the 1950s, Hollywood was under fierce pressures to bring novelty to its product, to ratchet up the tension between "tradition" and "new elements" that André Bazín famously noted in articulating the "genius of the system."[3] In other words, the early 1950s was a period of economic crisis for Hollywood, and the question of *Annie* or *Calamity*'s boundary transgression—sexual, generic, and otherwise—needs to be posed alongside another one: how might the majors (here, MGM and Warner Bros.) have supervised the mixing of the off-kilter and the mainstream to get the hits they needed? This chapter begins by considering *Annie Get Your Gun* and *Calamity Jane* as mixed-genre novelty A films and then explores how their songs operate alongside the conflicting demands for both novelty and tradition. Having female gunslingers who sang may have been a great new gimmick, but do the songs themselves contribute to the films' quirky status?

The Two Gal Gunslingers

Calamity Jane and *Annie Get Your Gun* both follow the familiar Pygmalion narrative of educating two skilled but naïve young white women into their proper class, ethnicity, and gender roles so they can be (implausibly) partnered with their male leads. Unlike most Pygmalion variations, however, Annie and Calamity retain the primary feature that exceptionalizes them and masculinizes them: their skills as westerners. In Annie's case, her shooting skills absolutely cannot be relinquished since they provide the raw material needed for the glitzy machinery of show business, whose sophisticated artifice Annie must also learn and adopt. The number that heralds that world, "There's No Business Like Show Business," also showcases the personal sacrifices that enhance the excitement of showbiz; other songs elaborate the roles that capital, class, white ethnicity, and heteronormativity play in Annie's transformation. When Frank Butler (Howard Keel) sings to a goofily smitten Annie of the "soft and pink" features of "The Girl That I Marry," he is oblivious to her despair over falling so short; but once their relationship begins, the film is at pains to show Annie striving to become that image through a comic montage sequence of her in curlers, scrubbing her face, learning to read.

Other aspects of *Annie*'s story are completely by the book. Buffalo Bill Cody (Louis Calhern) and manager Charlie Davenport (Keenan Wynn) falsely encourage Annie to believe that Frank, the show's star, would enjoy being surprised by her new specialty act in which Annie shoots targets upside down and backwards from a galloping horse. Furious at being upstaged and at what he considers an act of deceit from Annie, now his love interest, Frank quits to join Pawnee Bill's rival western show. The two characters' lovesickness (Annie's depicted, Frank's presumed) finds expression in the dire finances of

Figure 5.1 Annie Get Your Gun

the two struggling shows: each needs the other to survive, telegraphing how entwined the roots of capital, showbiz, and heterosexuality in fact are. After Frank and Annie challenge each other to a final sharpshooting contest ("Anything You Can Do"), Annie learns that if she wins the match, she will lose the man, and so throws the game.

Calamity's outsider status is less crushingly formulaic: Calamity is one of Deadwood's townsmen, a tomboy more than a gender outlaw, and her education is more quickly handled in a female–female makeover scene ("A Woman's Touch") that sets the stage for Calamity's eventual wedding—although the number's butch/femme dimensions make that ultimate pairing somewhat less than convincing. Col. Bill Hickok (Keel again) is introduced as Calamity's best friend and rival, and the competition number that musically establishes their relationship ("I Can Do Without You," modeled after *Annie*'s "Anything You Can Do") lacks any erotic energy whatsoever. Indeed, Hickok could be of any gender when he tells Calamity that if she "ever crawled out of that deer hide and dolled up a bit, I've got a hunch you'd be a passable pretty gal."

Style, Westerns, and Musicals

Stylistically, both films—western though they are—largely obey the rules and conventions of the Hollywood musical, a genre that, at first blush, seems a world apart from that of westerns, a genre stuffed with seriousness, of history-telling and nation-building, equipped with a stern sense of place and self-effacing style. It celebrates outcasts and outlaws, lone-wolf white men and few others. Human communication and expressivity are rare commodities, and pleasure is similarly kept in check, an affective logic that informs (and is informed by) the use of songs in western films. Indeed, the diegetic songs of A westerns rarely grant reprieve from this restrained emotionality, whether for characters or audience members. Typically songs introduce, establish, or celebrate community (even in *Calamity*'s "The Deadwood Stage" or "The Black Hills of Dakota") or articulate the affective links binding that community (the rural chauvinism of *Calamity*'s "Just Got in From the Windy City" whose lyrics boast of Deadwood's superior charms to those of Chicago). Emerging from small social groups and ritualized events (funerals, campfires, dances, church services), songs in the western convey subdued, communally agreed upon feelings and the sense that things are in their place. As Paul Rosenfeld wrote a propos of folksongs in 1940, one of their main objectives was "to waken fellow-feeling."[4] Songs commemorate social functions and public ritual, rather than the desire to move away from these things. And even when the songs are individualized, sung by peripheral figures, in A westerns or the singer stars of B westerns, such as Roy Rogers and Gene Autry, they announce the obvious, such as the joys of horseback riding, the solitude of cowboy life, the mysteries of the night. In short, songs of the film western usually announce or enhance setting; rarely do they break out of it to appeal for something new, or to suggest that something new might be needed.

Compare this to the musical, a genre that openly declares its status as fantasy text and celebrates pleasure, camaraderie, and the power of emotional expression. It trades in the tension between intense stylistic artifice and intense emotional sincerity, a sincerity that can be sung at the level of community ("Oklahoma!") as easily as at the level of individual characters ("I Whistle A Happy Tune"). As a genre of expressivity, musicals move toward—not away from— expression as a means to counter the suppressions and difficulties of daily life and work, not to accompany them as in the western. Appealing to the power of emotions themselves, musicals frequently suggest emotional alternatives to the dulling experience of everyday life, articulating unexpressed yearnings for difference and change.

It's no stretch to state that *Calamity Jane* and *Annie Get Your Gun* adhere to the conventions of Hollywood musicals more than those of the western, with their lavish sets and choreographed numbers (especially the extravaganza that is *Annie*'s "There's No Business Like Show Business" and "I'm an Indian Too"), their big singing stars (Hutton, Day, and Keel), and their propensity for comedic entertainment over lonesome, gritty tales of survival. Both MGM and Warner Bros. were literally banking on that blend of musical and western genres—as well as the seeming irregularity of featuring female gunslingers. Forget John Wayne (who actually sang a little in early westerns for Republic Pictures); even Gene Autry's assuring tones and muted black and white hues seem worlds away from these cowgirls.

Gender, Affect, and Fakery

Calamity Jane quickly establishes its deviation from standard western fare in its opening number, "The Deadwood Stage/Whip-crack Away." Although Day performs this from atop a stagecoach in buckskin jeans and riding crop, musically, despite its loping western rhythm, the song is more reminiscent of "Wells Fargo Wagon" from River City, Iowa than anything coming into or out of the OK Corral. As for *Annie's* numbers, most take already-exaggerated western icons, dialects, and characterizations to exaggerate them further, as in "Doin' What Comes Natur'lly" and "I'm an Indian Too," novelty numbers that use their ostensibly western settings and singers as comic material for the urban white audiences of Broadway, for whom it was originally written. (Songwriter Irving Berlin actually had to be persuaded to sign on for the show, famously saying "What do I know about hillbilly music?"[5]) Other numbers, notably from *Calamity*, appear to bypass Broadway—and western—musical conventions altogether. Songs such as "Secret Love," "A Woman's Touch" or even "My Heart is Higher than a Hawk" could have appeared in any 1950s film or succeeded as popular recordings not connected to any film.

In her 1992 study subtitled "the inner life of westerns," Jane Tompkins offers insights into the affective world of the western and the appeals it extended to outsiders reading and listening in. While Tompkins does not address music, her work will help as we consider these films whose fascinations were clearly filtered through gender as well as genre. Tompkins argues that the western was a highly popular early twentieth-century response to the heavily feminized sentimental novels popular in the nineteenth century. To her its appeal involved less an escape from the present, but an escape from the feminine, a term she uses not only to include women (of which there are plenty, with the westerns' many abandoned and heartbroken lovers, wives, and mothers), but of all things associated with womanliness: Christianity, domesticity, and "women's invasion of the public sphere between 1880 and 1920."[6] To her list we should add the emotional experiences of everyday life, routine, and, especially the routine of work:

> Though [the western] reproduces with amazing thoroughness and intensity the emotional experience of performing intolerable labor, it removes the feelings associated with doing work from their usual surroundings and places them in a locale and a set of circumstances that expand their meaning, endow them with an overriding purpose, and fill them with excitement.[7]

The fantasy of being in the physical present, of achieving meaningfulness through work, of re-wiring the numbing repetition of non-physical labor would not only have been meaningful for early twentieth-century consumers, but for audiences in the post-war era of *Annie* and *Calamity Jane*. For the white middle-class Americans who were the target audiences of these texts, the western might have offered a fantasy of a clearer moral time, a promise of renewal, of harmonious relations among law, settlement, and nature: that this fantasy utterly obscures ethnic difference, social disharmony and violence is part of its fraudulent potency. Still, with desk jobs replacing physical work and growing leisure time on their hands, middle-class Americans could readily have been drawn to the more elemental alternatives of the genre: facing life-and-death clashes with nature; confronting pure, uncompromised evil; having to struggle for survival itself.

In the western, Tompkins asserts that emotion is released through action and action alone. Otherwise put, the guiding emotional principle for characters of the genre is not to express any. Tompkins maintains that the burden is equitably discharged among men and women: "Women cannot express their rage because to do so marks them as unfeminine. Man cannot register their pain because to do so marks them as unmanly."[8] Still, if this is what characters endure, difference is more selectively meted out for the people actually consuming the stories: "The feelings that reading or seeing a Western excites are related to the principal messages it sends. Intended for men primarily, they are messages about what it means to be a successful adult in our [sic] society."[9] This may be the message of some western narratives, but it is not the message of all of them.

Calamity Jane's Deadwood is a western community filled with fraudulent performers. Saloon owner Henry Miller (Paul Harvey) hires Frances Fryer (Dick Wesson) sight unseen to entertain at the Golden Garter. When the "actress" arrives in the form of male performer Francis, Miller—himself called Milly— has Francis perform as the woman Milly believed him to be. Nervous at first, Francis quickly warms to it, flirting with the puzzled but happy men until a band member's sliding trombone removes his wig. Soon afterwards, Calamity goes to Chicago to fetch singing sensation Adelaid Adams for the Golden Garter and, unbeknownst to her, returns with Adelaid's maid, Katie Brown (Allyn McLerie), for whom Calamity's mistake affords an opportunity to perform. Katie's ruse is also exposed on stage, during her poor performance of "Keep It Under Your Hat." In both instances the saloon audience accepts the performers even after learning of their deception, and their acceptance is not simply a matter of tolerance but of embrace: Francis remains an active part of Deadwood, a prominent player in the town's otherwise nondescript group; Katie becomes an economically and erotically appreciated member. Such an affective scenario seldom plays out in westerns, where a lack of histrionics and full authenticity are normally read as compelling, unless said histrionics occur in action scenes. It is even rarer to find a communal, open-eyed willingness to buy into and accept a fake, knowing it is a fake, in westerns. *The Man Who Shot Liberty Valance* (1962) offers one example, but it is an individualized, rather than a communal, willingness to sustain a secret. Moreover, its lie is less one of deceptive gender roles but rather of keeping them firmly intact.

For American musical comedies, however, the sense of acceptance is deeply resonant and familiar. Unlike their vaudevillian predecessors of the 1920s and 1930s—or even the early book musicals of the 1930s and 1940s—musicals of the immediate post-war era took on more social themes and problems in which tolerance and acceptance—especially within some formation of a community— were depicted as desirable and valued. That liberal plea for tolerance[10] cuts a large swath of American musical history, from *South Pacific* ("You've Got to be Taught") in the middle of the century to *Avenue Q* ("It Sucks to Be Me") at the end. Of course western musicals such as *Calamity* and *Annie* hardly had serious targets in their sites and embrace Broadway's post-war focus on tolerance and acceptance uneasily. Their aim was to entertain and to use generic and gender strangeness to do so.

Singing the West on Screen

Vocal songs were never absent in the western, whether sung by a chorus of cowhands or churchgoers or by individuals such as Frenchy (Marlene Dietrich) in *Destry Rides Again* (1939). If, by the late studio era, female performers such as Dietrich took center stage in more of these non-musical westerns, it did not mean that gender rules shifted so dramatically that male performers would actually sing much. To paint in wide brush strokes, when A westerns of the late and early post-studio era associated songs with male leads, they usually did so through motivic underscoring utilizing song fragments, whereas the actually singing of songs, if any, usually went to females or peripheral males, such as Harry Carey, Jr. singing to the cattle in *Red River* (1948), a formula that helps explain the eventual disruptiveness of *Paint Your Wagon* (1969).[11] Even in Republic's somewhere-between-A-and-B film *Johnny Guitar*, music does not push too hard. Despite the expectations established by the film's title and its eponymous lead, *Guitar* never raises its voice in song. Vienna (Joan Crawford) performs the title song once on the piano while waiting for the town vigilantes to arrive at her saloon, yet only at the end is the torch-like number finally *sung*, by Peggy Lee, in a move that adhered to the growing practice of the time of releasing title songs performed by singers with no screen roles in the films themselves.

The history of the B western, with or without music, was much different. In the silent era, westerns accounted for a majority of American filmmaking ventures but with the advent of sound and the difficulties posed by recording on location—not to mention the major studios' decision to concentrate their efforts on the lucrative white, middle-class audience of big cities—other genres outpaced westerns by the early 1930s. The mass production of cowboy films was taken up by B studios such as Grand National, Monogram and Republic that churned out serialized westerns aimed at lower-class, immigrant and rural audiences. And some of their cowboys sang.

Scholars such as Peter Stanfield and Roderick McGillis have noted that the gender roles in these low-brow westerns were somewhat fluid, a fact overlooked even by feminist scholars such as Tompkins, who focus on the more middle-class narratives of the West. For instance, B westerns often featured female characters who were economically independent and unafraid of "physical action and violence,"[12] in general offering more relaxed models of western femininity and masculinity. McGillis goes so far as to argue that the B western "challenges the very hegemonic masculinity that [its heroes] most obviously promote."[13] Even A westerns can give insight into a less rigidified gender world. Consider the masculinity of heroes such as Clint Eastwood when becoming spectacles of masochistic humiliation in *The Beguiled* (1971) or heroes studiously avoiding domesticating sexual partnerships. As B. Ruby Rich notes, long before *Brokeback Mountain* (2005), the genre was a hotbed of queerness: of virile cowboys used for gay desires and queer counter-identifications. Cowboys appeared in gay porn and in art films such as *Midnight Cowboy* (1969) and *Lonesome Cowboy* (1968), where, as Rich adds, their erotic value was literalized in the form of turn-tricking characters.[14] Much more than gender boundaries are at stake here. When Stanfield and McGillis characterize B westerns for their focus on spectacle, non-psychologized heroes, and privileging action over narrative, they show how flimsy the boundaries between western and musical genres actually are.

Still, it must be stated that the overwhelming majority of singing cowhands were white and male, even in the B film. When women or people of color sang, their performances were downscale or novelty acts, occasional musical forays that provided commentary on the action at hand or to redirect attention to the central male characters. So cowgirls had their place, but with few exceptions, it was to support or entertain their cowboys.

A prominent exception is Dale Evans, the almost equal on- and off-screen partner to Roy Rogers. Another is recording artist Patsy Montana, a frequent guest star on Autry's radio show, and the first singing cowgirl to sell a million records. And during the 1930s, there was B picture star Dorothy Page, whose alluring contralto could handle elegiac ballads such as "Prairie Boy" as well as more rousing fare, and who was ordained by Grand National Pictures as "the singing cowgirl" after the title of her successful film for them, *The Singing Cowgirl* (1938). But Page's stardom was short lived; by 1939 Grand National had gone under. Whether these failures were due to a reluctance to accept singing cowgirls as leads, or to a general fatigue of the formula, is hard to say.

Recent scholarship of the western asks us to understand genre—and gender—as categories bereft of stability or impermeability. Even Tompkins, whose 1992 *West of Everything* works from second-wave feminist dichotomies of gender, writes that "What is most characteristic of these oppositions is that as soon as you put pressure on them they break down. Each time one element of a pair is driven into a corner, it changes shape and frequently turns into its opposite."[15] Tompkins argues that female characters are extensions of men, and indeed *Calamity* and *Annie* show that the men—especially those performing in traveling western shows—are not functionally different from the women. *Annie Get Your Gun* institutes difference less through sex than by body size, age, sophistication, and experience as showbiz professionals.

Moreover, the generic norms typically associated with the western—character development, attention to narrative emplotment, credibility, and verisimilitude (characteristics, it must be stressed, deemed antithetical to most musicals) were not always at the forefront of the film western, especially in B and in silent films. Yet rather than position *Annie* and *Calamity* as throwbacks to earlier, edgier film practices, or as forerunners of queer theory, I want to pursue how the singing Annie Oakley and Calamity Jane were very much figures of the period that produced them.

Queerness as Product Novelty

To maintain itself, any mass reproduced form, from film genres to social and gender identity, requires constant transformation. For the Hollywood film industry in the early 1950s the need for innovation was particularly intense. Struggling in the wake of the Paramount Decision, US filmmaking also had to re-invent itself to compete with its fast-moving rival, television. Many B studios folded. To differentiate its product from the small screen, Hollywood flirted openly with novelties that were technologically, morally, or legally unavailable to television, from innovations such as 3-D and color to challenging MPCC censorship through storyline, theme, or dialogue. Studios produced lavish spectacles that small screens could not, and new genres (e.g., social problem films) emerged along with other new fusions and subgenres, increasingly blurring the boundaries of A and B production at the time (e.g., sci-fi and horror).

As musicals and westerns tried new formulae to stay fresh, they adhered to a variety of different strategies, moving in overlapping, contradictory directions. None of that movement was unilateral, of course. Some screen musicals followed fiscally conservative paths. Producers hedged their bets by adapting established stage hits: after all, the 1950s was the decade of *Oklahoma!* (1955), *Call Me Madam* (1953), and *The King and I* (1956) in addition to *Annie Get Your Gun.* Broadway also took fewer risks as post-war production prices soared, something that affected musicals more than other shows. But there was also unexplored territory to pursue: the New York stage saw the vernacular *Guys and Dolls*, and the entrepreneurial Rogers and Hammerstein often created characters without stars in mind to insure longer runs and tours. Hollywood, for its part, slowly acknowledged youthful consumers in rock and roll musicals such as *Rock Around the Clock* (1956); both coasts embraced social issues musicals such as *West Side Story* and *South Pacific*—all changes that kept the form fresh.

The A western was no different. For French western critic Yves Kovacs, 1950 was "the 1789 of the western."[16] The unquestioned pre-war ethnic chauvinism and white heroism now received some scrutiny: studio westerns began to represent Native Americans with (patronizing) respect (*Broken Arrow*, 1950) and white male heroes became increasingly neurotic, feckless, or damaged (*Pursued*, 1947; *High Noon*, 1952) as Hollywood masculinities more generally were reconfigured. In the ensuing years, white western male heroes lost their pre-existing goodness, becoming tainted, even savage, in the next decades (*Ulzana's Raid*, 1972). Hollywood also began reflexively to pass the classical western itself into a legendary past (*The Man Who Shot Liberty Valance*, 1962).

As part of this generic movement, the 1950s cowgirls were no different, but they appear further off the grid than the shifting male heroes, due to the paucity of established female heroes from which to deviate. Compare Joan Crawford's high camp turn as Vienna in *Johnny Guitar* to Dean Martin's Dude in *Rio Bravo* (1959), for instance. Females in A westerns simply stood out, their very presence—enhanced by the star system, to be sure— often enough to sell a film such as *Calamity Jane* or *Annie Get Your Gun*.

For a motion picture industry struggling to secure its footing in a new legal and economic landscape, the strange brew mixing women, song, and westerns was not in actuality so strange. As Stanfield notes, when Gene Autry was listed as Hollywood's fourth biggest male box office star in 1940, the stunned majors took note and returned to the western genre, providing context for big-budget singing western fare such as *Calamity Jane* and *Annie Get Your Gun*.[17] Further context is offered by the fact that this was a time when cowgirls thrived in American popular culture, however briefly. From 1954 to 1957, a dramatic, non-singing television series, *Annie Oakley*, was broadcast, featuring Gail Davis, fresh from her work on Gene Autry's television show. *Annie Oakley* dropped the tomboy-to-femme arc of the film and, although the show was in her name, Annie was half of a team: her male partner Lofty, a deputy, did the heavy lifting and actual chasing of bad guys. Annie helped out when her shooting skills or knowledge about guns were needed. Instead of being a (gender) outcast who needs to be reined in, this Annie Oakley, with her blond hair in two impeccably kept braids, was an integrated community member, a family-friendly substitute parent to a young brother, not a gawking singing comedienne.

By the time *Annie Get Your Gun* and *Calamity Jane* hit the silver screen, B westerns were in the decline, their serial function absorbed by television. At the same time, popular music associated with the West was gaining ground in recording industries, especially as the relatively new BMI promoted folk, hillbilly, blues and other regional music to eager listeners. Producers of A westerns had merely to react. Although it is unlikely that MGM or Warner Bros. were trying to capitalize on the rise of western records (too new) with *Annie Get Your Gun* and *Calamity Jane*, they certainly redirected what B studios did not have the financial will to do: to put the woman in the lead and to make her colorful. That ostensible color was for not fitting in, either within the diegesis or within the representational contours of big-budget westerns. Even as the compass and conventions of the western changed, the cowgirl remained a one-off during the 1950s, treated in the industry and in the cultural imagination as an offbeat diversion.

Calamity Jane and Annie Oakley—Superstar Shooters

Like most icons of the Wild West, Calamity Jane (1852–1903) was at once a real person and a tall tale: a scout who rode and fought alongside men, eventually settling in Deadwood. Martha Jane Cannary Burke was linked, sometimes romantically, to Wild Bill Hickok, one of the men with whom she rode and shot. The nickname "Calamity" is of indeterminate origins (she claimed an army captain gave it to her; another version is that men who ignored Burke's observations of approaching calamity did so at their own risk).[18] After the early death of her parents, she supported her orphaned brothers and sister —and later herself—by dishwashing, laundry, and prostitution. Calamity ended her career as a performer, like Annie Oakley, in *Buffalo Bill's Wild West*.

Calamity Jane was famous for her tall tales and exaggerations; whether she and Hickok were lovers, or spouses, as she claimed, or that he fathered her daughter, is anybody's guess. Sources often claim Hickok could not stand her, and their survivors even buried Jane at his side to have a last laugh on him. (It is somewhat surprising that Warner Bros. did not use these biographical details to enhance the rivalry of the film's leads.) Calamity's fame had already entered the mass media well before she died. She was a character in a series of dime novels beginning with Edward Wheel's *Deadwood Dick* series in 1877; she wrote her own autobiography in 1896, and on her death, some of her unsent letters to her daughter were set to music in an art song cycle called *Songs From Letters* by Libby Larsen. From there, Calamity Jane went on to become the subject of popular songs from Adelyne Hood's "Calamity Jane" (1929) to "Deadwood Mountain" by Big & Rich (2004). She has also figured in stage plays, novels, cartoon strips, computer and video games, and Hollywood films such as *The Plainsman* (1936) and *Paleface* (1948).

Skilled sharpshooter Annie Oakley (1860–1926) appeared in Wild West shows and was a western superstar *avant la lettre*. A sharpshooter of humble origins in Ohio, Annie beat the touring performer Frank Butler in a Cincinnati sharpshooting contest and they married soon afterwards. Together Oakley and Butler appeared in *Buffalo Bill's Wild West* for most of their lives; even after subsequent debilitating accidents, Oakley kept working, promoting gunmanship for women, especially during wartime. Her life seems to have little of the rough and tumble of Calamity's, and offers a more genteel version of Wild West femininity. Dorothy Fields, who co-wrote the stage version's book, jokingly complained that "We did a lot of research on Annie Oakley and Frank Butler, and both of them apparently were about the dullest people in the world. Annie Oakley in real life used to sit in her tent and *knit*, for God's sake!"[19]

Oakley's career as a proto-mass media sensation was secured well before she died, and she seemed savvy to the demands show business placed upon her. At five feet tall, she was called "Little Sure Shot," a detail which the film musical preserves as a sign of affectionate condescension from the men in *Buffalo Bill's Wild West* but in actuality, Oakley used it to distinguish herself from older, established female performers in the shows. Oakley and Butler performed as stars in one of Thomas Edison's early Kinetoscope films, *The "Little Sure Shot" of the "Wild West"* (1894). Oakley performed in a 1902 stage play written for her, *The Western Girl*, where she used pistol, rifle, and rope to outsmart outlaws. Hollywood latched on to her story, notably in Stanwyck's non-musical *Annie Oakley*, but it was Irving Berlin's *Annie Get Your Gun* that put her on the pop culture map. The point here is that before these two cowgirls ever opened their mouths in song, they were part of a highly mediatized Wild West, rather than deviations from it.

Betty Hutton and Doris Day—American Songbirds

MGM paid a record-breaking $650,000 for the rights to the Broadway show.[20] Its early production, however—unlike Calamity's, which went seamlessly—was beset by problems. Frank Morgan, hired as Buffalo Bill, died soon after filming started; he was replaced by Calhern, wonderful but without Morgan's bluff and bluster. Garland shot two numbers as Annie before being let go for exhaustion; there has been speculation about the charisma she might have brought to the role ever since. Compared to Garland, Betty Hutton was not only a lesser presence but also more limited as a dancer, and so the film's choreographers (Busby Berkeley too was replaced, by Robert Alton) had to restrict her movements and directed focus away from her. Ironically, after having replaced Garland, Hutton would herself soon be branded as trouble.

After small roles on Broadway and in musical shorts for Warner Bros., Betty Hutton established herself as a comic screen actress in Morgan's Creek (1944), and in musical comedies such as Happy Go Lucky (1943), Incendiary Blond (1945), Perils of Pauline (1947), and Let's Dance (1950). By the time of Annie's casting, Hutton was big box office, and she even had top billing over Fred Astaire in Let's Dance. Her image had been secured in these musical comedies, which called for all-American womanhood with youthful zest. Chipper and sometimes naïve, Hutton's performances possessed less of the ribald or bulldozing energy than, say, Ethel Merman, who preceded her as the original Annie on stage and, earlier, the lead in Cole Porter's Panama Hattie (1942), in which Hutton had a supporting role. Her stage and screen roles had also established Hutton as a particular kind of vocalist; specifically, an extroverted singer and belter, concerned (as were Berlin's songs) with providing vocal characterization over finesse. First and foremost, Hutton was a singing comedienne.

By any Hollywood standard, Hutton was rather short, 5'4", and physically unimposing, as Annie dramatizes in scenes with the 6'3" Keel. Her earlier roles had hardly made it difficult for audiences to accept her as someone not quite adult. Incendiary Blond aside—based on the life of singer Texas Guinan—Hutton's attractiveness was neither promoted nor consumed as erotic, urbane, or glamorous, and it would not be controversial to say that Hutton epitomized the image of an upbeat, all-American white palliative that Hollywood finds useful during wartime. Her singing style enforced this image as well. Belters are associated with powerful femininities, but due to the conspicuous physicality of their vocal production, are rarely perceived as transcendently glamorous; even in contrast to Garland, Hutton's belt seemed eager, innocent, untried. Hutton was a Paramount player until 1952, when she resigned in a contract dispute and, several years later, saw her star power begin to wane.

Doris Day sang with big bands before going to Hollywood. Her 1945 recording of "Sentimental Journey" with Les Brown clinched her fame, and the piece would become associated with her for the rest of her life. That background—especially in contrast to Hutton's—is evident in her work for *Calamity Jane*, and was well served by Fain and Webster's songs for the show. Calamity's numbers—with exceptions such as "I Can Do Without You"—did not require her to be in character when singing, and Day/Calamity never appears quite the bumpkin that Hutton/Annie does, vocally or visually. Day's voice is also crisper and brighter than Hutton's, and exudes more control and confidence. Also unlike Hutton, Day continued her work as a recording star during and after her work for film and television.

Usually linked to male singers, crooning was also a popular singing style for white female singers such as Dinah Shore beginning in the early 1940s. Their popularity lasted well in the 1950s (e.g., Peggy Lee, Julie London) and, like male crooners, started waning as rock and roll displaced it and other popular singing styles. At the time of *Calamity Jane*, Day fit well in this crooning category, excelling at light swing and romantic ballads. Her vocal and overall image, as the relaxed girl next door, not a drama diva out to shock, burnished Day with a gentility and softness that she sustained even when playing a tousled tomboy. By contrast, belter Betty Hutton's image did not enjoy such gentility, since class, gender, and ethnic markers differentiated the two singing styles, along with the women who performed them. Hutton's belting style and delivery still suggested a woman from the wrong side of the tracks, even if she did not seem terribly sexualized or adult in the proceedings. Moreover, by the time of *Annie Get Your Gun*, Hutton's voice had acquired a certain huskiness as an early result of alcohol abuse.

Day's voice never had that grittiness. Instead, it was smooth and crisp, in keeping with other white pop singers of the 1940s and 1950s who stayed out of low registers and showed careful enunciation without much huskiness or depth. Yet unlike some of them (e.g., Shore), Day's voice was marked less by emotional intensity than by transparency, a sense of assurance over display. That feature probably helped Day enjoy longer and more cross-media success than Hutton. As Peter Kemp has maintained for Julie Andrews, Day had a vocal clarity that connoted emotional transparency and wholesomeness, whereas Hutton's voice, though not without transparency, lacked that crispness.[21] Berlin's songs for *Annie* reinforced this, demanding frequent gimmicks and characterizations, requiring Hutton to punch up rhythms and her overall delivery, whereas only a couple of *Calamity*'s songs ask that of Day: "Whip Crack Away" has occasional dropped "g's" and "I Can Do Without You" has her sock out her retorts to Keel/Hickok.

The songs of *Annie Get Your Gun* fully reveal their Broadway origins: rhythmically uncomplicated, with memorable refrains, easy to sing and easier to buy. Berlin's in particular are characterized by their limited range and memorability, and are rather simply written, at once enhancing the simplicity of the show's protagonist as well as facilitating audience access. *Calamity* adheres to the same formula, although as we shall see, with more deviations. Both films feature classic scene-setting numbers ("Colonial Buffalo Bill is Coming" and "Deadwood Stage"), competition numbers between sparring couples ("Anything You Can Do" and "I Can Do Without You"), and songs of confessional longing performed for the benefit of the audience ("My Defenses are Down" and "Secret Love").

Annie's songs serve primarily as vehicles to establish the traits and desires of the show's characters, not to showcase the singers' skills. Achieving that end, ironically, necessitates vocal flourishes and gimmicks. Annie required Betty Hutton to rough up her voice, to complement the dialect in Berlin's lyrics which she performed in a heavily caricatured western accent. In songs such as "You Can't Get a Man With a Gun," Hutton forces her breath out so hard that her effort nearly overwhelms the lyrics. "Doin' What Comes Nat'rly" is filled with vocal hiccups[22] and, like "Gun," has a nasal dialect built into it via Berlin's lyrics ("you cain't git a man"). The show's songs required extroverted, showy performance, something perfectly suited for theatrical musicals and singers such as Hutton, although less appropriate for film musicals. Indeed, it is no accident that the two songs MGM dropped from the original stage version, "Moonshine Lullaby" and "I Got Lost in His Arms," were romantic ballads.

The song list of Calamity is far less theatrical. Day performs as a singer, not as a character, delivering most of the western hick dialect through dialogue, not song, again giving her a confidence Annie withheld from Hutton. Indeed, Hutton's vocal performance in Annie can be described as trying too hard; in Calamity, Day's seems to strive not at all. Much of this is Day's singing style: she doesn't slug out her delivery, and is more restrained with showy techniques (such as belting), which has the additional effect of making her seem less eager to please. In other words, Day, as Calamity, seems indifferent to listeners accepting her, which in some ways makes her the more conventional western hero, since that hero's autonomy is secured partly by disinterest in the recognition of others.

In the end, however, Hutton's trying so hard to please and Day's hands-off approach lead to similar ends. Both reveal the artifice required to codify the West: Hutton achieves this by constantly performing westernness, Day by being its breezy visitor. Hutton acts and sings as if she were on a stage, whereas Day seems as if she would have been perfectly at ease performing in a night club or recording studio. Because both singers do not adhere to prevailing conventions for film musicals—much less for westerns—they further suggest one-off novelties.

Howard Keel's singing career was firmly tied to his work in the cinema. His performances in both Annie Get Your Gun and Calamity Jane are far less showy than either of his co-stars. His clear, strong baritone was like those of John Raitt and Gordon MacRae, also popular in stage and film musicals of the late 1940s and 1950s and presented relaxed yet confident, virile forms of masculinity reminiscent of the macho beefcakes of the 1940s (e.g., John Wayne, Robert Mitchum) but without their threat of volatility and violence. Keel's comforting baritone was boosted not just by how the characters of Frank Butler and Bill Hickok were written, but by how he inhabited them: his performance is assured without being over the top. At the same time, while Keel's voice, demeanor, and physical presence in *Annie* and *Calamity* may have offered a reassuring form of masculinity, it did not mesh with non-singing forms of masculinity emerging in Hollywood at the same time. Consider its gently neurotic forms (James Dean), its agitated time bombs (Robert Ryan), its downtrodden nerds (Jack Lemmon), and its heroic caricatures (Charleton Heston). In this regard, Keel's place in both *Annie* and *Calamity Jane*—no matter how lavishly outfitted (or, in *Calamity*, briefly cross dressed)—impressed with the assurance of established, perhaps vanishing gender convention, a counterweight to the stranger, newer territory enacted by his female co-stars.

Sung Signs of the American West

The songs of both films signal western idioms in overwhelmingly hackneyed ways. The accompaniment to "Just Blew in from the Windy City" in *Calamity* suggests a banjo, and "Deadwood Stage" uses the loping rhythms that Hollywood often employed to suggest the trotting of horses. The presence of Native Americans in both films is conveyed through the clichéd intimations of pentatonic scales, the vocal pulsation of the longer notes, and steady, punctuated tom-tom drumbeats—the first of every four accented. This is especially the case in "I'm An Indian Too," the extravagant novelty number in *Annie Get Your Gun*, which accompanies the ceremony in which Annie is adopted as the daughter of Sitting Bull, another performer in Wild Bill's show. The *mise en scène* serves to further the trite ethnic clichés. Alton's choreography, the homoeroticism of which is stunningly overt, showcases dozens of half-nude Indian men (played by white dancers). Hutton's movements are restricted to schticky, white-fear poses as she confronts individual men or tries clumsily to mimic their movements. For a 1950 musical number it is resoundingly vaudeville in its retro ethnic humor; for audiences at the beginning of the twenty-first century, it is far worse than that. In her study of Indian music in westerns, Claudia Gorbman puts it best: "Both narratively and musically, the Indians are reduced to ciphers, bits of local color."[23] Moreover, neither *Annie* nor *Calamity* contains any intimation of jazz, or any other non-white musical influence, except at arm's distance in *Annie*'s "I Got the Sun in the Morning."

"Any effort to convey the West," adds music critic James Reel, "comes mainly from the [two] singers, who sometimes adopt a nasal bumpkin twang and employ that Yosemite Sam dialect that seems to occur only in the environs of Hollywood."[24] This feature is strongest at the beginning, before Annie and Calamity shed their bumpkin status to achieve the "peaches and cream" that make them eligible gender partners. Again, Day deploys the hokey dialect primarily when speaking (Chicago is always "Chi-cahgee"), shedding it in song (exceptions include her elongated "n's" and dropped "g's" in "Windy City"). Hutton, by contrast, frequently deploys the faux-western dialect in speech and especially in song, but again, loses it as she progresses toward becoming the "peaches and cream" partner of Bill.

Interestingly, over the course of "Woman's Touch," the female–female number in which Calamity's persona and home are femmed up, the voice of both women shift. By the song's end, Day's has lost its initial masculine brashness, roughness, and forced twanginess, whereas McLerie's voice as Katie accumulates more twang and informality; by the end of the song the two are singing quite similarly. From that point on, Day's western idiolects drop out almost entirely from her songs, and even the diegetic music comments upon her gentrification. At the dance where Calamity, as Bill's date, is unveiled as glamorous femme, the band plays "It's Harry I'm Planning to Marry" (initially performed by the real Adelaid Adams).

Preserving musical signifiers of the West might seem important work for a western, even a musical one, yet shedding them is hardly surprising. These are Pygmalion narratives after all, stories intent on proper heterosexual pairing and needing music to match. Such effacement is not restricted to comic modalities such as Hollywood musicals, pre- or post-Paramount. As Susan McClary has argued in her analysis of Bizet's *Carmen*, whose hints of non-Anglo otherness and sexuality ideologically need to be "resolved" (i.e., destroyed) in the storyline, so too do they require musically resolution, and the opera does just that, by dispatching the chromatic elements that had been linked to the heavily sexualized Latina.[25]

Figure 5.2 *Calamity Jane*

Of the song lists considered here, only *Calamity*'s "Black Hills of Dakota" uses aspects of western music without kitsching them up. Western ballads are characterized by steady, uncomplicated rhythms, which "Black Hills" shares. Moreover, Day and Keel (and a chorus of townspeople) perform the tune with affective fondness—again, not passion—on their way to the dance, giving it a communal function typical of songs in westerns, its lyrics expressing their appreciation of the land around them: no clichéd dialect or delivery gimmicks to joke it up. At the other end of the scale, however, is Francis's "Hive Full of Honey," in which he/she is looking for the right kind of "honey bee." A historical throw-back to burlesque, complete with risqué lyrics and double entendres, it stands apart from all of *Calamity*'s other tunes (and from 1950s pop music), a lambent queer moment indeed. In many ways, the songs of both *Annie* and *Calamity* simply do not belong in a film western—or perhaps even in a film musical—since *Annie*'s song list derives from the original stage production and *Calamity*'s, arguably, has no connection to the movie at all.

Gender and Genre Inauthenticity

For fans of quirky and queer musicals, *Annie Get Your Gun* and, especially, *Calamity Jane* are rich for the picking. Part of their attraction, as Eric Savoy and Tamar McDonald have maintained vis-à-vis *Calamity*, is their emphasis on performativity, a focus that helps expose the instability of gender and posits queerer, unsettled gender production.[26] *Calamity*, a lesbian camp classic for decades, openly depicts gender as fluctuating and is a highly performative text. First is Francis as Frances, then Katie as Adelaid. Before Calamity mistakes Katie for Adelaid in her dressing room, Katie takes Calamity to be a young man; and Calamity, who had earlier attracted solicitous views from Chicago women, asks Katie, "How do you keep that dress up?" Even tough old Bill Hickok has his identity-in-flux moment when he appears as a Sioux woman complete with screaming infant after losing a bet to Calamity. (Bill's gender and ethnic confusion, of course, is a fleeting joke played for crude laughs, too much for the film to sustain.)

Calamity's iconic queer moments occur in "A Woman's Touch," in which Calamity and Katie playfully spruce up Calamity's cabin to live in, diegetically explained by Calamity's jealous protectiveness of Katie, whom Bill and her own heart-throb, Danny Gilmartin (Philip Carey), are pursuing. The women sing, clean, paint, and decorate the tiny shack in a dazzling butch/femme sequence. Calamity too moves from dirty buckskin to groomed hair, frilly blouse and wasp-waisted skirt. In contrast to Annie Oakley, who gentrifies herself in an earnest desire to please Frank Butler, Calamity is bemused by the whole affair, donning bloomers over her arms, later referring to them as Katie's "man-traps." Since her femming up is at the hands of—and for the partnership with—another woman, Calamity's final heterosexual domestication is diminished to say the least. Even narratively, the denouement doesn't settle things with much conviction. Spurned by Danny and Katie respectively (who have fallen in love with one another), Calamity and Bill realize their own "Secret Love" in a brief, unpersuasive scene. By concluding with the double wedding of both couples, *Calamity* scarcely defuses its other doublings and impersonations, even after the secret love has been defined and acted upon as a straight one.

Savoy lauds *Calamity Jane* for not shutting down its queer potentiality, especially during a decade he describes as the "most acutely homophobic era" of twentieth-century America.[27] Yet as his analysis attests, the same period was utterly incapable of maintaining a seamless illusion of heteronormativity. Like film genre, gender was undergoing no small upheaval in American culture at the time. Yet if *Calamity* enables "the possibility of a lesbian subject, tentative and evanescent . . . to emerge into visibility,"[28] it is important to recognize that that emergence was also facilitated by the Hollywood film industry, a risk-averse institution with no agenda to ameliorate representations of queer desires or subjects.

For as much as *Annie Get Your Gun* and *Calamity Jane* play with genre- and gender-bending, especially in *Calamity*, the music is not very adventurous. Significantly, the song that takes the most risks is the one celebrated for queer longing, "Secret Love," whose lyrics, like its music, are not even remotely frontier-driven. Unlike the other pieces scored in the simple, homophonic style of conventional Hollywood and Broadway musicals, the melody of "Secret Love" has chromatic elements, just enough to make it float free of typical harmonic structures, but not enough to have it wander off too far from conventions. It is as if its queerness were permitted some expression, but then instantly pulled back. The gently undulating melody of "Secret" is indeed written and delivered in keeping with a typical crooner song of the early 1950s, its orchestration lightly shimmering, but not sublimely transcendent. And interestingly in terms of affect, is that for all the yearning its lyrics first evoke, they finally tell of resolution, a lack of demand. In place of expressed yearning is unthreatening satisfaction, and the passion of Day's delivery is carefully controlled, a restraint in great contrast to the exuberance of, say, Gene Kelly's "Gotta dance!" in *Singin' in the Rain* the previous year. If lesbian and other non-mainstream, queer desires have been easily— and rightly—hitched to "Secret Love," then it is worth stressing that the music itself is not geared for truly unconventional hearings. In that regard, "Secret Love" insures the hailing of many desires and as many consumers as possible. Based on the awards and sales figures it received, it succeeded.

This aspect of "Secret Love" demonstrates one of Hollywood's strategies of the period: aim for as wide an audience as possible—women, children, families, demographics outside of the large urban centers, desires outside of the mainstream. Curiously, Peter Stanfield argues the same thing in relation to earlier B westerns: "The series western sought to be inclusive in its cross-generation and gender address, to exclude no one."[29] In the early to mid-1950s, Hollywood flailed in all directions, trying for mass appeal and targeting niche audiences. Some of its gimmicks were new, such as 3-D and color technologies; others were not, such as adopting aspects of B series singing westerns. So

although A films such as *Annie Get Your Gun* and *Calamity Jane* were fundamentally musicals, their self-conscious style, their singing cowhands and intense
performativity cannot be explained away entirely by their musical pedigrees.
Since Hollywood westerns had no choice but to be A westerns in the early to
mid-1950s, they had to be westerns with a difference, whether that be achieved
through shifting masculinities, odd casting choices, new moral compasses, genre
irregularities, or female leads. The performativity of *Annie Get Your Gun* and
Calamity Jane needs to be taken in this context. Major studios, moreover, were
aware of the stakes, announcing the gimmicks they used to grab back audiences
in ads boasting about production details (Warner Bros.' trailer for *Annie*
boasted of its "Technicolor!" and "Cast of Thousands!"), or more tacitly, by
the attention-grabbing techniques of the films themselves. It was as if
Hollywood genre films were screaming in all directions, "watch me." But with
Annie and *Calamity*, the music was not screaming out in the same way.

It might have. For film music was part of the overall sea change experienced
by the Hollywood industry of the time, seeing the hegemony of its classical neo-
romantic underscore diminishing along with the dismantling of in-house studio
orchestras. Scores now featured art music that broke with tonality (Leonard
Rosenmann), jazz (Elmer Bernstein), and, of course, pop, and rock and roll
tunes. Title songs were released as hits, helping Hollywood stay afloat by
diversifying its interests. Clearly the songs of *Annie Get Your Gun* and *Calamity
Jane* were a huge part of the films' success. Yet for as much as both movies played
with genre and gender, especially in *Calamity Jane*, musically, very little works
in that direction. The songs in *Annie* and *Calamity* remain by and large
conventional, scarcely working to challenge the generic parameters of
Hollywood musical form. There are exceptions, to be sure—Francis's burlesque
number, Day's lack of affect, and Hutton's excess of it.

Gender Irregularity for Sale

Faced with the crisis of post-Paramount restructuring, declining profits, new
media and changing audience interests, major studios needed enough instability
and innovation to market their projects, but not enough novelty to scare
anyone off. In that regard, *Annie and Calamity Jane* hardly seem like bold
experiments. Still, even if they are not as convention-busting as queer readings
might assert, they do speak to how queerness resides within heteronormativity
and within mainstream institutions such as Hollywood genre and heterosexuality. At the same time, they show how queerness can be yoked to commercial ends as easily as progressive academic ones. With *Annie Get Your Gun*
and *Calamity Jane*, MGM and Warner Bros. may have engineered an odd
marriage of genres and a fun new way of packaging heterosexual romance. But
that's where the innovation stopped. For precious little of the two films'
quirkiness is established through the songs themselves. True, they belong, not
belong, seem there, not there, momentarily queer, unconvincing in affect. But
peeled back just a bit, the songs reveal little more than regular and largely

regulatory structures executed musically. Their familiar conventions provided an assurance that the oddly gendered characters singing them did not. In the end, it is probably no surprise that producers wanted to corral the gender and genre-bending elements that *Annie* and *Calamity* might musically have offered to minimize the risk of simply going too far.

Notes

I would like to thank James Reel and especially Kathryn Kalinak, for being the fastest (and best) editor in the West.

1 http://www.enotes.com/topic/Secret_Love_(1953_song). Accessed March 24, 2011.
2 Eric Savoy, "'That Ain't All She Ain't': *Calamity Jane*" in *Out Takes: Essays on Queer Theory and Film*, ed. Ellis Hanson (Durham: Duke University Press 1999), 155.
3 André Bazín, "*La politique des auteurs*" in *The New Wave*, ed. Peter Graham (no translator) (Garden City, NY: Doubleday, 1968), 154.
4 Paul Rosenfeld, "Folksong and Culture-Politics," *Modern Music* 17, 4 (1940), 20.
5 Berlin quoted in Caryl Flinn, *Brass Diva: The Life and Legends of Ethel Merman* (Berkeley: University of California Press, 2007), 156.
6 Jane Tompkins, *West of Everything: The Inner Life of Westerns* (New York: Oxford University Press, 1992), 44.
7 Ibid., 12.
8 Ibid., 127.
9 Ibid., 210–11.
10 See especially the musicals of Richard Rodgers and Oscar Hammerstein.
11 See Kathryn Kalinak's analysis of the use of songs in underscoring in John Ford's *The Searchers*, in her *How the West Was Sung: Music in the Westerns of John Ford* (Berkeley: University of California Press, 2007), especially pages 163–79.
12 Roderick McGillis, *He was Some Kind of a Man: Masculinities in the B Western* (Waterloo: Wilfred Laurier University Press, 2009), 20.
13 Ibid., 1–2.
14 B. Ruby Rich, "Hello Cowboy," *The Guardian*, September 23, 2005, http://www.guardian.co/uk/film/2005/sept/23/3. Accessed October 27, 2010.
15 Tompkins, 48.
16 Kovac quoted in Claudia Gorbman, "Scoring the Indian: Music in the Liberal Western" in *Western Music and its Others: Difference, Representation and Appropriation in Music*, eds. Georgina Born and David Hesmondhalgh (Berkeley: University of California Press, 2000), 239.
17 Peter Stanfield, *Horse Opera: The Strange History of the 1930s Singing Cowboy* (Urbana: University of Illinois Press, 2002), 150.
18 http://en.wikipedia.org/wiki/Calamity_Jane. Accessed March 24, 2011.
19 Fields quoted in Flinn, 153.
20 Quoted in Flinn, 168.
21 See Peter Kemp, "How Do You Solve a 'Problem' Like Maria von Poppins?" in *Musicals: Hollywood and Beyond*, eds. Bill Marshall and Robyn Stilwell (Exeter: Intellect Press, 2000), 55–61.
22 This can best be described as a full glottal stop that produces a hiccup-like sound. Rock vocalists Buddy Holly and Michael Jackson used them to great acclaim.
23 Gorbman, 235.
24 Personal correspondence with the author, October 11, 2010.
25 Susan McClary, *Georges Bizet: Carmen* (Cambridge: Cambridge University Press, 1992).

26 See Savoy, and also Tamar Jeffers McDonald, "Carrying Concealed Weapons: Gendered Makeover in *Calamity Jane*," *Journal of Popular Film and Television* 34, 4 (Winter 2007), 179–87.
27 Savoy, 155.
28 Ibid., 153.
29 Stanfield, 45.

Part II

Westerns Outside Hollywood

Innovation and Imitation

An Analysis of the Soundscape of Akira Kurosawa's *Chambara* Westerns

Yuna de Lannoy

Introduction

Sound and music function in an intricate relationship to the visual in two of Akira Kurosawa's period films, *Yojimbo* (1961) and *Sanjuro* (1962). In particular, certain pieces of music from two American westerns, William Wyler's *The Big Country* (1958) and Howard Hawks's *Rio Bravo* (1959), inspired Kurosawa and the composer Masaru Sato in the making of *Yojimbo*, whose musical themes bind it to its sequel *Sanjuro*. Much has already been written about Kurosawa's artistic debt to the western and his influence in turn on the spaghetti western, but few scholars have investigated the music of Kurosawa's films. My purpose here is to illuminate audiovisual relationships in *Yojimbo* and *Sanjuro*, particularly the role of music, and show the connection between the musical themes of these *chambara* films and the scores of the two American westerns which inspired them.

Collaborating with Sato, arguably Japan's most prolific film composer in the last century, Kurosawa crafted a new type of soundscape for *chambara* (sword fight) films that would have a long-lasting impact both at home and abroad. Throughout this chapter I refer to Kurosawa's two films as *chambara* rather than *jidaigeki*, the latter being a more encompassing term meaning period drama in general. The word *chambara* describes period films which have swordfight sequences as the highlight of the narrative. It is a shortened form of the Japanese onomatopoetic "*chan-chan bara-bara*," representing the clinking sound of swords. *Chambara* films are closely associated with the Edo period (*c.*1600–1868), in which samurai were no longer real warriors accompanying their lords to battles but were rather working as bureaucrats while following their strict social and moral codes of *bushido*. The genre of the *chambara* is often compared to the western, since both share many characteristics in spite of cultural differences between their countries of origin.[1]

Kurosawa has been frequently referred to as the most Westernized Japanese filmmaker and, in making *Yojimbo*, in fact, Kurosawa stated that he "took lessons in the grammar of the western."[2] Many critics thus draw attention to the film's stylistic resemblance to the American western. Donald Richie, for example, points out that the town in *Yojimbo* is very similar to "those god-forsaken places in the middle of nowhere" in the westerns of John Ford or John Sturges,[3] an aspect that inspired David Desser's study of Kurosawa's period films.[4] Kurosawa himself said on several occasions that the western, especially Ford's films, significantly influenced his work.[5] In his later life, Kurosawa spoke at great length about the biography of Ford, *Pappy*, written by his grandson, Dan Ford, and expressed his sympathy with the American director for the hardships in his career.[6]

With regard to *Sanjuro*, however, critical opinion is divided as to whether or not it has also been influenced by the western. While Richie observes that *Sanjuro* is based on *Yojimbo* and Japanese period drama,[7] Burch dismisses the film as a mere concession to Japanese popular taste for swordfight movies.[8] Desser discusses in detail how *Sanjuro* borrows many elements from *Shane* (1953);[9] but Yoshimoto disagrees, asserting that the film is without any close relation to Stevens's film.[10] I will argue that genuine connections between *Sanjuro* and the western exist and are revealed through the music. As far as the swordfight is concerned, we will see that far from being a "mere concession" to popular taste, *Sanjuro* had instead a profound influence on the genre.

Different sources suggest Kurosawa's seemingly contradictory intentions in making *Yojimbo*. Richie writes that this was Kurosawa's first "full-length comedy."[11] Sato also recalls that Kurosawa was very eager to make a comic film, saying that the director was "laughing seriously" while shooting *Yojimbo*.[12] According to Yamada, however, Kurosawa desired instead to send a solemn message to the audience and to remind them of "the scariness of carrying a sword as well as the meaninglessness of killings."[13] Clearly Kurosawa aspired to challenge the conventional notion of *chambara*, a conservative genre saturated with audio and visual clichés.

Popular *chambara* films in the late 1950s were mass produced by Toei and Daiei, two of the four major studios of the time. Toei was particularly prolific in creating long-running series with their star actors, including Chiezo Kataoka and Utaemon Ichikawa. The action scenes of *chambara* were packed with what Philip Kemp calls "clean violence—no blood, no agony and certainly no severed limbs."[14] *Yojimbo* subverted the predictability of the genre by introducing fast and shocking sword fight scenes.[15] The protagonist is a master of *iai*, a Japanese fencing technique consisting in unsheathing a sword and killing one's opponent in a single movement. In addition, according to Yoshimoto, the film pioneered sound effects for the cutting of human flesh and bones, and severed hands and arms were clearly shown.[16] However, these were not the only innovations *Yojimbo* introduced.

Yojimbo and Music in the Western

In his memoirs, Sato gives a short but vivid account of his discussions with Kurosawa in the early stages of *Yojimbo*'s production. He claimed that Kurosawa first asked him if there were any novel contemporary ideas concerning music for period films. This might seem a rather unlikely request for a director known to make pointed and sometimes unreasonable demands of composers.[17] Giving a piece of well-known music as an example and requesting the composer to write "something similar but better" was a technique typically used by Kurosawa from his early career onwards.[18] Nonetheless, since it was Kurosawa's first time making *chambara*, he did in fact seek the composer's professional opinion.[19] Sato answered Kurosawa's query by giving two examples, *The Big Country* and *Rio Bravo*, saying that these films were both "masterpieces of the western."[20] Using a linguistic analogy, Sato described the music of the former film as "written style" and that of the latter as "spoken style," and commented on the music's ability to define the different tones of the respective films so effectively. Kurosawa agreed with him, and asked therefore what could be done for their film.

Sato's interpretation of the music of the two American films may become clearer if we replace what he referred to as "written" and "spoken" styles by "symphonic music" and "country and western." Indeed, the music in *The Big Country* is more formal and classical,[21] while *Rio Bravo* features music associated with the frontier, such as a Mexican cantina band as well as harmonica and guitar. Compared to *Rio Bravo*'s classical western structure, the music of *The Big Country* may have been a drastic departure from the western genre, but Sato brought these two films together and made a perceptive observation about contrasting characteristics of their music. It is very interesting that, for Sato and Kurosawa, it went without saying that the western was an appropriate source for innovative ideas for their *chambara* film.

The openings of the two American films underscore Sato's remark. In both, the music illustrates the arrival of key characters in town, although from two contrasting musical approaches. The orchestral main title heard during the opening sequence of *The Big Country* accompanies the title credits that are superimposed on shots of a stagecoach crossing the plains. The score conforms to the standard procedures of Hollywood orchestration: violins play the melody in the highest register of the orchestra, followed by trumpets which play magnificent fanfares that will recur throughout the film, and timpanis which anticipate the opening of a grand spectacle. This cue conveys the speed of the coach and a sense of freedom in the open air, and perhaps its composer, Jerome Moross, intended to illustrate the excitement of the protagonist, a former ship's captain, impatient to reach the town where his fiancée awaits him.

Rio Bravo also begins with shots of a travel. We see a wagon train, although this is accompanied by leisurely paced country music. The music is played with guitar, harmonica, and temple blocks, a percussion instrument that evokes the sound of horseshoes striking the ground. The characters shown in these opening shots are in fact not the two main characters, but a minor character, Pat Wheeler (Ward Bond) and his men. Among the wagon train's team is the young man, Colorado (Ricky Nelson), who will join the sheriff and his deputy and become their valued teammate.

Yojimbo similarly opens with the journey of its protagonist into town. The sequence is accompanied by the main title, comprising a musical theme known as *Sanjuro's Theme*. According to Kobayashi, a short introduction by timpani, bongo, maracas, and saxophone accompanies the Toho logo, followed by the Japanese characters representing the co-producers, that is, "Kurosawa Productions" and "Toho."[22] Then a harpsichord plays a phrase as we see the Japanese title *Yojimbo* on the screen with mountains as a backdrop. As soon as the back of a *ronin*, a masterless samurai named Sanjuro (Toshiro Mifune), appears, a trombone, trumpet, and tuba solemnly play long, low notes. The brass is then joined by percussion playing a rhythm that is syncopated at the end of the phrase (Figure 6.1) followed by the lush melody, played by low instruments in unison (Figure 6.2) played over the rhythm.

This opening sequence reveals how the Japanese filmmakers endeavored to emulate the achievements of their American counterparts. Indeed, the opening is clearly modeled on that of both *The Big Country* and *Rio Bravo*, introducing us to the protagonist as he travels from the frontier into the town. As in *The Big Country*, the credits are superimposed over this opening sequence, a departure from Kurosawa's past practice in earlier black and white films where the titles were not superimposed over the action. In both *The Big Country* and *Yojimbo* the music emphasizes the speed of travel: the fast pace of the stagecoach matched by the tempo of the music in *The Big Country*, and in *Yojimbo*, the casual and deliberate pace of the protagonist traveling on foot, without any motivation to go faster, accompanied by the slow tempo (*andante*) of *Sanjuro's Theme*. Moreover, although the medium close-ups, rear tracking, and low angles of *Yojimbo*'s opening contrast with the long shots, frontal perspective, and static camera of the wagon train in *Rio Bravo*, the music resonates between the two films. After *Yojimbo*'s main title ends, a short non-diegetic piece with banjo and woodwind plays a variation of *Sanjuro's Theme* as Sanjuro stands at a crossroads, wondering which way he should go. The banjo is clearly out of place in the setting but in referencing one of the western's iconic instruments, *Yojimbo* shares with *Rio Bravo* a dependence on instruments which connote westernness.

The outline of *Sanjuro's Theme* was originally written for a documentary film that was released in the same year as *Yojimbo* about the construction of a

Figure 6.1 Sanjuro's theme (rhythm)

Figure 6.2 Sanjuro's theme (melody)

dam.[23] Sato first used the cue from the documentary to accompany the trailer of *Yojimbo* and Kurosawa liked Sato's music so much that he asked the composer to use it as a basis for the protagonist's theme in *Yojimbo*.[24] Sato thus recycled the rhythm and rewrote the melody for Kurosawa's film. According to Whitmer, most of Moross's rhythms in the score of *The Big Country* are syncopated, an aspect that underscores the American composer's most distinctly "American" style.[25] Sato may have been aware of the association of syncopated rhythm and Americanness and that was probably why he retained the rhythm of the original cue. It may even have been the very reason for using it for the trailer in the first instance. Furthermore, Sato subverted the conventional orchestral scoring and reversed the roles of the respective parts.[26] The violin part was eliminated and the main theme was presented by low strings, with the viola playing in a lower register than the cello. In the brass part, the typical roles of the instruments were also reversed, with the trumpet playing in a lower register than the trombone. In addition, the percussion section was augmented to eight musicians.

Sanjuro's Theme generally appears when Sanjuro displays his brilliant sword skills. Compared to *Sanjuro's Theme*'s masculine qualities, suggested by the low registers and especially the role reversal of several instruments, as well as the breadth brought about by the melody played in unison by several parts, the second main theme, representing the *yakuza*, sounds comical and cowardly, acting as a metaphorical antithesis to that of the main character. In the *yakuza*'s theme, the xylophone's harsh dissonance suggests their comical absurdity as well as lack of organization and intellectual capacities.

The following dialogue, taken from Sato's memoirs, provides more information about the genesis of *Yojimbo*'s soundtrack:

[Kurosawa:] "If only Mifune could play the guitar!"
[Sato:] "Sanjuro and a guitar isn't a good match."
[K:] "But it would look awkward if he played 'pekôn' [Japanese onomatopoeia for strumming the *shamisen*] with *shamisen*."
[S:] "In the western, if somebody could do 'jaraaan' [Japanese onomatopoeia for strumming a guitar], that alone would make him cool."[27]

Three different issues emerge from this conversation. First and foremost, it shows that Kurosawa was aware of the essential role *diegetic* music plays in the western. Second, Kurosawa and Sato are concerned with the issue of the historical authenticity of music and musical instruments in period drama. Finally, the conversation indicates the contrasting relationships between the protagonist and music in Japanese and American films.

In *Rio Bravo*, music is performed diegetically in key sequences of the film, most notably *Degüello* and the two songs ("My Rifle, My Pony, and Me" and "[Get Along Home] Cindy, Cindy") sung by Dean Martin and teen idol Ricky Nelson. Otherwise, the music exists, in general, in the background, quite faint and subdued, making its status as non-diegetic or diegetic ambiguous. While holding out against hired guns who are trying to get Joe Burdette (Claude

Akins), a local thug, out of jail, Dude (Dean Martin) and Colorado perform two songs while Stumpy (Walter Brennan) plays the harmonica and Sheriff John T. Chance (John Wayne) listens to them. This is a highly memorable sequence, because the diegetic songs unite four diverse characters facing a common danger. In *The Big Country*, the diegetic chamber music in the party sequence at Terrill's sumptuous home functions effectively to portray the elegance of the town's privileged class, in sharp contrast with the roughness of Rufus Hannassey (Burl Ives), who interrupts the party, as well as with the brutality of Henry Terrill (Charles Bickford) earlier in the film.

The *Degüello*, the "cut-throat song," was originally played by the Mexican army to the Texans at the Battle of the Alamo in 1836, according to Colorado, and is first heard diegetically in *Rio Bravo* when Nathan Burdette (John Russell) requests the cantina band in the bar in Carlos's hotel to play the piece. (Incidentally, the hotel is called The Alamo). In a recent version of *The Alamo* (2004), we hear a totally different version of the *Degüello* played on bugle and drums. This 2004 piece is probably the authentic version actually played during the famous battle in 1836. The piece consists of repetitions of a bugle call, and the soldiers playing the piece are shown without discernible expressions, as if they were mechanical dolls. Tiomkin did access the score of the "authentic" version, but chose to compose his own *Degüello* for the cornet and the guitar.[28] Charles Leinberger's argument also supports the originality of Tiomkin's tune from a technical and historical viewpoint.[29]

Kalinak writes that guitars were deeply rooted in Mexican popular culture and often played a central role in the scoring of music in the western as one of "stereotypical musical markers" for Mexico.[30] It is important to note, however, that their link with western United States is more of a contrived one, since the instrument was not generally used by American cowboys in the nineteenth century.[31] Tiomkin's choice of the musical instruments for his *Degüello*, especially his use of the guitar, was thus in accordance with the prevailing trend in Hollywood film scoring. In Tiomkin's cue, the cornet alternates between long notes and ornaments in a minor key, sounding more melancholic and therefore more fitting to the scene than the dehumanized quality of the original melody. In both films, the band playing the *Degüello* emphasizes the otherness of the Mexicans. In *Rio Bravo*, it does so in the more traditional manner of presenting them as an exotic other, whereas in the 2004 *Alamo*, this otherness is conveyed through their dehumanized discipline contrasted with the loose egalitarian ethos of the Americans.

In *Yojimbo*, Kurosawa and Sato also struggled to fill the gap between an authentic music associated with nineteenth-century Japan and their desire to have music play a critical role in the film's diegesis. The conversation cited above shows that Sato and Kurosawa associated guitars with western heroes. As we have seen, this is not in fact historically accurate but a convention that became widespread and acquired a new authenticity in its own right in the early twentieth century with the development of the popular media. Of course, the Japanese filmmakers knew that it was not realistic to have their Japanese hero play a guitar. However, the *shamisen*, which might be regarded as an eastern version of the guitar, was not a viable choice either, because Kurosawa thought that the Japanese instrument was not aesthetically attractive enough, either aurally or visually. This is shown by the fact that in his conversation with Sato, he described the sound of *shamisen* using the onomatopoeic term "*pekôn*" which implies clumsiness, if not outright ludicrousness.

Another problem with musical authenticity occurred while Kurosawa and Sato were working on a scene, accompanied by the "prostitutes' theme," which crosses the border between the diegetic and the non-diegetic. It is first heard non-diegetically on harpsichord and percussion accompanying the women paying a visit to the local inspector. The theme itself was originally written to sound like the *yagi-bushi*, a genuine folk dance of Joshu (a contemporary Gunma prefecture near Tokyo) where the film was set.[32] Sato recalled, however, that what he wrote was simple traditional Japanese music that sounded rather boring. Kurosawa, too, did not like it at first, but then suggested a creative solution: he told the *shamisen* player to repeat the same phrase—a syncopated phrase consisting of E, B, and D—over and over again, and determined that the percussion should be improvised. The music was then pre-recorded, using electric *shamisen*, drums, *chanchiki* (a Japanese percussion instrument) and bongo, and the actors performed the sequence to the recorded music.[33] The end result was a powerfully grotesque scene, in which the dancers move quickly and energetically to keep up with the fast pace of the dynamic music. They make crude gestures, swaying their hips and lifting their legs. We even wonder if we hear a thump when their legs move up and down in front of Sanjuro's eyes.

Sanjuro's interpolated medium shot shows him frowning at the dancers' dangling legs. He looks unimpressed by their coarsely seductive dance and quickly leaves the room, telling Seibei (Seizaburo Kawazu) and his wife to keep the two captives secure. Sanjuro's indifference to the dance shows his wariness and cold-bloodedness: he is a perfectly focused warrior who is not distracted by amusements. His only apparent weakness, drinking, does not affect his capacity to fight. In *Rio Bravo* singing is a necessary distraction underlining the process of male bonding; the solitary drinking of Sanjuro, on the other hand, exposes his estrangement from those around him. Sanjuro's perfectly focused warrior is more comparable to Sheriff Chance, who enjoys a romance with a girl and appreciates his colleagues' songs without joining in, while sipping a cup of coffee off screen as his friends sing.

In *Rio Bravo*, the dominant trope is given by the repeated ups and downs of Dude whose alcohol addiction repeatedly leads to disaster but who, thanks to Chance's unfaltering support, regains his dignity through several heroic deeds. In an early scene in *Rio Bravo*, when Chance brutally knocks down Joe Burdette in a saloon and drags him away, a drum beat begins. This drum acts as a sound bridge to the next scene in which we see a funeral procession headed by a Mexican boy playing a drum, the source of the sound we heard in the previous scene. During the sound of the drum, Dude, leaning on a low pole, notices something coming toward him. Because the drum is heard off screen, we expect a reverse shot of the funeral procession for the next shot. Instead, Dude's point-of-view shows a wagon train arriving in town. The camera then focuses on Pat Wheeler on horseback, still accompanied by the drum sound. In the next shot Dude gets up and, lifting his right arm, walks to screen-left. While the camera follows Dude, the procession moves in the background to screen-right. Although taking place in broad daylight, this short scene appears somewhat ominous, as if suggesting Wheeler's imminent death through the editing which cuts between Wheeler's wagon train and the funeral, linking them both aurally by the drum sound and visually by Dude's presence. The connection of sound and the image through the editing effectively foreshadows narrative events as Wheeler does indeed get killed by a hired gun soon after this scene.

A similar Hawksian editing, also derived from the aesthetics of silent cinema, is found in *Yojimbo*, when the two fighting *yakuza* clans exchange their hostages. It is very likely that the idea of exchanging hostages comes directly from *Rio Bravo* where Dude and Joe Burdette are exchanged in an empty farm just outside the town. As Chance and Colorado on the one side and the Burdette clan on the other side observe the hostages moving toward each other, Dude suddenly attacks Joe, a movement that triggers Chance and Colorado to start shooting at the house in which the Burdette clan is holed up. In *Yojimbo*, a similar exchange occurs in two steps, as revealing of the treacherous nature and cruelty of both *yakuza* groups as the *Rio Bravo* exchange was revealing of Dude's heroic character. Initially Unosuke (Tatsuya Nakadai) kills the two gangsters held hostage by his enemy, while his group keeps Seibei's son. In return, Seibei immediately presents a new prisoner, Nui (Yoko Tsukasa), a beautiful woman. When the camera focuses on Nui's face, a piece of non-diegetic music begins and then the camera cuts back to Unosuke as he, startled, turns toward Nui and her captors. The music, "Nui's theme," played on the harpsichord "aiming to produce the effect of a balalaika,"[34] also continues into a medium shot of Unosuke, creating the impression that he has been emotionally affected and making the spectator wonder if the woman is Unosuke's girlfriend or wife. However, we discover in the following scene that she is the mistress of the business associate of the *yakuza* who took her from an unfortunate man who had lost everything because of gambling. The deeply poignant music accompanies alternate shots of Unosuke and close-ups of Nui, expressing Nui's misery and revealing by contrast that what appeared to be emotion in Unosuke's surprise was only an upset at a tactical setback, creating an intriguing uncertainty in the film's otherwise unambiguous plot.

Sanjuro and Beyond

The original script of *Sanjuro* was entitled *Nichi-nichi heian*, based on the novel of that title by Shugoro Yamamoto.[35] The original protagonist was a weak and comical *ronin* who nonetheless helps a group of young samurai who hope to obtain a position in their *han* (feudal domain). Due to the immense commercial and critical success of *Yojimbo*, however, Toho asked Kurosawa to make another film with the same hero. Kurosawa decided to rewrite the script of *Nichi-nichi* and replaced the weak protagonist with strong Sanjuro.[36] Casting the new young stars from Toho,[37] *Sanjuro* is a product of the compromise between the studio's wish to make a sequel with their own popular actors and Kurosawa's ambition to direct another film in the *chambara* genre. Instead of playing two *yakuza* clans off against each other as he does in *Yojimbo*, Sanjuro here aids a group of young samurai who are struggling in a good cause—they want to rid their *han* of financial corruption. Although reluctantly, Sanjuro acts as their mentor in order to help them fulfill their objectives.

The opening of the film reveals at once that the musical design of this film is more solemn and minimalist than that of *Yojimbo*. With the appearance of the Toho logo we hear a dry, eerie percussion sound and a series of short notes played in unison by drum, low strings, and piano. The percussion here is the *quijada*, a traditional Latin American instrument made out of a donkey jaw. The rattle sound is created by hitting the jawbones which makes the teeth in the jaw tremble. The random sound of woodwind and alto sax accompany the Japanese characters "Kurosawa Productions" and "Toho" followed by a melody accompanying the title credits. Unlike *Yojimbo*, there is no initial sequence showing Sanjuro's journey. The music is a variation of *Sanjuro's Theme* but lacking the rhythm that lent a wild and carefree nature to the theme as it appeared in *Yojimbo*. Instead, low strings, xylophone, and muted brass present the theme in a dignified manner, while the sound of *quijada* is frequently inserted. The melody begins with the same note, C, as *Sanjuro's Theme*, and followed by the same descending second (C to B flat) but instead of continuing the familiar tune sonorously, the new theme proceeds hesitantly, with semitones, suggesting that Sanjuro's carefree aspect is attenuated by a sense of restraint that was prevalent within the society of samurai, the ruling class of the Edo period. Sanjuro's fierce nature is also subdued as a result of his awkward interaction with the chamberlain's wife, who tells him quietly that he should not kill people indiscriminately. In the rest of the film, along with drums, the *quijada* is used diegetically as well as non-diegetically to bridge transitions between scenes, working as a musical punctuation mark. Sato does not explain if the idea of using the *quijada* was influenced by the western, nor does he elucidate the origin of this inspiration in any way. In fact, the *quijada* was not commonly used in the western, and Sato confirms that *Sanjuro* was the first Japanese film in which the *quijada* was played.[38] Nevertheless, *quijada* provides a clear musical link between *Sanjuro* and Latin American elements in the American West.

The diegetic soundscape of *Yojimbo* is most notably defined by the whistling sound of the dry wind, the cooper's hammers and the prayer drum. In *Sanjuro*, these dry and harsh sounds are replaced with the mellow and soothing sound of a brook and the chirping of bush warblers. However, the sound of swords cutting human flesh is heard more clearly in *Sanjuro* than in *Yojimbo*. Ichiro Minawa, who was in charge of the sound effects for both films, said that this novel sound effect had had to be used very discreetly at first as the use of sounds evoking violence was banned in Japan during the American post-war occupation, and Japanese filmmakers still had to be very careful about using such acoustic effects as late as the early 1960s.[39] In *Sanjuro* Kurosawa finally achieved a kind of sound effects in the Japanese period genre which was even more shocking than the sound of the gunshots in the western by its brutal evocation of pain.

Although absent from the opening music of *Sanjuro*, the characteristic rhythm of *Sanjuro's Theme* does occur later in the film. This theme, which connotes Sanjuro's great prowess and power, normally hidden behind his calm and impassive pose, is heard when Sanjuro's power is suddenly revealed and unleashed to dramatic effect. The theme's sharpness remains intact and unaffected by the generous tone of the melodic part (played separately in other scenes), and illustrates sudden outbursts of Sanjuro's impressive skills. This lively fragment is used, for example, in an accelerated tempo when Sanjuro attacks watchmen at the chamberlain's estate and kills two of them in an instant, and at the end of the film, after Sanjuro bids the young samurai farewell. Sanjuro liberates himself from all rigid formalities of samurai society, as well as from the young men, now so attached to him that they are on the verge of tears at his departure. The music begins as he turns away from the men and starts walking away, once again alone.

In contrast to the rhythm part of *Sanjuro's Theme* that evokes his aloofness as a lone warrior, the melody symbolizes Sanjuro's more humane aspect which, although apparently contrary to his humble appearance and mercenary attitude, will nonetheless be demonstrated by the outcome of his actions. We first hear this piece during a scene when the young samurai are gathered at the shrine. Affirming his resolute commitment to their righteous cause, one of the young men swears that they will fight together "for life or death." Sanjuro interrupts, declaring that he, too, will become the young men's ally. His declaration prompts the melody of *Sanjuro's Theme*, played by cello, double bass, and percussion, which connotes Sanjuro's genuine concern for the young men, although he is only able to express it verbally and visually in an apparently insolent manner. The same tune is heard again when Sanjuro gets angry at the young samurai who did not trust him and unnecessarily exposed themselves to danger. As a result of their actions, Sanjuro has to kill dozens of men in order to save them, and, after the killing is over, he says disgustedly, "What horrible cruelty I've had to commit, thanks to you," and strikes the young men across the face one by one.

The young samurai's theme (Figure 6.3) is comparable to *Sanjuro's Theme* in terms of intervals between notes. *Sanjuro's Theme* is built upon a combination

Figure 6.3 Young samurai's theme (melody)

of notes whose intervals consist of seconds (C and B-flat, D-flat and C) and minor thirds (C and E-flat, A-flat and F). The young samurai's theme also contains seconds (D and E, F-sharp and G) and descending minor thirds (G and E). Although in different keys (the former in F minor and the latter in G major), the young samurai's theme echoes *Sanjuro's Theme* through imitation of its melodic structure, and might be called the "offspring" of *Sanjuro's Theme*. A skeletal form of the young samurai's theme is first heard on xylophone when the group is saved by Sanjuro's intelligence and experience. The xylophone mirrors the viewer's visual experience, playing one note at a time as the young men show their faces one by one from below the wooden planks of the shrine floor. The melody then develops into an orchestral piece as they thank Sanjuro, bowing deeply. The theme is heard again when the group follows Sanjuro to investigate the situation at the missing chamberlain's estate. The young samurai do not know how to act in such a situation and follow Sanjuro in a single file, as if they were "goldfish faeces," to use Sanjuro's humorous terminology. In this sequence the theme, played by xylophone, brass, and low strings, appears softly and in a partial form, as though their courage is slowly kindling, waiting until it blazes out. This musical anticipation resolves as they split up and run in various directions to gather information about the chamberlain. Evoking the earlier scene, they show their heads above a wall, one by one, as the xylophone and woodwinds also play intermittently to echo the visual. Then, following the sound of the harp, the trumpet plays the theme loudly, announcing the emergence of a new psychological dimension to the young men who can now act more or less individually. The theme is once again heard non-diegetically when the young samurai dance in a restrained but joyous manner because they are overjoyed by the news that the villains have been tricked by Sanjuro's scheme. Sanjuro himself is absent from this comical yet emotional scene, not only because he is at the enemy's residence, waiting for a chance to send a signal that the young samurai should come and rescue the chamberlain, but also because he is an outsider and cannot share the excitement that the young men are feeling.

Conclusion

In *Yojimbo*, Kurosawa and Sato challenged the established conventions of Japanese period drama by borrowing the audio and visual grammar of the American western as well as by the introduction of a pioneering use of realistic sound effects. In particular, the music of the Hollywood western served as an aesthetic model on which Kurosawa and Sato constructed their own musical ideas. The comparison of scenes from *Rio Bravo* and *Yojimbo* demonstrates that both Hawks's and Kurosawa's cinemas draw upon the tradition of silent cinema through their emphasis on the aural and visual that frequently undermines the role of spoken words. The musical themes of *Yojimbo* and *Sanjuro* are closely related, and in the latter film we have seen the way *Sanjuro's Theme* is developed in order to connote two distinct sets of psychological characteristics of the protagonist. Similarly, the young samurai's theme derives from *Sanjuro's Theme*, symbolizing their mentor–student relation. Sato also discovered a perfect harmony between the sound of the *quijada* and the image of serene samurai, and thus launched a new musical tradition in Japanese cinema.

The audiovisual invocation of violence in *Yojimbo* had an immense impact on subsequent works in Japan and beyond: intense competition took place between studios to produce period films with ever more excessive graphic violence, each one trying to outdo its predecessor through an escalating display of cruelty and brutality.[40] It is also worth noting that no matter how powerful and influential Kurosawa's films were, Toei continued to produce their own style of conventional *chambara* for the mainstream audience. Popular heroes such as Mondonosuke Saotome in *Hatamoto taikutsu otoko* (1930) and Kinshiro Toyama, the tattooed magistrate in *Irezumi hangan* (1950), both of whom appeared long before the arrival of Sanjuro, are still alive today, having been interpreted by different actors over many generations. Outside Japan, *Yojimbo* was remade as the spaghetti western and stimulated the emergence of a new kind of hero, most notably portrayed by Clint Eastwood as the "Man with No Name." Nowadays the *quijada* and its recent version the vibraslap is ubiquitously employed in Japanese TV soap operas, such as *Abarenbo shogun*, a long-running series starring Ken Matsudaira that first began in 1978, and *Mito komon*, another popular series, about a vice-shogun traveling throughout Japan in disguise.[41] Television's cross-media borrowing is ironic considering Kurosawa's *chambara* westerns were made when cinema was in decline due to the growing popularity of television. Moreover, Kurosawa deplored the increasing representation of exacerbated violence prompted by *Yojimbo* and *Sanjuro*, attempting to counter the fervor for violence with *Red Beard* (1965), in which a humanistic doctor helps the poor and the deprived in the Edo period. But the trend had by then become irreversible.

Notes

Special thanks to Kathryn Kalinak, Charles Leinberger, Ed Carter, and Simon Humphries.

1 See, for instance, Hideyuki Kikuchi, "*Yatto to donpachi* [Period films and the Western]," *Chambara e no shotai* [*An Invitation to Chambara*], ed. Go Osaka, et al. (Tokyo: PHP Kenkyusho, 2004), 101–33. All the Japanese materials used in this chapter have been translated by me unless stated otherwise.
2 Koichi Yamada, "*Kaisetsu* [Commentary]", Explanatory notes to *Yojimbo*, Toho DVD (2002), 12.
3 Donald Richie, *The Films of Akira Kurosawa*, rev. ed. (Berkeley: University of California Press, 1984), 147.
4 Desser designated these films, including *Yojimbo* and *Seven Samurai*, "Samurai Films," and analyzed how the formulas of popular American cinema are transposed in Kurosawa's period dramas. David Desser, *The Samurai Films of Akira Kurosawa* (Essex: Bowker Publishing, 1983), 25.
5 Richie, 227.

6 Akira Kurosawa, *Kurosawa Akira: "Yume wa tensai de aru"* [*Akira Kurosawa: Dreams Are Geniuses*] (Tokyo: Bungei Shunju, 1999), 29.
7 Richie, 159.
8 Noël Burch, *To the Distant Observer: Form and Meaning in the Japanese Cinema* (Berkeley: University of California Press, 1979), 332.
9 David Desser, "Kurosawa's Eastern 'Western': Sanjuro and the Influence of Shane," *Film Criticism*, 8, 1 (Fall 1983), 54–65.
10 Mitsuhiro Yoshimoto, *Kurosawa: Film Studies and Japanese Cinema* (Durham: Duke University Press, 2000), 294, 423 n. 3.
11 Richie, 148.
12 Masaru Sato, *300/40: Sono e, oto, hito* [*300/40: The Picture, Sound and Person*] (Tokyo: Kinema Junpo, 1994). First Published in *Kinema Junpo* (Jan/Feb 1992–August 1993), 84.
13 Yamada, 13.
14 Kemp, Philip. Audio commentary in *Yojimbo*. Toho/Kurosawa Productions, 1961. BFI DVD (2000).
15 Tadao Sato, "Sakuhin kaidai" in Akira Kurosawa, *Zenshu Kurosawa Akira* [*Akira Kurosawa Complete Works*] Vol. 5 (Tokyo: Iwanami Shoten, 1988), 361–77, 366.
16 Yoshimoto, 289.
17 Teruyo Nogami, *Tenkimachi: kantoku Kurosawa Akira to tomoni* [*Waiting for Good Weather: With Director Akira Kurosawa*] (Tokyo: Bunshun, 2001), 248.
18 Nogami, 248.
19 Kurosawa had already made several period films by then, most notably *Seven Samurai* (1954), but they were different from what Japanese audiences usually thought of as *chambara*, because of either different period settings or lacking choreographed sword fights.
20 Masaru Sato, 83.
21 Mariana Whitmer discusses how the audience of the time was shocked by Jerome Moross's "big score" that was completely different from the conventional western film scores of the time. Whitmer argues that with this film Moross reverted the trend in the western film music that was moving away from symphonic orchestra and toward smaller ensembles and popular songs. See Mariana Whitmer, Chapter 3, "Reinventing the Western Film Score: Jerome Moross and *The Big Country*" this volume.
22 Atsushi Kobayashi, *Sato Masaru: ginmaku no shinfoni* [*Masaru Sato: Symphonies of the Silver Screen*] (Tokyo: Waizu Shuppan, 2007), 146.
23 Nogami (ed.), Special Feature in *Yojimbo*. Toho/Kurosawa Productions, 1961. Toho DVD 2002.
24 Ibid.
25 Whitmer.
26 Kobayashi, 147.
27 Masaru Sato, 83f.
28 Kathryn Kalinak shared documents with me that she found in the Warner Bros. archive which confirm that the *Degüello* heard in *Rio Bravo* was an original composition by Dimitri Tiomkin.
29 According to Charles Leinberger, military bugles traditionally do not have valves and therefore could not possibly play Tiomkin's tune. Leinberger argues that although brass instruments with valves already existed in the nineteenth century, there is no evidence to suggest that Santa Anna's buglers used them in Alamo in 1836. Charles Leinberger, Chapter 7, "The Dollars Trilogy: 'There are two kinds of western heroes, my friend'" this volume.
30 Kalinak, *How the West was Sung: Music in the Westerns of John Ford* (Berkeley: University of California Press, 2007), 186.

31   Seeman, quoted in Kalinak 2007. Kalinak writes that the popularity of guitars was promoted by country-and-western singers in the twentieth century. The instrument became widely used in western music accompanying singing cowboys on the radio and films, and, 'in a kind of projection backwards,' became inseparable with the nineteenth-century American West (Kalinak, 184).
32   Sato, 84.
33   Kobayashi, 155.
34   Kobayashi, 154.
35   Tadao Sato, 369.
36   Richie, 156.
37   Yoshimoto, 295.
38   Masaru Sato, 86.
39   Although American-led GHQ left mainland Japan in 1952, Okinawa remained under occupation until 1972, when the island was returned to Japanese sovereignty and the US presence became limited to a few bases around the country.
40   Tadao Sato, *Nihon eiga shi III 1960–1995* [*The History of Japanese Cinema vol. 3 1960–1995*] (Tokyo: Iwanami Shoten, 1995), 61.
41   The Mito Komon series first began on TV in 1969 and reached over 40% share of total viewing during its most popular period. It is indeed the longest running Toei period drama to date, which continued gathering audience support even after rival series such as *Lone Wolf and Cub* and *Abareno Shogun* disappeared from the regular repertoires of private TV channels.

In July 2011, however, the production company of Mito Komon announced that the series will be put to an end in December due to the decline in its viewing figures.

Warm thanks to Kinejapan for this piece of information. "An End to 42 Years of History: Low Viewing Figures of Mito Komon," accessed July 16, 2011, http://www.nikkansports.com/entertainment/news/f-et-tp0-20110715-805224.html.

Chapter 7

The Dollars Trilogy
"There are two kinds of western heroes, my friend!"

Charles Leinberger

The American movie audience had a long and fruitful love affair with the Hollywood western through much of the twentieth century. Directors in the sound era, such as John Ford and Howard Hawks, stars such as the singing cowboys Roy Rogers and Gene Autry, and box office mega-stars such as John Wayne, built their careers on the loyal and predictable American audience's appetite for stories of the pioneer days of the American West. Audiences relished above all the satisfaction that came with knowing that the villain would be captured or killed, peace would be restored, order would replace disorder, and justice would prevail.

As Robin Wood has observed, there are typically three main sections to the architecture of many Hollywood westerns: the exposition, which introduces the characters; the development, where disorder and conflict occurs; and the recapitulation, the eventual restoration of order.[1] Nowhere is the restoration of order more obvious than in the final scene in *Chisum* (1970) as John Chisum (John Wayne) rides his horse to the top of a hill where he looks over his vast spread, re-enacting the film's opening shot.

This formal design served much the same function as the main sections of the classical sonata form of Haydn and Mozart, including the obligatory return of stability after a period of ambiguity. Just as the traditional tonal forms of classical music eventually gave way to more unrestricted modern musical forms, so did the form of the classic Hollywood western give way to less predictable and occasionally unsettling innovations of non-traditional, and often non-Hollywood, westerns. Italian filmmakers played a major role in this paradigm shift. Ennio Morricone is arguably the composer most responsible for accelerating this shift through his innovative scores for the westerns of Sergio Leone.

The Model of the Hollywood Western

Although the western genre had been in existence since the days of silent films, one need only consider two key Hollywood westerns—and their music—to appreciate the significance of the impending paradigm shift. *The Searchers* (1956), one of the finest Hollywood westerns ever made according to many film scholars,[2] follows the model of the genre that Wood outlines. In the opening scenes, the stability of a nuclear family is soon disrupted by the arrival of Ethan

Edwards (John Wayne), only to be disrupted further by an attack by the principal antagonists (a renegade group of Comanche warriors). Two of those who survive, Ethan and Martin Pauley (Jeffrey Hunter), endanger their lives for what they believe is morally right. In the end, order is mostly restored and the surviving family members are reunited in a scene much like the film's opening scene in which Ethan first returned home from the Civil War. Ethan, however, is seen walking off into the distance, as the outsider he was at the beginning of the film. The fact that Ethan is represented as the outsider bears a slight resemblance to the Clint Eastwood characters of later westerns, characters who, as will be seen, ultimately ride off into the unknown place from which they came.

Max Steiner's music for *The Searchers* likewise follows many of the formal conventions of the period. The music for this film begins with an original instrumental introduction that features easily recognizable Native American rhythmic motifs which then smoothly transitions into Stan Jones's western song "The Searchers."[3] This song is heard during the opening titles of the film (exposition) as well as in the film's closing credits (resolution). However, as Kathryn Kalinak has explained, of the eight verses of the song, Ford chose only the second verse for the main titles, and only the seventh verse for the closing credits.[4] Throughout the film, Steiner does an outstanding job of evoking a wide range of moods, from the somber and serious, to the fast and exciting, and from the triumphant to the comical. He does this, quite skillfully, while using what is, for all practical purposes, the instrumental timbres of the standard symphony orchestra (strings, woodwinds, brass, and percussion), occasionally adding an acoustic guitar. The audience sees characters in the film playing guitar and fiddle. His compositional style is firmly rooted in the nineteenth-century Germanic operatic tradition, often displaying the influence of Richard Wagner.

Rio Bravo (1959) similarly follows many of the same classical conventions. Sherriff John T. Chance (John Wayne) is the protagonist who symbolizes authority and order. He upholds the law and risks his life to see that the law is enforced, and those who break it are incarcerated. A murder, the subsequent arrest of Joe Burdette (Claude Akins), the attempt to break him out of jail by his brother Nathan Burdette (John Russell) and his gang, and his deputy, Dude's (Dean Martin) problems with alcohol all bring disorder to Presidio County. In the end, the escape attempt is foiled, the Burdettes and their gang are in jail, Dude conquers his inner demons, and order is restored. Chance even ends up with the girl, Feathers (Angie Dickinson).

Dimitri Tiomkin's music for *Rio Bravo*, much like Steiner's music for *The Searchers*, is a reflection of the classical formal structure of order, disorder, and the eventual restoration of order. The film opens with an instrumental version of a theme that is later reprised in the film's closing scene, sung by Dean Martin in the latter. Also like Steiner's *Searchers* score, Tiomkin's score employs a standard orchestra, occasionally adding acoustic guitar, but the appearance of the harmonica is quite noticeable in the opening sequence. Both guitar and harmonica are instruments that might be heard in the world created by the film's narrative. In the film, Colorado Ryan (Ricky Nelson) is seen playing guitar and Stumpy (Walter Brennan) is seen playing harmonica.

What makes Tiomkin's score for *Rio Bravo* so noteworthy is his diegetic use of a tune called "Degüello" (Figure 7.1), which is a theme that Tiomkin created for the film.[5] The fact that this theme bears a remarkable resemblance to a musical device that Morricone will later make part of his signature style is almost certainly not coincidental. During a scene in a saloon, one of the antagonists, Nathan Burdette, asks a cornet[6] player to play a tune.[7] Later, Colorado explains to Chance, and presumably to the audience as well, its significance. He elucidates that it is the "cut-throat song, the Mexicans played it for those Texas boys when they had them bottled up in the Alamo. [They] played it day and night till it was all over." [8] Chance elaborates, "No quarter. No mercy for the losers." As it turns out, it is Burdette, not Chance, who will eventually be the loser in this case.[9]

This theme is in a minor key (A minor, which explains the occasional F-sharp and G-sharp) and features some rhythmic devices that give it a quasi-improvised quality, such as the syncopated figures and the occasional division of the beat into seven unequal note values.

Both Steiner's score for *The Searchers* and Tiomkin's score for *Rio Bravo* compliment the Hollywood model of exposition, development, and resolution (recapitulation), each one ending with music similar to what was heard in the exposition. These themes, which do not diverge from the melodic, harmonic, and orchestral conventions of the day, provide the viewer with a sense of closure and a return to the comfort and security of something musically familiar.

The Italian Westerns

The European perspective on the western would inevitably be a departure from the formal designs of the Hollywood western. According to Sir Christopher Frayling,

Figure 7.1 Tiomkin, cornet melody of "Degüello" from *Rio Bravo*

Between the early 1950s and the mid-1960s, Italian (and later, Spanish) producers working at Cinecittà Studios had made various attempts to anticipate (or exploit) the taste of Italian urban cinemagoers, by hi-jacking entire film genres—the most notable being the "film fumetto" (1948–54), the farcical comedy, often of a dialect kind (1955–8), the "sword and sandal" epic (1958–64), the horror film (1959–63), the *World by Night* or *Mondo Cane* genre (1962–4), and the spy story derived from James Bond (1964–7).[10]

It would be only a matter of time before the western genre was likewise "hi-jacked." Italian filmmakers would find the means to create low-budget westerns, with exterior scenes often filmed in Spain with Spanish-speaking actors, interior scenes filmed in Rome with Italian-speaking actors, and, to give the films an American appearance, English-speaking actors from Hollywood. According to Frayling, "Well over 300 Spaghetti Westerns were released in Italy between 1963 and 1969 alone."[11] Surprisingly, these "spaghetti westerns,"[12] which required voice-overs by additional actors to be viewed in any single language, created a subgenre that would change the way westerns were made and viewed worldwide. These revisionist westerns from Italy gave American audiences a seemingly unfamiliar and alternative perspective on the American West, one that deconstructed the elements of the classical Hollywood western, primarily the hero/villain dichotomy, and reassembled them in a way that some found original and refreshing while others, including many American film critics, found distasteful.[13]

There may be no such thing as a typical Italian western. Each one has some unusual twist that sets it apart from others. But there are certain recurring themes throughout the subgenre that should be mentioned. Like many Hollywood westerns, an Italian western often has at least two protagonists. Each is introduced to the audience early in the film, like themes being introduced in the exposition of a musical form. Unlike a Hollywood western, however, when each protagonist is introduced, he is usually about to kill somebody, sometimes one or two other gunmen, but killing three gunmen at once seems to occur quite often.[14] Such protagonists often live outside the law, following their own moral code of right and wrong. Also, unlike a Hollywood western, it is often unclear until the end of the film, typically after a surprise twist in the narrative, which protagonist is evil and which one, if any, is good. In the revisionist Italian western, and in particular those of director Sergio Leone, all protagonists are part evil and usually, but not always, part good. Cynicism abounds. There is almost always some large monetary prize, usually gold or cash, sometimes buried, for which the protagonists compete. Transporting the loot across the Texas–Mexico border, in either direction, is a familiar subplot.[15] Mistaken identity is also an occasional subplot, especially when twins are concerned.[16] Beautiful women and children can be an integral part of the formula, but are not required. When they appear, they often are minor characters who remain nameless. Often, there is a male character, a bartender or shopkeeper, who risks his life to help the protagonist for no apparent reason.[17] Honest lawmen are usually characters that exist in the background and are always expendable. There must be a final conflict between the mostly good protagonist and the mostly evil one, but a complete return to order is normally frustrated.

Just as the formal structure of the Hollywood western had been recast in these Italian films, disrupting the pursuit of the eventual restoration of order, so was the formal design of the musical score recast. Rather than providing emotional music to accompany the on-screen action, music in the Italian western, and the scores of Morricone in particular, became a foreground event demanding the attention of even the most inattentive viewer. No longer a device to reinforce the on-screen drama, music became part of the narrative, often indistinguishable from the blaring sound effects of gunfire, cannon fire, and locomotives.

It was much more than the unconventional production methodology that made these films the antithesis of their Hollywood counterparts. These revisionist films redefined the roles of good and evil, order and disorder, law and lawlessness. Even more surprising is the fact that these films, in spite of their superficial American appearances, were never meant for American audiences. The idea, according to Frayling, was to make Italian audiences believe that they were watching an American film.[18] Their eventual importation to the United States coincided with another cultural phenomenon taking place in the 1960s, the British Invasion.[19] Like many aspects of the American culture of the 1960s, rock and roll in particular, the western would never again be the exclusive province of the United States, but would inescapably become a part of the emerging international popular culture.

Sergio Leone

Of the hundreds of Italian westerns made, most Americans will only see those of director Sergio Leone.[20] This is at once fortunate because these films represent the peak in the evolution of this subgenre. This is likewise unfortunate because it is by viewing the works of his contemporaries that one can truly appreciate his revisionist contribution to this subgenre. As Frayling explains, "Sergio Leone's 'Dollars' trilogy comprises a two-level detachment from the Hollywood Western genre. Firstly, as a type of European critical cinema which, using an established cinematic tradition, and without shedding its popular character, can deconstruct and rearrange the images and themes which exemplify the *reverence* of puritan–liberal Hollywood Westerns, the established bases of the genre."[21] Unlike the quintessential Hollywood hero figure, who was the personification of the American values of life, liberty, and the pursuit of happiness, the typical Italian western protagonist is not all-righteous by any means, but is, however, almost always all-knowing and all-powerful. This hero/antihero dichotomy is one of the key distinguishing features of the Italian western, in which the apparent hero figure is astonishingly lacking in traditional heroic qualities. Additionally, not all Italian westerns feature the breathtaking panoramic vistas juxtaposed with extreme close-ups (usually of blue-eyed actors) or the influences of Italian neo-realism (long uncut shots of characters doing ordinary things) as the Leone westerns do.

Leone's A Fistful of Dollars (Per un pugno di dollari, 1964), the first of the three films in the so-called Dollars trilogy, is a perfect example of this deconstruction and rearrangement. Just as John Sturges's The Magnificent Seven (1960) was a remake of Japanese director Akira Kurosawa's Seven Samurai (1954), A Fistful of Dollars was similarly a remake of Kurosawa's Yojimbo (1960). In Fistful, a drifter, the so-called "man with no name" (Clint Eastwood), arrives in a town divided into two feuding factions, the Rojos and the Baxters. This story was an ideal choice for Leone's first revisionist western, due to its dissimilarity with the Hollywood western in which there must be eventual resolution. The only resolution comes as the man with no name (Eastwood) kills Ramón Rojo (Gian Maria Volanté), the film's main antagonist, in the film's final confrontation. Eventually, the man with no name rides out of town, leaving behind not a restoration of order, but a trail of death and destruction. Unlike the classical Hollywood protagonist, the central character in these narratives, both the Japanese and Italian productions, is a stranger who seems to come out of nowhere, only to eventually return to that unknown place in the films' conclusions.

Unlike Fistful, Leone's second film in this trilogy, For a Few Dollars More (Per qualche dollaro in più, 1965), does offer the audience a slightly greater sense of resolution. The protagonists, Monco (Clint Eastwood) and Mortimer (Lee Van Cleef), are bounty hunters. As the opening caption makes clear, "Where life had no value, death, sometimes, had its price. That is why the bounty killers appeared."[22] Having set up the film's protagonists as killers for profit, the audience knows that these are not the archetypical Hollywood western heroes, and the film's exposition confirms this, as the audience sees each protagonist kill a wanted man. Mortimer kills Calloway (José Terrón), but Monco kills the clichéd three gunmen before killing his target, Cavanaugh (José Marco). In the end, there is some restoration of order as Mortimer finally satisfies his quest for revenge in the death of his sister, the result of an attack by El Indio (Gian Maria Volanté).

Leone's final film of this trilogy, The Good, the Bad and the Ugly (Il buono, il bruto, il cattivo, 1966), is more complex in that there appears to be three protagonists, but in fact, they are each a different component of the same multifaceted Leone character. Although all of the protagonists are essentially selfish, each one is shown to be partly good, with the possible exception of il cattivo (Lee Van Cleef), partly bad, and partly ugly. As will be seen, Morricone's music for this film builds on this concept; just as these are three facets of one character, his score incorporated three distinct timbres of the same easily recognizable leitmotif. The audience has no purely righteous figure with which to identify, like the quintessential John Wayne characters of the Hollywood westerns, but rather is manipulated into identifying with the character that is the least evil. In the end, it is that character that is seen riding off into the distance with the loot.

Although not part of the Dollars trilogy, Leone's next western is certainly deserving of some mention here. The panoramic vistas of the Dollars trilogy could only be superseded in *Once Upon a Time in the West* (*C'era una volta il West*, 1968), by using as its backdrop the breathtaking Monument Valley of northeastern Arizona, as John Ford did in *The Searchers*. A man with no name, who everyone calls Harmonica (Charles Bronson), is the best candidate for the protagonist, but is he really? Cheyenne (Jason Robards) could be the central figure, but he's in handcuffs when first seen and dies at the film's conclusion, as does Frank (Henry Fonda). In a characterization distinct from the Dollars trilogy, there is a female protagonist as well, Jill McBain (Claudia Cardinale). Unlike the films of the Dollars trilogy, this film ends with a great sense of resolution and optimism, as the new train line from Flagstone finally reaches the nearly complete Sweetwater Station.

According to Patrick Ehresmann, irony is also a key component in the narrative of many of Leone's westerns: "A fundamental characteristic of the Leonian cinema has always been to maintain a certain irony, even in the most dramatic scenes, in total opposition with the usual approach of the American cinema producing either comical westerns or dramatic westerns, but very seldom mixing both kinds."[23] These ironic twists include, for example, discovering Mortimer's motivation for killing El Indio in *For a Few Dollars More*, or discovering the $200,000 is not in Arch Stanton's grave in *The Good, the Bad and the Ugly*. These ironic twists further distinguish the Italian westerns, particularly those of Leone, from their more predictable Hollywood counterparts.

Ennio Morricone and a Fistful of Aerophones

When Ennio Morricone began composing for Italian films in 1961, he not only brought to the profession all of the modern compositional techniques he had learned as a young student of Goffredo Petrassi at the Santa Cecilia Conservatory in Rome, but he also brought his experience as a record producer of Italian popular music for RCA. Most intriguing is his work for American singer Peter Tevis, a practically unknown performer in the United States. Tevis's cover version of Woody Guthrie's *Pastures of Plenty*, arranged by Morricone, features many of the unusual devices that Leone wanted to hear in his westerns.

Before Sergio Leone approached Ennio Morricone to write music for *A Fistful of Dollars*, Morricone had composed (as Dan Savio) music for the western *Gunfight at Red Sands* (*Duello nel Texas*, 1963) for director Ricardo Blasco. Like many Italian westerns, in *Gunfight at Red Sands* there is a surprise twist: the audience learns late in the film that the sheriff, Lance Corbett (Richard Harrison), is actually the leader of the gang planning to steal the gold and land from the Martinez family. Morricone wrote a pleasant but rather unremarkable score for *Gunfight at Red Sands*. The title song, "A Gringo like Me," is a vocal piece, which was a common practice for title music in both Hollywood and Italian westerns. Morricone reprises the tune in an instrumental version throughout the film. Noticeably absent are many of the stylistic traits that would later become associated with his signature style for scoring westerns, such as the prominent harmonica, whistling, solo trumpet, and percussion. The silence that accompanies the final showdown in this film, however, is strikingly uncharacteristic of Morricone's mature western film-scoring style. The stylistic differences between Morricone's music for *Gunfight at Red Sands* and his score for *A Fistful of Dollars* (again as Dan Savio) are numerous and noteworthy.

Among Morricone's preferred compositional techniques are his orchestrations that feature, among numerous timbres, aerophones, musical instruments that produce sound when air is blown into them. Aerophones that Morricone featured in his western scores include the soprano recorder, English horn, harmonica, trumpet, and in one film, the bass ocarina (arghilofono). This is not to say that he is not fluent when scoring for keyboard, guitar, strings, and percussion; rather, it is his use of aerophones that helps to make his style so easily distinguishable among film composers.

For the melody of the main title from *A Fistful of Dollars*, Morricone features the sound of a human whistle. Cumbow has observed, however, that Tiomkin had previously used this timbre in his main title to *The High and the Mighty* (1954),[24] yet it is Morricone who has become associated with this device. Those who have heard Morricone's arrangement of *Pastures of Plenty* will recognize the accompaniment of the main title as a note-for-note duplication of that song's accompaniment (the acoustic guitar, the five-note descending scale on the flute, the tubular bells, the whip cracks, the triangle, and the male background vocal parts), only the whistled melody being completely original. According to Ehresmann, Leone liked the arrangement of *Pastures of Plenty*, but did not care for the vocal part sung by Tevis.[25] Also featured in the main title and throughout the film is the electric guitar. At the time, the electric guitar had been featured in hits by such recording artists as Duane Eddy[26] and the Ventures. Hollywood film composers, on the other hand, had not yet incorporated such ubiquitous pop sounds into their film scores.

Morricone's score for *The Good, the Bad and the Ugly* cleverly incorporates the concept of each protagonist being part of a more complex mega-character on a musical level. As alluded to earlier, rather than giving each protagonist their own theme, as a traditional leitmotif composer would do (Steiner comes to mind), Morricone gave all three protagonists the same leitmotif, but each with a distinctive timbre: soprano recorder for the Good (Clint Eastwood), falsetto voice for the Ugly (Eli Wallach), and bass ocarina for the Bad (Lee Van Cleef).[27] He consistently and cleverly uses these timbres throughout the film as an identifier of each protagonist.

Another distinguishing compositional technique employed by Morricone throughout many of his western scores is his use of a six-note scale, an otherwise diatonic (seven-note) scale that omits the sixth degree of the scale, in the creation of many of the main themes (Figure 7.2).

The whistled melody of the main title from *A Fistful of Dollars* is such a melody, based on the pitches D, E, F, G, A, and C (Figure 7.3). This scale

Figure 7.2 Morricone's six-note scales on D and A (the starting note repeated an octave higher)

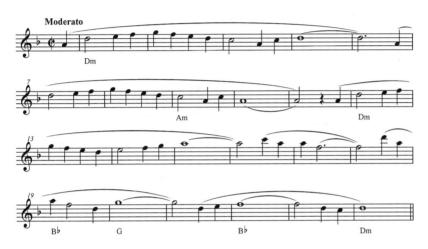

Figure 7.3 Morricone, whistled melody of main title from *A Fistful of Dollars*[28]

suggests the key of D Aeolian, but could also be interpreted as being in D Dorian. The missing scale degree (B-flat or B-natural) is the distinguishing note. Morricone's fondness for this scale helps to disguise the true modality of many of his themes. The missing scale degree appears in the accompaniment (B-flat in measure 19) and is followed by its chromatic counterpart (B-natural in measure 20) before returning to its original pitch (B-flat in measure 22),[29] perpetuating the vagueness of the cue's true modality.

The haunting English horn melody that begins "The Ecstasy of Gold" ("L'estasi dell'oro") from *The Good, the Bad and the Ugly* uses the same six-note scale, this time on A: A, B, C, D, E, and G (Figure 7.4). The English horn melody appears to be in A Aeolian or A Dorian. The missing scale degree appears in the accompaniment in measure 12 (F-sharp), but its chromatic counterpart (F-natural) appears in the accompaniment in measure 14.[30]

The combined effect of a melody based on this six-note scale and the appearance of both possible complementary scale degrees in the accompaniment give many of Morricone's themes an unusual modality, which musicologist Philip Tagg describes as "Celtic" in nature.[31] The use of such a modal scale makes these melodies memorable and easy to sing. This unique modality, combined with the composer's eclectic choice of instrumental timbres, aerophones in particular, helps to position his scores as the antithesis of the classic Hollywood western score.

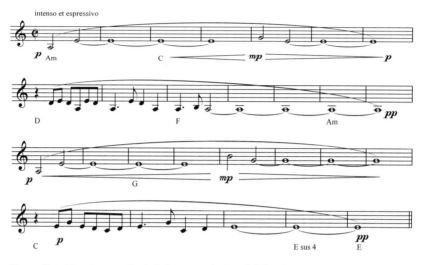

Figure 7.4 Morricone, English horn melody of "The Ecstasy of Gold" from *The Good, the Bad and the Ugly*

Morricone's scores resemble Hollywood scores in one respect, however. Although order may not be restored in the films' narrative, music from the main title ("Titoli") returns at the end of each of the films in the Dollars trilogy, as Eastwood's character rides off into the distance. In the classic Hollywood western, the return of music from the beginning signifies a return to order, that life has returned to normal for most of the surviving protagonists. In the westerns of Leone, however, the return of music from the beginning, as the stranger rides of into the distance at the films' conclusions, signifies that he is returning to the unknown place from which he came, and that he does so after successfully absconding with the loot and leaving a trail of dead bodies in his wake. Morricone's themes for the Dollars trilogy are able to serve as a different type of signifier because they are inherently different, as Leone wanted them to be, from the symphonic sounds of Steiner, Tiomkin, and Elmer Bernstein. The starting point of the music for the trilogy was a style that was whimsical, picaresque, and unlike anything audiences had heard previously. By contrast, Morricone's main theme for *Once Upon a Time in the West* (aka "Jill's Theme") is firmly in D major and appropriately signifies a return to order, not a protagonist riding off into the unknown,[32] at the film's conclusion. As mentioned earlier, this film ends with newfound prosperity coming to Sweetwater Station, and not the omnipresent death and destruction of *Fistful*. It is possible that Morricone chose a theme that was much more Hollywood in style (major key and a more traditional orchestration) as a signifier of a more conventional ending to the narrative, a restoration of order.

Another device that quickly became part of the Morricone sound is the mariachi-style trumpet solo during the final confrontation between the protagonist (mostly good) and the antagonist (mostly or completely evil). These solos have a distinct and authentic southwestern-American sound to them, and, as eluded to earlier, are reminiscent of Tiomkin's "Degüello" tune featured in *Rio Bravo*. This did not happen accidentally. According to multiple sources, this was done by Leone's request.[33] In Leone's Dollars trilogy, as in *Rio Bravo* score, there is "no mercy for the losers." Unlike Tiomkin's score, the solo in Morricone's score is non-diegetic; the solo instrument is an unseen trumpet and not the cornet seen in *Rio Bravo*. In *A Fistful of Dollars*, the man with no name confronts Ramón Rojo (Gian Maria Volonté) as the fateful trumpet sounds (Figure 7.5). Like Tiomkin's "Degüello," this solo is in a minor key, features rhythms (the occasional division of the beat into seven unequal note values) unique to Latin American folk music, and as a result, has a quasi-improvised quality to it. In *For a Few Dollars More*, it is Mortimer who confronts El Indio accompanied by the solo trumpet (Figure 7.6). In *The Good, the Bad and the Ugly*, the trumpet sounds once again as the three protagonists, the Good, the Ugly, and the Bad, face off in the film's climax (Figure 7.7). The fateful trumpet sounds yet once more in *Once Upon a Time in the West* as the antagonist Frank approaches on horseback moments before his final confrontation with Harmonica (Figure 7.8). These memorable trumpet melodies have some noteworthy characteristics in common. They are all in minor keys and use the Aeolian mode (natural minor scale) almost exclusively (except for an occasional chromatic note). They are all in common time, which itself is not so unusual, but divide the beat in significant ways. Each subsequent trumpet melody is less and less similar to Tiomkin's "Degüello" theme, as Morricone's style evolved beyond that of his most clever Hollywood contemporaries. These

Figure 7.5 Morricone, trumpet melody from *A Fistful of Dollars*

Figure 7.6 Morricone, trumpet melody from *For a Few Dollars More*

Figure 7.7 Morricone, trumpet melody from *The Good, the Bad and the Ugly*

Figure 7.8 Morricone, trumpet melody from *Once Upon a Time in the West*

solos serve to advance the significance of these confrontational scenes in the films' narrative. In doing so, such a device has come to be a signifier of the ultimate conflicts that are cornerstones of westerns, both Italian and Hollywood.

After the Dollars trilogy, Morricone continued to compose for westerns, both in Italy and occasionally in Hollywood, including director Sergio Corbucci's *Navajo Joe*, aka *Navajo's Land* (1966), starring Burt Reynolds, and Giulio Petroni's *Death Rides a Horse*, aka *As Man to Man* (*Da uomo a uomo*, 1967), starring Lee Van Cleef. For Sergio Leone's *Once Upon a Time in the West*, he wrote a clever score that incorporated the harmonica, which he had used before, but now it is a diegetic device associated with a character. For *Duck you Sucker* (*Giù la testa*), aka *A Fistful of Dynamite* (1971), perhaps Leone's darkest and most somber film, Morricone wrote a surprisingly whimsical score, even quoting Mozart's light-hearted *Eine Kleine Nachtmusik*.[34] Other westerns include Don Siegel's *Two Mules for Sister Sara* (1970), and Tonino Valerii's *My Name is Nobody* (*Il mio nome è Nessuno*), aka *Lonesome Gun* (1973). His contributions to other genres are too numerous to mention here.

The challenges for any composer scoring for Clint Eastwood westerns after the Dollars trilogy would be formidable. As a result of the American release of the Leone films, Eastwood not only became an international star, but he quickly developed a particular on-screen persona, and audiences had established certain expectations from his characters in subsequent westerns. Eastwood's first post-Dollars western was *Hang 'Em High* (1968). Jed Cooper (Clint Eastwood) in this film is more like the traditional Hollywood protagonist; he is clean-shaven, has a first and last name, has a love interest, wears a badge, and does not operate outside the law. Dominic Frontiere's score is likewise very much in the Hollywood tradition. It does, however, betray some influence of Morricone's music for Leone. For Cooper's theme, he composed a catchy Dorian-mode melody that occurs throughout the film. There is the electric guitar, harmonica, and tubular bells. Surprisingly, there is no mariachi-style trumpet for the final confrontation between Cooper and his antagonists. Frontiere must have been familiar with this device, however, as he used it, albeit two years later, in *Barquero* (1970), as the confrontation between Travis (Lee Van Cleef) and Jake Remy (Warren Oats) is about to occur.

For Eastwood's next Hollywood western, *Two Mules for Sister Sara*, director Don Siegel was fortunate enough to collaborate with *il maestro del cinema Italiano*, Ennio Morricone. Hogan (Clint Eastwood) is more reminiscent of the protagonist in the Dollars trilogy as well. He is an unshaven mercenary, motivated only by money, and has no regard for the law, love, or the church. Early in the film, he shoots three gunmen who are attacking Sara (Shirley MacLaine). Morricone's clever score for this film is representative of his music for the Italian westerns and features numerous aerophones (oboe, bassoon, and flute). The introduction to the main title features a high-register solo bassoon, reminiscent of Stravinsky's *The Rite of Spring*. The theme is based on the same six-note scale used in the Dollars trilogy, suggesting either the Dorian or Aeolian mode. He composed a religious-sounding vocal theme for Sara, and cleverly imitates the hee-haw sound of a mule throughout the score. Morricone was careful, however, not to re-use all of the musical devices that distinguish his scores for Leone from his other scores. There is no mariachi-style fateful trumpet melody in the film's climax. There is, nonetheless, a bugler at the French garrison who signals an alert when Hogan, Sara, Beltran, and his men attack, until he is silenced by a bullet.[35] Perhaps this was Morricone's way of killing-off this musical device as well.

Morricone's influence on other composers of music for westerns is significant. Little-known composer and Morricone collaborator Amedeo Tommasi wrote a score for *This Man Can't Die*, aka *Long Days of Hate* (*I lunghi giorni dell'odio*, 1967) that not only displays the influence of Morricone, but even includes "Without Pity" ("Senza Pietà"), a cue lifted note-for-note straight out of Morricone's score for *A Fistful of Dollars*. As already mentioned, Frontiere's score for *Hang 'Em High* includes a theme for the protagonist in the Dorian mode, a practice unheard of in pre-Dollars Hollywood westerns. Both Lalo Schifrin in *Joe Kidd* (1972) and Dee Barton in *High Plains Drifter* (1973) used themes in the Aeolian mode, whereas Hollywood composers had previously used major and minor keys much like the beloved classical composers they emulated. Like Frontiere and his score for *Barquero*, Bruno Nicolai, a long-time Morricone collaborator (conductor on *For a Few Dollars More* and *The Good,* the Bad and the Ugly), wrote a very enjoyable score for *The Fighting Fists of Shanghai Joe* , aka *My Name is Shanghai Joe* (*Il mio nome è Shanghai Joe*, 1972) that includes one of the most lyrical trumpet melodies found in the genre (in E-flat Aeolian).

Hollywood composer Alan Silvestri resisted the lure to imitate Morricone's music for the Dollars trilogy-influenced *Back to the Future: Part III* (1990). However, for *The Quick and the Dead* (1995), an apparent Hollywood tribute to the tradition of the Italian western,[36] Silvestri composed a memorable minor key trumpet tune, very reminiscent of Morricone's trumpet themes for the Dollars trilogy, for the scenes in which "the Kid" (Leonardo DiCaprio) prepares for his gunfights with Gutzon (Sven-Ole Thorsen), and later with Herod (Gene Hackman). The theme appears once more in the film's closing credits, after the "woman with no name" (Sharon Stone) rides off into the distance. Additionally, there is a whistled theme for Stone's character. For the animated film *Rango* (2011), Hans Zimmer not only composed music reminiscent of the Dollars trilogy, but asked the trumpet soloist to play "a la Ennio Morricone."[37]

More recent tributes to the Italian western go far beyond Hollywood, demonstrating the subgenre's international stature as well as its place in the international popular culture. Japan's *Sukiyaki Western Django* (2007) is based on *A Fistful of Dollars* which, as has been mentioned, is a remake of the samurai film *Yojimbo*. *Sukiyaki Western Django* has visual references to the westerns of Leone that are far too numerous to mention here. Musical references to Italian westerns, however, are few and far between. One notable exception is an on-screen cornet soloist playing a minor key melody that begins with the ascending perfect fifth, one of Morricone's favorite melodic intervals (see the opening notes of Figures 7.4, 7.5, and 7.8). The Korean film, *The Good, the Bad, the Weird* (2008) is a whimsical, fast-paced, and very violent tribute to Leone's *The Good, the Bad and the Ugly*, to the point of being too predictable. Much of the music, however, is more like the big-band music John Barry composed for the James Bond films than anything Morricone ever composed for westerns. There is, however, a whistled theme with banjo accompaniment for some of the desert-crossing scenes that is reminiscent of "Cheyenne's Theme" from *Once Upon a Time in the West*.

Morricone's themes from his western scores have subsequently been used in numerous films, including children's films from Disney,[38] to represent a confrontation or competition. On numerous occasions, director Quentin Tarentino has expressed his fondness for Morricone's music; however, Morricone has yet to compose any original music for Tarentino's films. Morricone's music from his western scores does appear, and rather cleverly so, in Tarentino's *Kill Bill Vol. 1* (2003), *Kill Bill Vol. 2* (2004), and *Inglourious Basterds* (2009).

To say that many of the compositional techniques Morricone introduced into, or developed more thoroughly for, music for westerns have been assimilated by composers around the world would be an understatement. Before Morricone's music for the Dollars trilogy, music for Hollywood westerns consisted of a symphony orchestra, occasionally complemented with guitar or harmonica, playing beautiful melodies in major and minor keys. Since the trilogy, it is not unusual for composers of music for westerns to use electric guitar, solo trumpet, human whistling, and tubular bells while writing in modes such as Aeolian and Dorian. As can be heard in westerns since the Dollars trilogy, whether an apparent homage to the Italian westerns such as *The Quick and the Dead*, *Sukiyaki Western Django*, or *The Good, the Bad, the Weird*, or a mainstream Hollywood western that reflects his influence such as *Hang 'Em High*, Morricone's contribution to the craft of film music is immeasurable. Although he is, and always will be, best-known for his western scores, he has also composed numerous scores for other genres, including: science fiction—*The Thing* (1982) and *Mission to Mars* (2000); gangster films—*Once Upon a Time in America* (1984), *Bugsy* (1991), and *The Untouchables* (1987); dramas—*Disclosure* (1994) and *In the Line of Fire* (1993); historical dramas—*The Mission* (1986) and *Casualties of War* (1989); and more recently, Italian romances for director Giuseppe Tornatore—*Cinema Paradiso* (1988) and *Malèna* (2000), to mention only a few.

As of this writing, Ennio Morricone is still active as a composer, writing mostly for Italian film and television, but in recent years most of his time and energy has been dedicated to conducting concerts of his film music at venues around the world. His music for westerns continues to be re-used in American films, television, and, more recently, in video games as well. In 2007, Ennio Morricone was presented with an Honorary Academy Award for his numerous contributions to film music during his long and prolific career. In his acceptance speech, he graciously acknowledged all of the film composers who work as hard as he has, but who have not been fortunate enough to enjoy the same level of recognition. Bravo, Maestro!

Notes

Special thanks go to Robert C. Cumbow, Patrick Ehresmann, Kathryn Kalinak, Yuna de Lannoy, Sergio Miceli, and William Rosar.

1 Here, I refer to the classical or Viennese sonata form, also known as sonata-allegro form. This form consists of three main sections: exposition, development, and recapitulation. The term "resolution" is also appropriate here. The dissonant relationship between musical themes and keys in the exposition requires a resolution. This occurs in the recapitulation when all themes return in the home key (tonic). See Robin Wood, *Rio Bravo* (London: BFI Publishing, 2003) 25, 42, 76.
2 Peter Lehman describes *The Searchers* as "a masterpiece and one of the greatest films ever made." Peter Lehman, *The Searchers: Essays and Reflections on John Ford's Classic Western* (Detroit: Wayne State University Press, 2004), xv.
3 Incidentally, many of Max Steiner's film scores for Warner Bros. begin with his "Warner Brothers Fanfare" which can be heard at the beginning of *Jezebel* (1938), *Now, Voyager* (1942), *Casablanca* (1943), *Mildred Pierce* (1945), *The Big Sleep* (1946), *Key Largo* (1948), and others.
4 Kathryn Kalinak, *How the West Was Sung: Music in the Westerns of John Ford* (Berkeley and Los Angeles CA: University of California Press, 2007), 158–59.
5 This is an original Tiomkin theme, and not the "Degüello" bugle call that many sources indicate was played by Santa Anna's buglers at the Alamo.

6 Several sources identify the instrument being played as a trumpet, but the audience sees a man with a cornet on-screen. In the author's opinion, it is a cornet that is heard.
7 A trumpet or cornet soloist had been featured in a Hollywood western before *Rio Bravo*. In the Mexican cantina scene from the film *Cowboy* (1958), legendary trumpeter Rafael Méndez is seen playing a solo version of the tune "El Gitano" during a confrontation between Frank Harris (Jack Lemmon) and several other men.
8 *Rio Bravo*, DVD, directed by Howard Hawks (1959; Burbank, CA: Warner Home Video, 2007).
9 It most likely came as no surprise to audiences when, about a year and a half later, Tiomkin cleverly incorporated the same "Degüello" tune into his score for John Wayne's *The Alamo* (1960).
10 Christopher Frayling, *Spaghetti Westerns: Cowboys and Europeans from Karl May to Sergio Leone* (London: I. B. Tauris, 2006), 68.
11 Ibid., 256.
12 Ennio Morricone considers the term "spaghetti western" to be "both annoying and unpleasant." Ennio Morricone, fax sent to the author, translated by Albert Balesh, MD, March 26, 2004.
13 Charles Leinberger, *Ennio Morricone's The Good, the Bad and the Ugly: A Film Score Guide* (Lanham, MD: The Scarecrow Press, 2004), 43–44.
14 In *Johnny Yuma*, Mark Damon's character kills three gunmen in the first scene. Early in *A Fistful of Dollars*, Clint Eastwood's character plans to kill three gunmen (he asks the undertaker for three coffins), but actually kills four. In the first scene of *The Big Gundown* (*La resa dei conti*), Lee Van Cleef's character kills three gunmen. In *The Good, the Bad and the Ugly*, each protagonist kills (or shoots) three people before receiving their on-screen epithet. In the opening sequence of *Once Upon a Time in the West*, Charles Bronson's character kills three gunmen at the train station. In later Hollywood films, Clint Eastwood's character kills three gunmen early in Don Siegel's *Two Mules for Sister Sara* (1970) and in Eastwood's own *High Plains Drifter* (1973).
15 Money is buried in *The Good, the Bad and the Ugly*. Retrieving the buried or otherwise hidden loot and transporting it across the border is a subplot in *A Reason to Live, a Reason to Die* (1972), *Red Sun* (1972), and *God's Gun* (1975).
16 Lee Van Cleef plays twins in *God's Gun* (1975) and William Shatner plays twins in the Spanish-made western *White Comanche* (1968).
17 José Calvo plays Silvanito, an overly-helpful bartender/restaurateur in *A Fistful of Dollars* (1964).
18 Frayling, 147.
19 During the 1960s, America fell in love with all things British: pop music, fashion, art, and movies. United Artists was enjoying financial success by importing the first of the James Bond films, starring Sean Connery, to the US. It was merely a matter of time before United Artists would look for another foreign commodity that was ripe for importing, the Italian westerns.
20 He is credited as director of only five westerns.
21 Frayling, 160.
22 *For a Few Dollars More*, DVD, directed by Sergio Leone (1965; MGM Home Entertainment, 1998).
23 Patrick Ehresmann, *Western Italian Style*. http://www.chimai.com/. Accessed December 12, 2010.
24 Robert Cumbow, *Once Upon a Time: The Films of Sergio Leone* (Lanham MD: The Scarecrow Press, 1987), 203.
25 Ehresmann, *Western Italian Style*. http://www.chimai.com/. Accessed December 12, 2010.

26 Frayling, 165.

27 In the film's opening, this leitmotif is heard with these three timbres in this order. The reason behind the ordering is simple. The Italian title of the film is *Il buono, il bruto, il cattivo*, which translates literally as *The Good, the Ugly, the Bad*.

28 The key signature of D minor is included for clarity, to identify the tonal center as D, even though the only flat in the key signature, B-flat, applies to the scale degree that does not appear in this melody.

29 B-flat is the root of the chord in measures 19 and 22–23. B-natural is part of the G major chord in measures 20–21. A chromatic mediant (two major chords with roots a third apart) exists between these two chords, which function respectively as VI, IV, and VI in D minor. Morricone will use a similar progression in the cue "The Ecstasy of Gold."

30 F-sharp is part of the D major chord in measure 12. F-natural is the root of the chord in measure 14. A chromatic mediant exists between these two chords, which function respectively as IV and VI in A minor. A chromatic mediant also exists between the C major chord in measures 27–29 and the E major chord in measures 30–31, which function respectively as III and V in A minor.

31 Ennio Morricone, interview by author, translated by Albert Balesh, MD, Rome, July 26, 2003.

32 If Harmonica does indeed ride off into the unknown, it is unseen by the audience. The last time he is seen, he is bringing Cheyenne's body back to Sweetwater.

33 Ehresmann. Also, Philip Tagg and Bob Clarida, "The Virginian—Life, liberty and the US pursuit of happiness" in *Ten Little Title Tunes* (New York, NY: The Mass Media Music Scholars' Press, 2003) 371.

34 Morricone likewise quoted Richard Wagner's *The Valkyrie* (*Die Walküre*) in *My Name is Nobody* (*Il mio nome è Nessuno*), aka *Lonesome Gun*, and Beethoven's *"Für Elise"* in *The Big Gundown* (*La resa dei conti*).

35 A bugler is also silenced by a bullet in *The Good, the Bad, the Weird* (2008), the Korean tribute to *The Good, the Bad and the Ugly*.

36 The most recognizable visual reference to the westerns of Leone comes in two scenes, one involving Cort (Russell Crowe), and one, a flashback involving the marshal (Gary Sinise), where a man with a noose around his neck is standing on a chair. Herod (Gene Hackman) shoots the legs off the chair; much like Tuco (Eli Wallach) is about to do in *The Good, the Bad and the Ugly*, until a cannon ball interrupts his scheme.

37 Rick Baptist, email to the author, March 13, 2011.

38 Disney films that use Morricone's music from the main title of *The Good, the Bad and the Ugly* include *Lion King 1½* (2004), during a slug-swallowing contest between Timon and Pumbaa, and *Racing Stripes* (2005), during a race between Stripes the zebra and a mail truck. Main title music from *The Good, the Bad and the Ugly* is also heard in DreamWorks's *Madagascar: Escape 2 Africa* (2008), during a confrontation between Alex the lion and Nana.

Chapter 8

Europe Cannibalizes the Western

Ravenous

K. J. Donnelly

The Canadian documentary *Beaver People* (1928) is not only of anthropological and historical value, but also features the only notable footage of North American Indian luminary Grey Owl, who toured Britain in the 1930s giving lectures about the Canadian wilderness and First Nation culture. He became something of a celebrity and his talks were as popular as his best-selling books, which included *The Last Men of the Frontier* and *Tales of an Empty Cabin*. One of his principal attractions was his authentic exoticism as a classic noble savage bedecked in Native American costume. However, he was in fact born in Hastings in England, as Archibald Belaney, and had come to Canada nearly thirty years before his return to England. Although now feted as a champion of early naturalism and conservation, his life had been full of fabrications and deceptions.[1]

There is also a cinematic tradition of fabricating America and Americans, through making westerns in Europe and with predominantly European casts. As Grey Owl's life and success visiting Europe as an ambassador for the First Nation illustrates, there has been a fascination in Europe with the American West and perhaps more with its representation on film. Westerns are the most characteristic of American film genres, yet there was a thriving European industry producing westerns in the 1960s and 1970s, most of which are often commonly referred to as "spaghetti westerns."[2] European film industries, when not subsidized heavily by their state, regularly have aimed at popular success in the substantial American market as much as, if not more so, than the home. The flip side to the dominance of US films abroad is that Europe feels it knows American culture only too well, and is able unproblematically to fabricate as quintessentially an American film genre as the western.

"British" western *Ravenous* (1999) was partially produced by a Hollywood studio, yet was a British production and registered as an international co-production between USA/UK/Czech Republic/Slovakia/Mexico. It was produced by a British producer (David Hayman), written by an American screenwriter (Ted Griffin), and directed by a British director (Antonia Bird). *Ravenous* was largely shot in the Czech and Slovak Republics (some in Poland and Mexico), and starred an Australian (Guy Pearce) and a Scotsman (Robert Carlyle). Two weeks into the production, Yugoslavian/Macedonian director

Milcho Manchevski was replaced by Bird. The film had music written by English musicians Damon Albarn (best known as the singer in pop group Blur) and Michael Nyman, an experienced film composer who is also known for writing art music. Pop star Albarn and scholar turned film music composer Nyman created music of a highly singular character, and attempted to supply the film with some credentials. Albarn's music at times is pop influenced but also embraces and is influenced by Native American music, thus appealing to the reality of ethnic North American music. Similarly, Nyman's music also appeals to the reality of the time and space the film represents, with a degree of historical and scholarly approach to music that might have been played at the time, including the limitations on performance of amateur musicians. These world music and avant-garde approaches mark responses to the universality of the Hollywood standard film score. Despite similar attempts to revise music for westerns, here, despite the surface of Americana, there remains something stoically and determinedly European. While *Ravenous* is highly singular, its music is also extremely characteristic and furnishes a large part of the film's distinctive character, and the film at least partly endeavors to negotiate the minefield of film and cultural tradition through its music.

 Ravenous is a black comedy about cannibalism rejuvenating individuals through their being possessed by a spirit the Native Americans call the "Weendigo."[3] Captain Boyd has discovered the life-giving powers of human meat in the Mexican–American War and has been sent to the isolated Fort Spencer in the western Sierra Nevadas in California. The appearance of a mysterious figure calling himself "Colquhoun" leads to a party from the fort making an expedition to a cave where he claims cannibalism has been taking place. It turns out that Colquhoun is the cannibal and he attacks and kills the whole party apart from Boyd who dives off a cliff and remains in a hole in the ground until he rejuvenates himself through partaking of the flesh of one of his dead colleagues. Upon his return to Fort Spencer, Colquhoun, now calling himself Colonel Ives, takes up residence at the fort. The two have a final and lengthy confrontation which culminates in both being caught in a bear trap

Figure 8.1

and seemingly expiring. It is an unusual story and has a strong cast, with Jeffrey Jones as Colonel Hart and David Arquette as Cleaves. The exteriors for *Ravenous* were shot at Tatranska National Park in Slovakia, with its evergreen forests and snow-capped mountains making a fairly convincing replacement for the Sierra Nevadas. Hollywood majors still dominate international film distribution, and *Ravenous* was released by Twentieth Century-Fox, although the soundtrack album was released by the British corporation EMI.

Westerns and Musicians

Writers such as Jim Kitses in *Horizons West* have ennobled the western, deeming it amongst other things the epitome of Americana,[4] and consequently many film scores for westerns have drawn upon self-consciously American orchestral music, particularly that by Aaron Copland and Virgil Thomson.[5] The distinctiveness of musical Americana has been held within Hollywood's industrial structure, which led to scores sounding fairly standard, being orchestral, by and large functional, and with often stereotypical music for chases or Indians.[6] Hollywood western scores broadly conformed to Kathryn Kalinak's formulation of the industrial and aesthetic pattern of the classical film score,[7] although they often contained some distinctive elements. One of these was the regular use of expansive melody, particularly in the opening titles or for sequences of open landscape.[8] A good example of this was Jerome Moross's main theme for *The Big Country* (1958), which also included another characteristic: repetitive kinetic rhythm (with the suggestion of horses running quickly), which opens the film.[9] Scores can often exploit what has become accepted as characteristic western timbres: harmonicas, tom-toms, Spanish guitars, and jaw harp. There is a degree of historical veracity for the use of these instruments, as they were popular during the frontier period, and they were woven into orchestral film scores increasingly from the 1930s onwards. The revisionist western made some significant changes to the film music model established by the classical Hollywood cinema. *A Man Called Horse* (1970) had a score by Leonard Rosenman that included Native American music alongside dissonant music inspired by Modernist art music, and Arthur Penn's *Little Big Man* (1970) had a soundtrack, by John Hammond, of delta blues music. Delta blues had no clear relationship to the western and works as something of a commentary in a film that might easily be construed as a commentary on the western and its version of American history.

The European western, however, arguably had more impact on the aural repertoire of the western.[10] Ennio Morricone's music for Sergio Leone's trilogy and other Italian westerns became highly celebrated and appeared to emphasize a more "Mexican" aspect with use of the shrill mariachi trumpet, although Morricone used many disparate but characteristic elements, such as whistling and other vocal effects, whip cracks, organ, and electric guitars.[11] For instance, *For a Few Dollars More* (*Per qualche dollaro in piu*, 1965) had a main theme that mixes the sound of a chiming music box melody with twangy electric guitar and Gothic organ perhaps inspired by Bach's *Toccata and Fugue in D Minor*. Morricone's influence cannot be underestimated, [12] yet much in the way of music for westerns sounds like we might expect music for westerns to sound— that is, traditional film score, with specific western aspects to it. There is an Italian tradition of bold film music, mixed loud in post-production, while Christopher Wagstaff notes that, "[t]he music of the spaghetti western was important in signaling to inattentive viewers the moments when they should pay attention."[13] Leone and Morricone went on to a larger budget western, shot in the US, *Once Upon a Time in the West* (*C'era una volta il west*, 1968). Uniquely, this had different themes representing the film's three principal characters, each with a distinctive timbre: high soaring wordless female vocal, banjo, and harmonica (with some artificial reverb). The music was written before shooting began and was played constantly on set, and then the film images were cut to the pieces of music.

Generally speaking, the Hollywood tradition for incidental music in westerns involved the use of broad, sweeping melodies, with bold uncomplicated harmonies. Many of the melodies were either derived from, or inspired by, Presbyterian hymns or Appalachian folk songs often of Anglo–Scots–Irish origin, while occasional instrumental timbres were the sort of thing that might have been found on the prairie (jaw harps, harmonicas, or acoustic guitars). However, *Ravenous* has some musical aspects alien to the broad tradition, of both the Hollywood mainstream and the spaghetti western. These comprise playing out of tune—a taboo in almost all recorded music—and electronic music, which traditionally has been corralled into modern or futuristic films rather than those set in the middle of the nineteenth century in the American West.[14] The choice of two distinctive musicians indicated that the producers were aiming at a non-standard product rather than an unremarkable "invisible" Hollywood-style score. Indeed, the two musicians were an inspired choice as composers for the film. Albarn was engaged initially but was thought to need aid from a more seasoned film composer.[15] Nyman had worked with Albarn recently and the score for *Ravenous* was a partnership, although it seems that

Figure 8.2

each cue was written by one or the other rather than the project being a full collaboration. Albarn began working on the film before Nyman, choosing his scenes and writing music, leaving Nyman to write the remaining cues.[16] There was separate writing but collaborative rehearsal and recording. Nyman conducted the Michael Nyman Orchestra, which provided a sense of sonic unity to the film's music. Even when the band of session musicians playing country instruments is used, the appearance of orchestral instruments manages to impart a sound reminiscent of Nyman's other musical recordings.[17]

At the time of *Ravenous*, Michael Nyman was an established film score composer, albeit one with a reputation for producing highly distinctive music. Initially at least, he had an art music reputation.[18] As a film composer, he has tended not to be commissioned to write music that sounded like a traditional film score, and, as Ap Sion notes, has a "belief that film music is central rather than incidental."[19] Instead, filmmakers desired music in his own highly idiosyncratic style, which was based on the repetitive character of minimalism allied to modifying elements derived from elsewhere, or at least using them as a basis for his musical variations.[20] His establishing scores were for Peter Greenaway's films, most notably *The Draughtsman's Contract* (1982), which reworked many motifs from restoration baroque composer Henry Purcell,[21] and *Drowning By Numbers* (1988), which made variations upon elements derived from the slow movement of Mozart's *Sinfonia Concertante* for violin and viola. His score for Jane Campion's *The Piano* (1993) was massively successful and added a rare piece of film music to concert hall repertoire, as well as establishing him as a top rung composer for the cinema. Despite success, Nyman retained his strong view on film music and has not significantly altered his style to fit the expectations of mainstream films. For instance, Nyman has stated his distaste for "indulging in the pointless activity of musical pastiche usually found in the soundtracks of films located in the 'historical past.'"[22] He also appears to have little interest in genre music. Both of these aspects feed directly into his music for *Ravenous*, which avoids genre convention as well as film music traditions for representing the past.

Ravenous includes some music that aims to set a sense of time and place strongly, namely some brass band music. The first is "O Columbia" (aka "Columbia, The Gem of the Ocean"), which plays as Boyd is given his award, and then Stephen Foster's "The Old Folks at Home" (aka "Way Down Upon the Swanee River"), which appears quietly under dialogue between Boyd and Colonel Hart. Nyman is responsible for these pieces, which are played in a shoddy, amateurish manner. (The second is performed by Foster's Social Orchestra.) On the one hand, this gives a strong sense of the sort of music that might well have been played at that time and in that place. On the other, it engages with Nyman's connections with out-of-tune-sounding experimental music ensembles in Britain in the 1970s, such as the Portsmouth Sinfonia and the Scratch Orchestra, both of which were premised upon musicians playing instruments to which they were not accustomed.[23] The Michael Nyman Band also effected a degree of "shoddiness," which gave their music a rough and ready character inspired by rock and folk music and in stark contrast to what some might characterize as the arid, polished performances endemic in art music circles. Nyman manages to deal with what in most films would have been a fairly functional requirement for diegetic music by infusing his interest in non-professional musicianship into music that works as a historical signifier.

Damon Albarn initially had come to prominence as the singer in flagship Britpop group Blur in the 1990s, which was eclipsed internationally by his success as part of the group Gorillaz in the 2000s. As is often the case with aging pop stars, there is a tendency to want to diversify into other activities. He acted in the gangster film *Face* (1997), which was directed by *Ravenous* director Antonia Bird, and became involved in other musical activities, including music for films. He contributed a song ("Closet Romantic") as well as Blur's evocative "Sing" to *Trainspotting* (1996) and after *Ravenous* provided some music for the film *Ordinary Decent Criminal* (2000) and shared the score for *101 Reykjavik* in 2002 with Einar Örn Benediktsson (once of the Sugarcubes). Albarn had already worked with Nyman on a version of Noel Coward's "London Pride" for the album *Twentieth Century Blues: The Songs of Noel Coward*, a project that reworked Coward's songs using contemporary pop stars.[24] Although some might imagine Albarn was a naïve musical *ingénue* on a project such as this, his work with Blur was often subtle and complex, and apparently as a youth he had won a regional competition for young composers.[25]

A film set in America in the middle of the eighteenth century might be approached through having a seemingly neutral score that merely becomes an unobtrusive aspect of the film's narration. On the other hand, the time and the place are potentially a fertile ground for an anthropological impetus to a film's music. Albarn has exhibited an interest in so-called world music, releasing an album of musical field recordings *Mali Music* in 2002, and collaborating on Chinese opera *Monkey: Journey to the West* in 2007. Elements of the music for *Ravenous* betray an interest in ethnic music, which had already translated to a few westerns. Claudia Gorbman discusses Ry Cooder's music for *Geronimo: An American Legend* (1993) and goes on to note: "In the 1980s, as exotic ethnic musics became raw materials to pass through the mills of global media commodification and consumption by western markets, a world music soundtrack began to stand for a style in itself, defining the film audience as much as the film."[26] While on the one hand there had been an increasing interest in consuming ethnic music, on the other there was a desire for anthropological documentation of a reality of what was being represented. For *Ravenous*, Albarn completed research into Appalachian folk music, listening to recordings at the Smithsonian Institution in Washington DC. Following the typical musical division in westerns, he divided the film's music into music inspired by white folk music and Native American music. For the latter, he enlisted Milton 'Quiltman' Sahmi (with help from his wife), both of whom he recorded on a reservation performing traditional singing.[27] This appears in *Ravenous* when Native American Martha is looking for the arriving men. The chant is traditional, and a similar one is also used when Boyd is wandering around the fort in the snow supporting himself with a stick. Indeed, Albarn says that he felt like a custodian of culture after anthropological dealings with Quiltman and the reality of Native American culture.[28]

Ravenous Music

The incidental music for *Ravenous* was performed by the Michael Nyman Orchestra, conducted by Nyman alongside a small band of musicians playing country or folk instruments, including violin, guitar, jaw harp, banjo, percussion, accordion, and dulcimer. In addition to this, there are some contributions from a female singer and the London Voices ensemble, as well as a couple of cues of Native American singing by Quiltman.

The score for the film includes a wealth of traditional western instrumentation, which imparts a strong ethnic and historical flavor to the film. However, Albarn pointed out that the dulcimer, which features prominently, was not an instrument used to any degree in the American West of the time of depiction, but was used in the score because of Morricone's use of it in spaghetti western scores.[29] The use of the Michael Nyman Orchestra means that the sound of the incidental music is often orchestral. However, the score for the film also includes instrumental sounds that are extremely uncharacteristic of westerns, namely electronic sounds and looped digital sound samples. Some of the most obvious samples, such as the strange repeated phrase as the party enter the cannibal cave, have a distinctly inorganic quality. Albarn created the sound through manipulating a sample of an oboe with pitch shifting software to give an almost vocal tone. On this and other occasions, digital samples, when not treated with electronic reverb or echo, have a strikingly rapid release time; they die immediately, which is a key characteristic of the sharp cutting points in digital audio editing. The film's use of electric keyboards is also a far cry from tradition in the western film. However, it is an instrument that Albarn has given some prominence to in his previous music, particularly in its most synthetic manifestation. For instance, Blur's best-selling album *Parklife* (1994) has pieces such as the instrumental "The Debt Collector," a fairground waltz with cheap organ sound (and session saxophonists, flautist, and trombonist) and the organ start of the subsequent track "Far Out" and the opening of the album's closing track "Lot 105." The tendency is to use organs as sustained chords, exploiting their particular static timbre over their melodic and harmonic capabilities.

The film's principal theme exploits electronic keyboards as well as more traditional instruments,[30] although in its initial appearance it is played by acoustic instruments. This piece provides the main aural character of the film, appearing at the start, finish and a significant point in the middle of *Ravenous*. It is a striking piece of music. As the pre-title sequence concludes with Boyd vomiting when faced with eating bloody-rare meat, regular, almost mechanical plucks of the banjo alternating between E and D-sharp a minor seventh higher, with the first note in a bar of $\frac{6}{8}$ and the second a bar of $\frac{7}{8}$. This is ambiguous and an unusual musical foundation for the principal theme of a film, which often will have something defining for the character of the film and an indication of what audiences might expect. This bed of banjo is joined by the accordion playing a pentatonic melody. However, the structures of the music are uneven and work across each other. This piece is in E major but the banjo suggests more of a modal rather than tonal usage.[31] After a time, a solo high trumpet enters playing the melody of "O Columbia," the music we have already heard played diegetically by the brass band in dubious tune and timing at Boyd's presentation and dinner. The melody has a rustic character but its structure is not even, indicating a jagged eccentricity in the film. This theme makes a spectacular return later in the film when Boyd emerges reborn from the hole in the ground having become rejuvenated through eating human flesh. This subsequent arrangement is slightly different. Its regular drum beat is more easily related to popular music beats. The mechanical plucking is now played by the dulcimer and the melody is played by an electric organ rather than the acoustic accordion. Thus it is less folky and a more ebullient, rock-inspired alternative (perhaps extremely alternative).

With this piece, we expect regularity but the structure is not straightforward. The whole is twelve and a half bars long and breaks down into four-bar, three-bar and five-bar phrases. In contradistinction, some of the music in *Ravenous* has utter regularity of structure. For instance, the most evident example of digital looping in the film is the striking music that accompanies Colquhoun's narration (an extended flashback sequence with voice-over) about the mis-adventures of a wagon train and the onset of cannibalism as they sheltered starving in a cave. This music was produced by Albarn making a loop of one bar of an Appalachian-style jig, and then adding a dulcimer melody with some flute accompaniment entering later.[32] Despite the digital loop being in A-flat major, the two instruments occupy themselves between the major and minor key of A-flat: the dulcimer melody is in minor, while the flute moves between major and minor.[33] After the flute additions, monotone strings enter and build in density (sounding very characteristic of Nyman's work). There are broad dynamic changes in the music matched directly through film editing to events in the story being narrated and changes in the image track. At the point where the visuals change from the face of the narrating Colquhoun to the images of the flashback, the dulcimer enters with its slow deliberate melody and the point where he notes that "things got out of hand" as human flesh was eaten, the

Figure 8.3 Principal theme

orchestra enters dramatically, and the music ceases precisely at the point where he stops narrating the story. Despite the successive musical additions, the music is very static and a strong sense of movement is added by the orchestra providing some loud and strident syncopated chords behind the accumulation of sounds. Nevertheless, the piece remains a repeated loop, of eight bars of $\frac{4}{4}$, its regularity expressing some of the inevitability of disaster in the events being narrated. The piece has a formalistic character, with something emotionally cold about the music's indifference to the events depicted and its regular unfurling irrespective of the shocking events that Colquhoun is illuminating. This indifference is a musical characteristic across the film, and although the piece is by Albarn, such criticism has been leveled at some of Nyman's film music, which seems to have a coldness not evident in most emotionally manipulative Hollywood film music.

A notable moment where the music's indifference meets the film's uncertain black comedy takes place at the cave when Colquhoun has attacked the soldiers from Fort Spencer and then chases one of them, Toffler (Jeremy Davies), through the woods. This is accompanied by a fiddle-led country jig with yodeling. This is a striking instance, as a grave situation is accompanied by ironic and happy music, inviting the audience to involvement with the energy of the chase but remaining anempathetic, as Claudia Gorbman and Michel Chion put it, to the plight of the soldier who is about to die.[34] This dislocation of emotional tenor between the event and the music can often rouse an enhanced emotional effect. Yet here it does not. In dynamic terms, this marks a release of the pent-up energy that has been built up by the extremely dramatic previous sequence of finding bodies in the cave and the revelation of the real and protean nature of Colquhoun. The music plays a valuable role in this process and while it arguably has the character of a throw away piece of music in the context of the film, it is also an almost anthropological showcase for the authentic style and timbre of American folk music in the middle of the nineteenth century.

The charge of emotional disconnection or anempathy might also be leveled at the music during the film's climactic sequence. This is a repeated loop of eight bars of $\frac{3}{4}$ and runs for over nine minutes—for the whole denouement of the film, the confrontation between Boyd and Colquhoun/Ives whereupon at the conclusion they both die. The music is an additive waltz, including electronic keyboards, electronic drums, with synthesizer drones and sustained deep bass notes. The onset of the confrontation is startling in that the music

Figure 8.4 Dulcimer theme

repeats with absolutely no development for nearly two minutes. The sound of electronic keyboards with a distinctive wobbly pitch begins (1.19:43) during dialogue between Boyd and Hart. At the point where the latter asks the former, "Can you be trusted?" to which Boyd replies "Of course not," there is the regular pulse of three notes of the waltz backing, which continues without development as Boyd cuts Colonel Hart's throat and then goes looking for Colquhoun/Ives.[35] It is almost two minutes before the first change to the musical ostinato, when some echoed percussion and dulcimer enters. The piece again follows an additive logic, with each new layer of music accumulating density for the repetitive piece. In succession, there is a deep synthesizer drone (on E-flat) with a very modern-sounding filter sweep (sounding like a wah wah pedal) which accompanies the sword fight between the two characters, a descending high synthesizer line,[36] dulcimer, and finally vocal chorus. The entry of the dulcimer matches the dramatic appearance in close-up of Colquhoun/Ives with a red cross painted on his forehead, with the image track again exploiting the structure of the music. Indeed, this procedure has been evident throughout *Ravenous*, where dramatic events are underscored by being cut to the entry of a particular instrument in a repetitive (and usually additive) piece of music. The building of drama in the music is through an additive process that also exploits the cumulative effect of extreme repetition. The conclusion of the duel, at 1.28:56, is when a large bear trap shuts loudly, trapping both of the characters in a deadly embrace. The music that has been building stops precisely at this moment but a deep synthesizer drone remains and continues through the ensuing sequence, joined by solo deep Native American wail, as the arriving general eats the stew containing human meat (and presumably the weendigo spirit enters him).

During this sequence, the music develops very slowly. Each successive addition is a musical loop that builds the density of the music. The image track is interesting, including big close-ups, moving camera work and point of view shots. However, as the list below indicates, the broad sweeps of development are keyed to progress in the additive piece of music.

Figure 8.5

Concluding Confrontation between Boyd and Colquhoun/Ives

1.19: 43 During dialog between Boyd and Hart three notes rising in pitch and in waltz time begin as Boyd says, "Of course not." The texture is sparing at this point. Dialog continues.

1.21:40 Echoed percussion hits and dulcimer tremolos are added.

1.22:45 A deep droning synthesizer tone enters as Boyd cuts Hart's throat. The continuous pitch is elaborated through filter sweeping which accompanied the sword fight between Boyd and Colquhoun/Ives.

1.23:34 A sustained high note enters as Boyd goes out into the fort's yard looking for Colquhoun/Ives; this develops into a loop of high synthesizer notes sounding like a female voice playing a descending melody.

1.25:08 A loud dulcimer is added at the precise point of cutting to a dramatic close-up shot of Colquhoun/Ives turning to reveal he has a cross daubed in blood on his forehead.

1.25:39 The music becomes louder, rhythmic triplets in the voices are added as the dueling pair begin re-engagement.

1.27:45 Voices clearly enounce the words "Save Our Souls Lissa."

1.28: 56 The bear trap shuts loudly and the music stops at precisely the same moment but the deep synthesizer drone remains.

This listing illustrates how close the structure of the action is interlocked with the structure of the music. The music also has a highly logical structure, developing almost automatically with additions of successive layers to the existing piece.[37] Narrative developments parallel musical developments. Changes in music match changes in activity, rather than the situation in most mainstream films, where impacts and important words are underscored and emphasized musically. This sequence of confrontation has some moments of distinct inspiration from Sergio Leone's westerns, with the dramatic facial close-ups and slow build-up to a duel being reminiscent of the denouements of *The Good, the Bad and the Ugly* (1967) and *Once Upon a Time in the West* (1968). This piece, like some of the rest of the music in the film, includes a number of elements that betray Albarn's origins as a pop musician, yet the music nevertheless remains highly effective within the context of the film.

Ravenous contains some extremely long sequences of image and loud music with no dialogue. For example, there is a sequence of over eight and a half minutes from where Boyd jumps off the cliff, is prostrate in the hole in the ground, after agonizing eats some of his dead comrade, and then emerges rejuvenated and re-enters Fort Spencer. Music dominates the soundtrack, with few incidences of diegetic sound, with just a couple of spoken lines from characters. At 43:09, in one of the most impressive sequences in the film, Boyd leaps from the cliff to escape Colquhoun and falls down a slope and into a hole in the ground. At 44:27 Colquhoun gazes off the cliff and a waltz begins, which is an additive piece with harp and eerie strings and short motifs, and described by Albarn as highly romantic.[38] It accompanies a slow montage of the passing of time with Boyd setting his broken leg, Colquhoun looking for Boyd, and his final surrender to the urge to survive by eating his dead comrade. At 49:55, the music changes as Boyd emerges from the hole and wanders back to Fort Spencer. The waltz recedes and the principal theme begins with the mechanical plucking on dulcimer rather than banjo, while percussion creates a beat emphasizing the third beat of the measure. Electric organ plays the main melody and after a while strings join in punctuating the piece, which fades out as Cleaves exclaims, "Boyd?" at 51:43. While the waltz does indeed have something of a romantic character, it is also rather dislocated and anempathetic in its relation to the action, through its relentlessness and inward-looking character. The return of the principal theme, despite its mechanical character, appears much more emotional, particularly allied with the images of the film's protagonist triumphantly leaving the hole and returning in a dramatic resurrection from the dead. The waltz suggests inevitable fate, and like the overwhelming majority of the film's music retains a repetitive stasis rather than movement toward a satisfying closure.

Overall, the film's music is premised upon repetition, sometimes with a mechanical character and in terms of structure is usually additive and modular. There is a tendency to use uneven time structures. Rather than introducing a human element, this suggests a cold mathematical logic. The principal theme has banjo playing in alternating bars of $\frac{6}{8}$ and $\frac{7}{8}$, and has an uneven structure of phrases. The cue that accompanies the first appearance of Colquhoun at the window has an additive time structure, starting with a bar of $\frac{4}{4}$ followed by a bar of $\frac{5}{4}$ then an alternation of two bars of $\frac{6}{4}$ followed by two bars of $\frac{5}{4}$. It settles into the last alternation and is a bass monody of E and then an octave higher followed by descending notes, and embodies the strategy of musical indifference that is evident in *Ravenous*. However, on the other hand, some pieces use very strict regular structures based on unerring pulses (such as the two prominent waltzes). There is a tendency toward heavy pulses and beats. Nyman's music is often heavily rhythmic and based on thumping beats, while Albarn's pop background has meant that he is accustomed to music that is based on dance beats. The music is based upon dynamic progression rather than musical development as such. It lacks cadences and closure and usually builds in intensity through addition rather than changes and development of musical material. The clear structures owe something to minimalism and seem to suggest music (and drama) that is going nowhere.[39] This is a rarity in film scores, where the Hollywood model is based on less rigid structures and more unobtrusive forms of expansion. Nyman would not mickey mouse or match action and is partial to music which retains its own integrity. This, of course, can be a problem in films, where music has to fit the film's requirements rather than its own. Albarn was not accustomed to writing to the image and tended to stay with an approach that had proven successful for him in popular music. Both Nyman's and Albarn's tendencies lead to music that retains its own integrity.

However, while this situation may not have been evident in many Hollywood westerns, in Italian westerns music often consists of distinct pieces, at times appearing almost unrelated to image dynamics, rather than being unobtrusive cues written precisely to aid and fit with on-screen developments.[40] Indeed, most musical cues occupy the foreground, giving the film a strong sense of musical depth. Loud music usually works to aestheticize images more, rendering them more acceptable and the audience more impressionable. On a couple of occasions, there is striking music mixed low to allow a prominence to dialogue and sound effects. Most clearly in the case of Colquhoun's story, the fact that the music is forced into the background is, as Albarn admits, due to his lack of experience scoring films.[41] Indeed, this would be one of the only moments where *Ravenous* would have benefited from a DVD "score only" option.

Conclusion—European America

The mix of scholarly and historical with the prism of modern technology, looking at the real past, is a curious mix. The dominant character of the film score, embracing repetitive structures, additive and modular development, allied to regular pulses but uneven temporal structures, is exceptional in any film let alone in a western. The music tends to be quite sustained pieces with their own integrity rather than music responding momentarily to film activity. Indeed, there is little clear evidence of a substantial influence on the music in *Ravenous* from Hollywood genre traditions, although there is definitely some from European westerns. However, across the score, there are a number of tunes that are either historical or pastiches of melodies that might almost be recognized as music from the American West. When Colquhoun/Ives cuts onions for the stew there is a quiet non-diegetic accordion and banjo country-style waltz that sounds very similar to "There's No Place Like Home" (aka "Home Sweet Home," a song dating from the 1820s). Earlier, when the party make ready to leave the fort to find the cave, the incidental music consists of a banjo and violin playing a melody country-style that sounds similar to Stephen Foster's "Oh! Susanna." Foster has been known as the "Father of American Music," writing such classic songs as "The Old Folks at Home," "Camptown Races," "Jeanie with the Light Brown Hair," "Old Black Joe," and "Beautiful Dreamer." He was writing in the middle of the nineteenth century—slightly after the film's historical setting.[42] Also, perhaps signaled by the seemingly assumed name of one of the film's protagonists, a partial shadow is cast upon the film's music by American composer Charles Ives. His orchestral music used folk songs and hymn tunes to establish a musical Americana, a similar raw material which regularly formed the basis of later film scores for westerns. His music not only included substantial quotations from song melodies but also used Stephen Foster's songs.[43]

The film begins with an epigram, which cuts to a fluttering US flag accompanied by "O Columbia," which was an effective national anthem for America. This very patriotic inauguration of the film informs the audience that the action takes place in 1847 during the Mexican War. The film's very clear metaphor is of the US as cannibalistic, promoting the eating of, rather than loving and respecting, your fellow man. Cannibalism is presented as something Native Americans understand as an ancient evil they have avoided, while whites find it more difficult to resist temptation. The corrupting spirit added to the notion of Manifest Destiny suggests something evil and contagious about America. The logic of the film, though, is that it is Boyd's fantasy, but might equally be approached as a European fantasy of America.[44]

As a film, *Ravenous* is very much a mixture of European and American impulses, while the music is more European in inspiration than following the traditions of Hollywood westerns. Damon Albarn thought that director Antonia Bird "brought a real European sensibility to it."[45] Bird herself said that many of the people in America during this period would have been Europeans and that the US was a "country made out of a lot of lost Europeans" and that Americans fail to see their past as being European.[46] *Ravenous* depicts North America as an amalgam of European and Native American as well as containing elements more recognizable as contemporary American. This melting pot of culture is represented as an ideal by the music—not simply the inclusion of authentic music but mixing genres/types of music (art music, pop style, folk, traditional instruments, ethnic world music, and electronics).

Notes

1 He was not a total sham and had lived with Ojibwa and Mohawk Iroquois and cared deeply about the land, its people and its animals, working for the Dominion Parks Service. Grey Owl was married three times without legal annulments and joined the Canadian Army during World War One but supplied them with false information (including informing them that he had been a Mexican scout for the US Army and was also half-Indian). He is depicted in Richard Attenborough's film *Grey Owl* (2000) by Pierce Brosnan.

2 Initially, Karl May's western novels were adapted by German-dominated international productions but these increasingly were outnumbered by Italian productions of western films as the 1960s progressed. Tim Bergfelder, *International Adventures: German Popular Cinema and European Co-Productions in the 1960s* (Oxford: Berghahn, 2005), 67.

3 In *The Six-Gun Mystique*, John Cawelti suggests the western is limited to seven archetypal plots: the Union Pacific story, the ranch story, the revenge story, the empire story, the cavalry and Indians story, the outlaw story, and the marshal story. While *Ravenous* has some aspects of "the Union Pacific story," with its implications that cannibalism is a component of expansion westwards, it probably has more in common with "the cavalry and Indians" western. The military in this case are not opposed directly to the Indians but to an Indian spirit that possesses their number. (One might say that some whites "go native.") John Cawelti, *The Six-Gun Mystique* (Bowling Green: Bowling Green State University Press, 1971, 1999), 19.

4 Jim Kitses, *Horizons West* (London: BFI/Thames and Hudson, 1969).

5 Neil Lerner, "Copland's Music of Wide Open Spaces: Surveying the Pastoral Trope in Hollywood" in *The Musical Quarterly*, 82, 2 (Fall 2001), 499.

6 Claudia Gorbman, "Scoring the Indian: Music in the Liberal Western" in *Western Music and its Others: Difference, Representations, and Appropriations in Music*, eds.

David Hesmondhalgh and Georgina Born (Berkeley: University of California Press, 2000), 235.

7 Kathryn Kalinak discusses the Hollywood film score as an industrial-based aesthetic standard in *Settling The Score: Narrative Film Music* (Madison: University of Wisconsin Press, 1992), xv–xvi.

8 Lerner, 486.

9 There was also, from time to time, the use of relaxed loping horse rhythm, which approximated the mood and leisurely pace of the cowboy in the saddle.

10 Although Christopher Frayling notes that Italian westerns did not aim explicitly to revise the Hollywood western tradition. *Spaghetti Westerns: Cowboys and Europeans from Karl May to Sergio Leone* (London: I. B.Tauris, 1998), xxiii. See also Charles Leinberger, Chapter 7, "The Dollars Trilogy: 'There are two kinds of western heroes, my friend!'" in this volume for a history of Italian westerns and their music.

11 For more analysis of Morricone's scores for Leone westerns, see Charles Leinberger, Chapter 7, "The Dollars Trilogy: 'There are two kinds of western heroes, my friend!'" in this volume.

12 An example of Morricone's influence would be a recent Hollywood western, *The Quick and the Dead* (1995), which contained a score by Alan Silvestri that doubles the film's references to Leone's westerns with music that references Morricone in terms of instrumentation as well as melodic and harmonic inflection.

13 Christopher Wagstaff, "A Forkful of Westerns – Industry, Audiences and the Italian Western" in *Popular European Cinema*, eds. Richard Dyer and Ginette Vincendeau (London: Routledge, 1992), 254.

14 There are no notable electronic scores for American westerns as far as I am aware, although *Breakheart Pass* (1975) includes a short burst of electronic music. Musical anachronisms in the genre are often played as such, with rock group ZZ Top appearing in *Back to the Future, Part III* (1990) and Neil Young's electric guitar score for the exceptional western *Dead Man* (1995), directed by Jim Jarmusch.

15 Albarn notes this on the DVD commentary, including the fact that some of the music had to be turned down to allow dialogue to be heard. *Ravenous*, Twentieth Century-Fox Home Entertainment, F1-SGB 00323DVD.

16 "Interview—Michael Nyman" on *Soundtracknet*, www.soundtrack.net/features/article/?id=53. Accessed April 28, 2010.

17 While Albarn used a digital sequencer, some of his music survives in a similar form in the film while other cues were orchestrated by Gary Carpenter who Nyman introduced to Albarn. "Interview—Michael Nyman," Ibid.

18 In the 1970s, he wrote the influential book *Experimental Music* (Cambridge: Cambridge University Press, 1974), the first book to chart developments in the wake of John Cage in the sort of music that regularly failed to be accepted in art music circles as it was often confrontational or conceptual in nature. Nyman's own musical activities included playing and conducting on EG Records, which showcased many marginal and experimental musical pieces.

19 Pwyll Ap Sion, *The Music of Michael Nyman: Texts, Contexts and Intertexts* (Aldershot, Hants: Ashgate, 2007), 185.

20 Ap Sion points to Nyman's *In Re Don Giovanni* as the origin of his mature musical style, noting compositional practices relating to musicological analysis and stylistic inspiration from pop and rock music. Ibid., 10–12.

21 This derived from scholarly research done by Nyman with Thurston Dart at King's College, London in the 1960s. Ibid., 22–23.

22 Michael Nyman from sleeve notes to *The Draughtsman's Contract* CD (Virgin CASCD1158, released in 1989).

23 Self-consciously amateurish playing characterized the Portsmouth Sinfonia, of which Nyman was a member and also fed into his own ensemble, Foster's Social Orchestra, which performed rough and ready versions of Stephen Foster tunes.

24 *Twentieth Century Blues: The Songs of Noel Coward* (1998, EMI7243 49463127).
25 Ria Higgins, "Relative Values: Damon's Albarn and his Sister Jessica," *The Sunday Times*, May 30, 2010. http://women.timesonline.co.uk/tol/life_and_style/women/families/article7133293.ece. Accessed September 28, 2010.
26 Gorbman, op. cit., 250.
27 According to Timothy Brennan, world music "remains a flight from the Euro-self at the very moment of that self's suffocating hegemony." "World Music Does Not Exist," *Discourse* 23,1 (2001), 46. It is telling that Quiltman's singing is associated negatively with the cannibalistic Weendigo spirit to the point where it might be conceived as an embodiment of that native spirit.
28 Albarn, DVD commentary, op. cit.
29 Ibid.
30 The main theme has a sense of irony about it that is slightly reminiscent of Nyman's music for *The Draughtsman's Contract* (1982) and *Drowning by Numbers* (1988).
31 The chords are primary (I, IV, V, and VI (relative minor)). This is more like folk or popular music without notable directional harmonic development.
32 The dulcimer tune appears later unaccompanied when Boyd and Ives/Colquhoun talk before they fight.
33 The play is upon the defining third note of the scale. Such attention to mixing major and minor thirds is a notable characteristic of the blues, like its parent black culture, an important American tradition absent from the film.
34 For discussions of anempathetic music, see Claudia Gorbman, "Anempathy: *Hangover Square*," in her *Unheard Melodies: Narrative Film Music* (London: BFI, 1987), 151–61, and Michel Chion, *Audio-Vision: Sound on Screen*, ed. and trans. Claudia Gorbman (New York: Columbia University Press, 1994), 123.
35 E-flat followed by B-flat a fifth higher and then E-flat a fourth higher than that, with each on the downbeat of the looped bar of $\frac{3}{4}$.
36 It sounds a little like a female voice and runs down a minor scale, including a chromatic sixth, from E-flat to B-flat (E-flat, D-flat, C, C-flat, B-flat). This melodic motif (in different rhythmic formation) appeared earlier in the film for the first appearance of Colquhoun, who puts his face to the window.
37 Musical pieces across the film tend to be structured in this way. Whilst pop music and Nyman's particular form of orchestral music often have structures like this, electronic softstudios also encourage the construction of music in this way, as witnessed by much electronic dance music.
38 Albarn, DVD commentary, op. cit.
39 Repetition in culture is thought to negate teleological desire, be non-dialectical, antithetical to Eros and goal-directed patterns of release that define the ego-creating life instinct. Robert Fink, *Repeating Ourselves: American Minimal Music as Cultural Practice* (Berkeley: University of California Press, 2005), 5.
40 Indeed, the tradition in Italian genre films is that music can be bold and mixed loudly, often aiming to sound distinctive rather than aim toward the model sound of high-quality but similar-sounding film scores such as in Hollywood films.
41 Albarn, DVD commentary, op. cit.
42 One piece by the Foster's Social Orchestra appears on the soundtrack CD but not in the film. This suggests that it originally was to be used but was removed in the latter stages of post-production. Interestingly, this piece is the only piece from the film discussed in Ap Sion, 51.
43 For example, the melody from Foster's "Camptown Races" appears in Ives's Symphony No. 2 (1901), Symphony No. 4 (1916) and *Washington's Birthday*. Ives's Symphony No. 4 not only includes Foster's "Camptown Races," but also his "Massa's in de Cold Ground" and "Old Black Joe." His Symphony No. 2 also

included a rousing version of "Columbia, the Gem of the Ocean" and the hymn "Bringing in the Sheaves."

44 Or perhaps even an American fantasy of immigrants being corrupted by something ancient that "turns them native."

45 Albarn, DVD commentary, op. cit.

46 Ibid.

Chapter 9

"How . . . were we going to make a picture that's better than this?"
Crossing Borders from East to West in *Rashomon* and *The Outrage*

Kathryn Kalinak

Introduction

Remakes have exploded onto American screens recently, becoming a staple of studio output. Nothing is sacred and even canonical texts such as *Psycho* (1960) and *The Manchurian Candidate* (1962) have been remade. Remakes have a long history both in Hollywood and outside it when it comes to westerns. I am interested in what happens to the music when a remake crosses generic and national borders. One of the most iconic western film scores of all time is Elmer Bernstein's for *The Magnificent Seven* (1960). But of course, it first saw light as a samurai film, *Seven Samurai* (1954) directed by Akira Kurosawa and scored by Fumio Hayasaka in Japan. Sergio Leone remade another Kurosawa samurai masterpiece, *Yojimbo* (1961), scored by Masuro Sato,[1] as a so-called spaghetti western in Italy, *A Fistful of Dollars* (1964), with a Hollywood star in its lead and Ennio Morricone composing its iconic score. I will be focusing here on another pair of films which begin with a Japanese genre film and end with a Hollywood one: Kurosawa's *jidaigeki* drama *Rashomon* (1950), scored by Hayasaka, and Martin Ritt's western *The Outrage* (1964), scored by Alex North.

In engaging the genre of the western, these remakes raise a number of questions about the relationship between genre, nation, and music. What happens when a "typically American" western does not begin its life as either a western or an American film? It is a well-established principle in contemporary film studies scholarship that a film score can encode gender, ethnicity, race, and nation. Part of the underlying rationale of the present volume is that film music can also encode genre. What can a film score tell us then about crossing borders between genres and across national cinemas?

Rashomon was the film that thrust Kurosawa into the newly developing international film community as a late entry and surprise winner of the Venice Film Festival in 1951. Marked as uniquely Japanese by its subject matter (the plot revolves around a samurai, his wife, and a bandit) and its production (produced at the Japanese Daiei Kyoto Studios), *Rashomon* is nonetheless also marked as, and in fact becomes, a model for the international art film. So it exists in an interesting cultural space to begin with, straddling two kinds of institutional practices: within the nation (the Japanese studio system primarily targeting Japanese audiences) as well as transcending the nation (the juried international film festival, the international art film audience, and the development of distribution networks that targeted audiences in the West). Noël Burch has described Kurosawa's ultimate achievement "as operating within and beyond the Western mode of filmic representation."[2] I will be arguing along these lines for *Rashomon*'s score: it is both uniquely Japanese and fundamentally western at the same time.

"I should have studied composing"

Akira Kurosawa had very specific desires when it came to the musical scores for his films and he took an active hand in their creation. Long-time collaborator composer Masuro Sato said of him, "If he had the talent, he probably would have done it himself."[3] Kurosawa himself proclaimed, "I should have studied composing."[4] He figured out how to do the next best thing. One way that he exerted control was by choosing music himself: "The Cuckoo Waltz" for *Drunken Angel* (1948) or the samurai theme for *Seven Samurai* (which Kurosawa claimed to have retrieved from composer Hayasaka's waste basket).[5]

Another was giving his composers musical models to follow. Kurosawa liked to listen to phonograph recordings—in pre-production as he was writing a script, and during production as he was shooting—to find musical models to pass on to his composers. Early in his career he played these pre-selected recordings for his composers and later, when the technology permitted, screened a rough cut for them synched up with his pre-selected recordings: Lizst's *Second Hungarian Rhapsody* for *Yojimbo* (1961) and *Sanjuro* (1962); Haydn's Symphony 101, "The Clock," and Beethoven's Ninth Symphony for *Red Beard* (1965), and Mahler's First Symphony for *Ran* (1985). Composers were generally not happy about this situation. For *Quiet Duel* (1949), Kurosawa played for composer Akira Ifukube Juventino Rossi's "Over the Waves" as the musical model to copy. Ifukube felt so compromised by the experience that he refused to work for Kurosawa again. Some composers wondered why Kurosawa simply did not use the original. (For the record, Kurosawa thought that if the audience actually recognized a famous piece of music it would distract them.) A notorious example comes from *Dodes' ka-den* (1970), where Kurosawa gave Tōru Takemitsu, Japan's most high-profile concert hall composer, Bizet's *L'Arlesienne* as the musical prototype. When Takemitsu responded that if Kurosawa wanted Bizet, he should hire Bizet, Kurosawa, perhaps stunned by such unexpected insubordination, acted uncharacteristically and allowed Takemitsu to compose original music instead.[6] Takemitsu would describe his typical collaboration with Kurosawa as a fight which Kurosawa invariably won.[7]

Fumio Hayasaka and Composing for Kurosawa

Kurosawa's interest in western and western-style music, a distinctive feature of his career before *Rashomon*, operated in contradistinction to a powerful musical aesthetic shaped in Japan in response to sound film. The first Japanese sound films in the 1930s depended upon popular songs to fill the soundtrack and the use of western-style music was typical of many films of this period. However, a rise in Japanese nationalism during this period fostered interest in Japanese music (under the Meiji era, Japanese music had been repressed by the government which promoted western music as more modern). Lively debates over the place of western musical elements ensued. Concert hall composers such as Yamada Kosaku and Kami Kyosuke were soon drawn to film scoring where the debate continued. An important figure here is Fumio Hayasaka. Trained and fluent in western classical musical traditions, Hayasaka advocated for the importance of Japanese music.[8] Hayasaka's concert music is characterized by a fusion of traditional Japanese musical elements and western classical music traditions. Timothy Koozin writes of him that he "intermingled elements of Japanese *gagaku* music, contemporary French and Russian orchestral music, and elements of jazz and popular music."[9] David Neumeyer compares Hayasaka to two of his contemporaries, nationalist composers who similarly integrated national music idioms and styles into their concert hall music: Ralph Vaughan-Williams in the UK and Aaron Copland in the US.[10] For Hayasaka, it was even more important that Japanese films should incorporate Japanese music. His score for Mizoguchi's *Ugetsu* (1954) uses *geza* music of Kabuki theater and his score for Mizoguchi's *The Crucified Lovers* (1954) features prominent use of Japanese percussion, fusing the boundary between music and sound. Hayasaka scored a series of films for Kurosawa so it should come as no surprise that Hayasaka found himself in conflict with the director over Kurosawa's preference for western music over Japanese music.

The Genesis of *Rashomon*'s Score

The genesis of the score for *Rashomon* revolves around the conflict of western and Japanese music and between Kurosawa and Hayasaka. Although in his autobiography, Kurosawa writes that he "asked Hayasaka to write a bolero kind of music,"[11] other sources suggest that Kurosawa played Ravel's *Boléro* for Hayasaka.[12] I suspect that it was not so much the bolero that attracted Kurosawa but rather what Ravel did with it, refracting a seed rhythm and melody through a series of variations. It must have seemed to Kurosawa the perfect accompaniment to a filmic exploration of the nature of truth and the variations of it practiced by human beings.[13]

Hayasaka was vehemently opposed to its use and protested to Kurosawa—to no avail. Hayasaka had very little room to maneuver here and gave Kurosawa *Boléro*-esque music which, in one variation or another, comprises the majority of the score. But Hayasaka was also able to incorporate *gagaku* music, although in a limited way: in the main title and during the closing moments of the film bridging into the end title. Classical music associated with the Japanese imperial court, *gagaku*, is based on the pentatonic scale and performed on traditional Japanese wind, string, and percussion instruments including the *gagaku sho* (a kind of mouth organ comprising a series of bamboo pipes, multiple reeds, and a central mouthpiece) and the *wagon* (a stringed instrument similar to a zither). It is interesting to consider whether Kurosawa was willing to accede to Hayasaka about using *gagaku* music because he felt that it lent authenticity to the film's depiction of medieval Japan. (And the *gagaku* amounts to less than three minutes of music in a score of nearly forty-six minutes.) Hayasaka was also able to incorporate elements of traditional Japanese music into other parts of the score. The cue for the woodcutter's walk, for example, while definitely derived from the bolero source, also carries the traces of traditional Japanese orchestration: the use of a solo woodwind with the accompaniment of percussion.[14] And thus we have a score crossing musical borders from East to West, germinating as it did from roots in a Japanese musical aesthetic as well as a western one.

The model for how that music would be used in the film crosses another kind of border. There were several models for musical accompaniment that had developed throughout the world as a response to sound film: indigenous popular music, both diegetic and non-diegetic, deployed throughout the film (perhaps the most typical early response to sound film internationally); the classical Hollywood film score; the *bricolage* models of Chinese-language, Iranian, Egyptian, and Hindi film industries which mixed indigenous traditional and popular music with western-style film scoring; and the disjunctive scores of early Soviet sound film. Kurosawa was much influenced by the Soviet model where disjunctions between the soundtrack (and especially the music) and the image track were designed to undercut conventional bourgeois emotional attachments in the audience, opening up viewers to the revolutionary aesthetic of these early Soviet sound films. Kurosawa was obviously thinking along these lines: "Hearing a piece of sad music in a sad scene is not necessarily good, because if the movie and the music pursue the same goal, the result would be flimsy and lack profundity."[15] Several of Kurosawa's features are marked by what Kurosawa described as "oppositional handling of music and performance,"[16] often involving western music: a life and death telephone call accompanied by a Latin American pop song or a tense confrontation between cop and criminal accompanied by a woman practicing Mozart on the piano in *Stray Dog* (1949); the use of the cheery "Cuckoo Waltz" assailing the gangster who has just learned he has lost a crucial power struggle in *Drunken Angel*;[17] the shock effect of traditional Shinto music paired with Wagner's "*Wedding March*" during a traditional Japanese bridal ceremony or mambo-esque pop music combined with a Buddhist monk's chanting at a funeral in *The Bad Sleep Well* (1960)[18]; a jazzy saxophone riff accompanying bumbling medieval peasants in *The Hidden Fortress* (1958); Takemitsu's lush Mahleresque Romanticism for the graphic battle sequence in *Ran* (1985); Schubert's *Heidenröslein* sung non-diegetically by a children's choir during a violent thunderstorm at the end of

Rhapsody in August (1991). Or a Japanese composer's version of a French composer's take on a dance piece of Spanish origin, itself inflected by North African influences, as accompaniment to a film taking place in medieval Japan. The use of music in disjunction with the images became so commonplace in Kurosawa's films that Kurosawa and Hayasaka devised a code word to describe it: "sniper," a reference to a 1931 Soviet film, *Sniper*.[19]

Rashomon and Modernism

Kurosawa was influenced by Soviet theories of musical accompaniment for *Rashomon*, but the score was also influenced by the filmic Modernism that was developing mid-century in the international art film community. In fact, many critics in the West responded to the film in the context of Modernism. Parker Tyler famously compared the film to Picasso's cubist painting *Girl Before Mirror*,[20] and Donald Richie to Klee and Matisse.[21] The film comes by its Modernism honestly. It is based on two short stories written in 1927 by the Japanese writer Akutagawa. Influenced by Modernist experiments in point of view and the representation of consciousness, Akutagawa fused two sources from different cultures and eras: an acknowledged source—a twelfth-century Japanese story concerning a man, a woman, and a bandit who tricks the man and rapes the woman—and an unacknowledged source, an American short story, Ambrose Bierce's "In the Moonlight" in which a crime is described from the multiple perspectives of the participants, including the murder victim who speaks through a medium, without any resolution of those perspectives or any indication of which version actually happened. [22]

Rashomon's score, however, has not been considered in terms of Modernism. I would argue that the score for *Rashomon* actually anticipates the distinctive scores of the 1960s generated in the films of directors such as Alan Resnais, Jean-Luc Goddard, Claude Chabrol, Ingmar Bergman, Michaelangelo Antonioni, Luis Buñuel, and Carlos Saura which embody a new and Modernist aesthetic: symphonic orchestration is avoided; music is used very sparingly; many of film music's traditional functions are ignored such as establishing time and place, mood, and atmosphere, and responding to narrative action on-screen. Above all, Modernist scores are characterized by the avoidance of music to evoke emotion, producing something akin to Brecht's distanciation effect with scores devoid of emotional triggers for the audience. In the cinema of the new auteurs and in the international film community where they circulated, the Modernist film score became a mark of authenticity, a sign of the suspicion of and refusal to adopt normative filmic conventions which manipulate the viewer. Perhaps the most striking examples can be heard in several Godard films: Michel Legrand's theme and variations for *My Life to Live* (1962), which abruptly and arbitrarily stop mid-phrase; Antoine Duhamel's score for *Weekend* (1967), which features a concert pianist in a barnyard and Gabriel Yared's for *Every Man for Himself* (1980), where characters in a shoot-out run past the musicians playing the score.

The score for *Rashomon* can be termed Modernist in this same way: it avoids many of the conventional functions of musical accompaniment that developed in the West. With the exception of the main title, and the very last moments of the film bridging to the end title, music is not designed to establish authenticity through the musical creation of time and place. In *Rashomon*, a Spanish dance form is the predominant accompaniment for a story set in medieval Japan, setting up inevitable disjunctiveness whenever the music is used. Music creates moods in *Rashomon* but often those moods are at odds with visuals. For instance, Kurosawa described the effect of first seeing the wife's story synched to Hayasaka's score as "positively eerie," "strange," and "overwhelming," an oddly interesting but disjunctive mood given the filmic context, the wife's emotionally powerful flashback.[23] The score lacks individual leitmotifs, a traditional method for fleshing out characters, and instead largely depends upon the same musical motifs and rhythms for most of the characters. Music occasionally responds to the action (the stingers which accompany the woodcutter's discovery of the elements of the crime scene, for example, or some of the swordplay), but it is more characteristic of the score to operate independent of the action or even in contradiction to the action creating more disjunctive effects. Yuna de Lannoy points out that the *Boléro*-esque music accompanying the woodcutter's walk is quite disorienting, serving "to confuse the viewer because it is in triple time, an unusual accompaniment to a shot of someone marching."[24] Neumeyer points out the wife's story's "strongly affecting, realistically compelling moments are flatly contradicted by the music, which continues on its repetitious, slowly arching way without any concern at all for immediate screen action."[25] Music does function to bridge sequences, covering the edits between the interrogations in the police station and the flashbacks in the forest, for example. But it rarely triggers the audience's emotions: in the suspenseful revelation scene, for instance, where the woodcutter comes upon the successive evidence of the crime, the music actually modulates down, not up, an extremely atypical musical strategy for building tension.[26]

Kurosawa and Hayasaka not only largely ignored the conventions of film scoring that had developed in the West, they also ignored the musical conventions of the genre that were developing in Japan. I would define *Rashomon* as a period drama, or *jidaigeki*, which also exhibits some elements of the *chambara*, a subgenre of the *jidaigeki* involving swordplay (what in the West is often described as a samurai film). The score resists the conventions of both, largely failing to use music to sustain authenticity of time and place, to establish character (as Hayasaka will do just a few years later in *Seven Samurai* with multiple leitmotifs helping to identify the different characters), to respond to and heighten the action, including the swordplay (again, so in evidence in *Seven Samurai*), or to intensify the audience's emotional connection to the film. What the score does instead is set up its own internal logic and add another layer of meaning to the film.

The Score for *Rashomon*

The score for *Rashomon* engages with the thematic terrain of the film, functioning as a key component in the creation of subjectivity and in the undermining of objectivity. Music accompanies the main title and bridges the last moments of the film to the end title. But otherwise, with some interesting exceptions (more on these later), music is relegated to the multiple flashbacks that comprise most of the film. Of course whether these are flashbacks, fantasies, or deliberate misrepresentations is the film's open question. The term "flashbacks" does not do justice to the ambiguous nature of these recollections or to the complexity of the film's flashbacks-within-flashbacks narrative structure, but for the sake of simplicity, I will refer to them as flashbacks here. Like later Modernist film scores, the score for *Rashomon* shuns the more typical functions of musical accompaniment, even those associated with the genre it represents, and engages with the film's thematics: music both signals subjectivity, indicating to the audience that they have entered a character's consciousness, and comments on that subjectivity. David Desser has argued of *Rashomon* that "[t]he dialectic between . . . objectivity and subjectivity, between fact and fabulation are thus constantly reintroduced and reinforced. The differentiation between the cinematic styles used to relate the three planes of action further deny us any certainty."[27] I would point out that the score participates in this process, undercutting the veracity of the flashbacks and impeding the audience's attempts to evaluate them. Thus music participates in the film's elaborate refusal to help the audience come to a definitive conclusion about what happened in the grove.

We start with the woodcutter (Takashi Shimura). There is no music at all in the opening sequence under the town gate where the woodcutter, priest, and thief gather to avoid a rainstorm, nor in the beginning of the woodcutter's flashback when he recalls his testimony to the police. Music appears for the first time in the film proper only when the woodcutter enters the subjectivity of his flashback, a trip to the woods for firewood that results in his discovery of a body. When his flashback ends and we find the woodcutter in the police station, the music disappears after bridging the temporal and spatial transition. Similarly, the flashback of the priest (Minoru Chiaki) is also accompanied by music, but not his interrogation (and interestingly, his music is at the farthest removed from the identifying characteristics of the bolero.) And so it goes. The man who captures the bandit Tajomaru (Toshiro Mifune) is accompanied by music during his short flashback but not during his equally short police interrogation. Taromaru's flashback is much longer than any of the preceding flashbacks and it is intercut several times with shots of his interrogation by the police. His flashbacks are accompanied by music; his interactions at the police station are not, with one exception—his final testimony where the music from the flashback bridges the cut back to the police station and remains in the film for the short final scene with Tajomaru.

When the interrogation turns to the wife (Machiko Kyo), the pattern changes. Her police interrogation as well as her flashback are accompanied by music. The same is true of the female medium (Noriko Honma) whose inter-rogation by the police is underscored as is her dramatization of the dead husband's testimony. The final flashback belongs to the woodcutter who once again tells his story, but this time it is not the official version given to the police but a revised version delivered to the priest and the thief under the Rasho gate. Unlike his earlier flashback, this one is unaccompanied by music. Music returns to the film only in the final moments, as the woodcutter walks out of the shelter of the gate with an abandoned baby and the film ends.

Music is very carefully calibrated here to connote subjectivity. It is as if the music is trying to signal us to be wary of each of the characters whose individual desires and fears, revelations and subterfuges cloud their narratives. Tajomaru's flashback is the most filled with music and with the loudest, most bombastic cues. In a film which up to this point contains so little music, the presence of so much music raises our suspicions about Tajomaru's veracity. It is almost as if the score is signaling that Tajomaru is romanticizing the events in the grove and we should not trust him.

Then there are the women: the wife and the medium. The women are the only participants whose interrogations by the police are scored. Intriguingly, Kurosawa said that he originally envisioned a bolero as the accompaniment to the wife's testimony and flashback.[28] The film seems to bear this out as the version of the bolero for the wife comes closer to the Ravel than in any of its other iterations. This is the bolero motif at its most sensuous, with its insinu-atingly exotic rhythm. The wife's extreme emotionalism and irrationality in her flashback and police interrogation signal her untrustworthiness, and the music with its exoticism and sensuality reinforces that perception. The film does not trust the female medium either; like the wife's, "her" entire police interrogation as well as "her" flashback are scored.

The woodcutter himself recants his initial flashback. His second and revised flashback is the inverse of Tajomaru's: it is presented without any music at all. If we suspect Tajomaru of prevarication because of the presence of so much music, we are tempted to accept the woodcutter's final version as truthful because of the absence of music. But we know that the woodcutter is lying: he deliberately leaves out his stealing of the dagger, revealed when he is caught in the lie by the thief. The "deception" of the score reminds us that what we were led to believe is the truth, is not; that nothing is to be trusted; that there is no answer. Ultimately, the score for *Rashomon* shakes off its generic constraints, creating a musical hybrid informed by Japanese traditional music, European art music, and early Soviet sound practice, and anticipates the Modernist film scores that would soon develop in the international art film. And, as Koozin points out, Hayasaka's exploration of "pan-cultural styles" looks forward to musical approaches that would develop later in the twentieth century, specifi-cally a "postmodern musical rhetoric, in which transhistorical stylistic markers interact as agents of expressive meaning." [29]

Seven Samurai and The Magnificent Seven

What happened when this complex film and particularly its innovative and unusual musical score was transplanted in Hollywood and remade as a western? I would like to start by briefly considering another, more successful transplant, the box office smash John Sturges's *The Magnificent Seven*, the Hollywood remake of Kurosawa's *Seven Samurai*. As I have suggested earlier, *Seven Samurai* was a much clearer expression of its genre, the *chambara*, than *Rashomon* was of its. I would say the same for its score. Hayasaka is less off the playbook here than he was in *Rashomon*, more drawn to the action sequences, using more generic action-film devices (lots of percussion here especially for the bandits), exploiting more Japanese instruments (watch and listen for the actual appearance of a shamisen early in the film) and musical structures (such as the pentatonic scale) and more clearly using music to create atmosphere and sustain mood. It is also a leitmotivic score with identifiable melodies to characterize participants (bandits, samurai, villagers, lovers) and activities (fighting, farming, rice planting) and manipulate our sympathies in response to them. This is not to say that *Seven Samurai* is oblivious to western musical influences; listen for the bongo drums amidst the Japanese percussion during Kikuchiyo's (Toshiro Mifune) drunken rampage and note the *Boléro*-esque love theme. And Kurosawa being Kurosawa, the ultimate swordfight in the rain is unscored. Hayasaka, in fact, attributed the score's success to its simplicity: "it was extremely simple and clear, I think."[30] I would agree and point out that part of that simplicity emanates from its genre specificity.

The Magnificent Seven was scored, famously, by Elmer Bernstein who reacts not as Hayasaka did to *Rashomon* with a genre-bending score, or with the jazz-inflected idiom of some of his earlier work (such as *Man with the Golden Arm* (1955) or *Sweet Smell of Success* (1957)), but with generic western musical elements rendered in symphonic form. Bernstein's iconic opening leitmotif, with its harmonic and melodic debt to Copland, enshrines the western landscape as American; his deployment of the conventions of Mexican music in a dark minor mode for the villains and in a brighter major mode for the villagers is working with long-standing conventions for structuring the score and for representing character and geography; and his score delivers some of its biggest moments in the cues for the action sequences. Despite the fact that *Seven Samurai* and *The Magnificent Seven* come out of very different national cinemas and very different genres, certain assumptions on the part of both sets of filmmakers about genre, including the function of music in relation to genre and nation, have to be considered as part of the successful transplant. (Of course, the line-up of stars does not hurt it either: imagine signing Steve McQueen, Charles Bronson, James Coburn, and Robert Vaughn before they became major stars. Yul Brynner already had his Oscar.)

"How . . . were we going to make a picture that's better than this?"

Rashomon and *The Outrage* would prove a different story. In the wake of the success of *The Magnificent Seven*, Kurosawa's films were given a good looking over by Hollywood (and other film industries—Sergio Leone jumped on *Yojimbo* at about this same time). *The Outrage* featured one of Hollywood's hottest leading men, Paul Newman, was directed by a man with a liberal pedigree, Martin Ritt, and was composed by the man who turned down *The Magnificent Seven*, Alex North. According to Hollywood logic, it could not miss. However, as we have seen, *Rashomon*, both as a film and as a score, lacked the kind of genre specificity that made for easy translation. And *The Outrage* was helmed by a director who had never directed a western and was scored by a composer whose vision for the film was ignored. Although *The Outrage* did not succeed either with the critics or at the box office (frankly, it is a wonder it did not ruin Paul Newman's career), it has much to tell us about crossing generic and national borders.

Transposed to the American West, the film became the story of a displaced Southern aristocrat (Laurence Harvey) and his wife (Claire Bloom), traveling in the American Southwest and victimized by a Mexican *bandito* Juan Carrasco (Paul Newman), told through the testimonies of four witnesses to the crime. As in *Rashomon*, it is framed by the story of three men, here a preacher, a prospector, and a con man, who amuse themselves with retelling the stories while they escape the rain in an abandoned train depot. On the face of it, *The Outrage* does not seem a natural fit for Ritt and the transposition of the source material to the nineteenth-century American West makes it seem even less conducive to Ritt's strengths as a director. Ritt came out of the Group Theater in New York, had been blacklisted in the 1950s, and professed an interest in making films with humanist themes, frequently focusing on stories set in the contemporary US which featured labor unrest and racial discrimination. Said Ritt: "Implicit in all of my films is a very strong and deep feeling for the minorities, the disenfranchised, the dispossessed, be they Blacks, Mexicans, Jews, or working people."[31] Yet Ritt professed to being intrigued by *Rashomon*, first by the intellectual challenge of adapting it, and then by the contemporary relevance of its theme: its "treatise on the nature of truth became a contemporary and social issue especially valid today."[32] Cinematographer James Wong Howe, on the other hand, confessed trepidation: "How, I thought, were we going to make a picture that's better than this?"[33]

It was the screenwriter, Michael Kanin, author of the play on which *The Outrage* was based, who set the film in the American West, although he initially considered the Middle East: ultimately, the West "transposed itself perfectly in every respect."[34] (The producer, A. Ronald Lubin, tells the story a bit differently claiming he steered Kanin to the western "because a western is more lucrative."[35]) In any event, the West did give Ritt the opportunity to address some familiar territory; race comes to the forefront when the robber was reconceived across racial lines, a dark skinned Mexican *bandito* played by Anglo Newman in brown-face and heavy Mexican accent.

Alex North and the Modernist Score

Alex North was asked to score the film. Known as a Modernist composer, he came to Hollywood from the New York dance and theater world where he had worked with Elia Kazan and helped to update classical Hollywood scoring practices in the 1950s, composing in a musical idiom that was relatively new to Hollywood at that time—Modernism—and incorporating jazz and traditional ethnic music in his scores long before it became popular to do so. North was classically trained—he had studied with Aaron Copland and Mexican Modernist Silvestre Revueltas—and was one of Hollywood's go-to composers for edgy, psychological dramas. He scored a string of them including *A Streetcar Named Desire* (1951), *Death of a Salesman* (1951), *The Bad Seed* (1955), *The Misfits* (1961), *The Children's Hour* (1961), and *Who's Afraid of Virginia Woolf* (1966). North had worked with Ritt before on two well-received films: *The Long Hot Summer* (1958) and *The Sound and the Fury* (1959). He was also developing a reputation for scoring unconventional westerns: *Viva Zapata* (1952) which blends Modernism with traditional Mexican folk music and *Cheyenne Autumn* (1964), dark and broodingly Modernist, which he asserted was inspired by actual Cheyenne music. He claimed to have turned down *The Magnificent Seven* because he felt the film "strayed too far from the original."[36]

The Genesis of the Score for *The Outrage*

Once he agreed to score *The Outrage*, North began work on his own, creating a master plan for how music would function in the film, using the rough cut to spot the places where he felt it belonged, and even composing a few themes and sample cues *before* he met with Ritt. His description of his vision is strikingly similar to the musical design of *Rashomon*:

> I had . . . decided that the scenes at the train station did not need any music. I thought it would be interesting to try and encompass . . . a certain mood which would be a variation on a main theme—what I called the "truth " theme—which would be broad enough to expand in any direction in order to capture the flavor of the . . . episode. I could begin the flashback with this theme, then expand it into . . . the story, and then return to the main theme to end the flashback. . . . I wanted to frame each flashback, to start with a piece of music that helped to convey the sense that this was the past but which, at the same time, was related to the personalities of the characters.[37]

North's vision departed from the generic functions of the western film score: music to establish authenticity, to emphasize or create mood and atmosphere, to underscore action, and to respond to the landscape. North even ignored newer conventions, such as the inclusion of a western theme song. Instead, he envisioned music only as accompaniment to the flashbacks from the four witnesses. Music would come in on the cut to the flashbacks and be used throughout each flashback, although not necessarily continuously, and would stop when the witness had finished. North had planned on using a single musical theme, a "truth" theme, for all of the flashbacks, varied in terms of rhythm, instrumentation, and harmony. He had estimated that there would be approximately thirty-five minutes of music in the completed score. Whether by design or happenstance, North reproduced Hayasaka's musical blueprint, confining music to the flashbacks and thus using music to flesh out the sub-jectivities of the participants.[38] Further, North's intention to use the same music throughout, a "truth" theme which he could repeat and vary to flesh out the subjectivities of the participants, sounds very much like Kurosawa's objective in choosing Boléro.

However, when North first sat down with Ritt, he learned that Ritt's vision was radically different from his own. Ritt thought that the film was "top notch"[39] and did not need much music. He cut almost all of North's proposed cues. Ritt did not share North's vision and Ritt was the director. A film score that North envisioned as comprising thirty-five minutes of music became eight minutes in Ritt's reconception. (Compare to the Rashomon score's running time of almost forty-six minutes.) North disagreed with Ritt, but apparently to no avail. Upon seeing the film at a preview, North expressed "mixed feelings,"[40] about as close to criticism as perhaps he dared to come. He would not work with Ritt again.

The Score for *The Outrage*

The score is very, very sparse. There is no main title. There is no music during the prospector's version of events, the first flashback of the film, not even during his extended walk through the woods, a sequence that proved such a showpiece for the Boléro-esque music in Rashomon. In fact, music makes no appearance until well into Carrasco's flashback, almost twenty-one minutes into the film and at the moment when Carrasco describes the breeze that he says caused the crime. The music for Carrasco, titled "Carrasco" in North's sketches, is heavily coded as Mexican—the Mexico of Copland's El Salon Mexico to which this piece of music is clearly indebted. It features, in addition to a small ensemble of strings and woodwinds, marimba, tambourine, maracas, timbales, guiro, and claves, all instruments used in Mexican and more generally Latin American music. The cue entitled "Carrasco" is marked "pizzicato" in the score, resulting in a sharper, less lyrical sound.

After Carrasco glimpses the wife, the music drops out for an extended period. It returns for the wife, a lushly orchestrated piece of music, titled "The Wife," featuring violins, cellos, bass cellos, and an *oboe d'amore* marked "plaintively" and heard as she waits for her husband to return. An edgier, more Modernist piece, "The Struggle," dissonant and antiphonal, is heard when she runs through the forest, discovers her husband, and struggles with Carrasco. The remainder of Carrasco's flashback is unscored.

Music's next appearance is at the very end of the wife's flashback immediately after she has stabbed her husband. Scored for strings and marked "*dolce*" in the score, this cue is related musically to the earlier musical motif for the wife. When she almost drowns after throwing herself into a river, she is accompanied by a short cue with turbulent strings, dissonant harmonies, and unsettling rhythms, reminiscent of "The Struggle."

An ancient Indian medicine man channels the spirit of the dead husband and relates his version of events. As in the other flashbacks, this one is largely unaccompanied. Only at the very end of the medicine's man's flashback, at the point when both the wife and Carrasco have left and the husband kills himself, is there music. Entitled "The Husband," this cue is scored for a small ensemble featuring violins and violas, cellos, and woodwinds playing *rubato* and *con animato*. As in *Rashomon*, there is no music during the prospector's second, revised flashback and the music returns only in the final moments of the film, bridging to the end title, a reprise of the wife's music.

Hayasaka's score is instrumental in creating a sense of past-ness and signaling to the audience the subjectivity of that past. North's score, because so little of it is left in the film, does not serve this function. There is just not enough music nor is it placed in such a way as to set the past apart from the present or to function as a cue for the audience to understand that they are entering a character's consciousness. Thus the score cannot sustain the idea that the flashbacks are a subjective reality in opposition to the objective present of the film. As we have seen, this is what North had intended to do.

Ritt has said that he wanted the film to be American and that he saw the West as the way to make it so. With so little music, and such drastic changes to North's overall design, I would find it difficult to argue that North's score helped Ritt much in this regard either. North's score abandons most of the conventions of the classical western film score. There is no music to react to the landscape, to establish mood and atmosphere, to underscore action. Western film scores in the classical Hollywood studio system have traditionally been called upon to identify the genre and attest to its authenticity. While there is the one musical cue featuring Mexican-inflected music, there is nothing else in the score which functions to establish a specific historical time (the nineteenth century) and geographic space (the American Southwest).

What is left of his score is character driven. Music is limited to accompanying the three main actors in the central drama, and sparse though the musical accompaniment may be, there is clearly some attempt by North to characterize the participants through the music: Mexican music for *bandito* Carrasco, lyrical violins for the wife, occasionally spirited but otherwise rather nondescript music for the husband. With such an economy of means forced upon him and to get the job done efficiently, North resorts to stereotypes of gender ("plaintively" and *dolce* for the wife whose music is played on violins, and the *oboe d'amore*, *con animato* for the husband) and race (the Otherness of the music with its Latin percussion and exotic rhythms for the Mexican *bandito*).

Conclusion

Rashomon after its international release was the most famous Japanese film in the world, its score a recognizable component of its reputation. *The Outrage* was neither a commercial nor a critical success and it created a permanent rift between Martin Ritt and Alex North, ending a thriving collaboration between them. Films are not made in cultural isolation, and how the music ends up in a film and how it operates once it gets there can be the result of a number of forces at work. In terms of these two films, the failure of *The Outrage* to successfully adapt *Rashomon* as a western may be less the result of incompatible genres steeped in national and cultural idioms untranslatable outside the nation, and more the result of the pressures of institutional practices both within and outside the nation that figured into the production of both films: the studio systems which privileged the directors' vision over the composers' as well as the international art film community which hovered over them both. It is tempting to ponder to what extent it was *Rashomon*'s genre-fluidity in terms of the film's structure and its genre-bending score in combination with North's discarded vision and disinterest in western musical conventions that helped to spell disaster for *The Outrage*.

Notes

Thanks to Yuna de Lannoy for sending me material from her unpublished dissertation and for her thoughtful and insightful criticism of this chapter.

1 Masuro Sato was Hayasaka's orchestrator for *Seven Samurai* and would go on to score a series of films for Kurosawa after Hayasaka's untimely death. For more on Sato's relationship with Kurosawa, see Yuna de Lannoy, Chapter 6, "Innovation and Imitation: An Analysis of the Soundscape of Akira Kurosawa's *Chambara* Westerns" in this volume.
2 Noël Burch, *To the Distant Observer: Form and Meaning in the Japanese Cinema* (Berkeley: University of California Press, 1979), 296.
3 Sato quoted in Stuart Galbraith IV, *The Emperor and the Wolf* (New York: Faber and Faber, 2001), 261.
4 Kurosawa quoted in Teruyo Nagami, *Waiting on the Weather: Making Movies with Akira Kurosawa*, trans. Juliet Winters Carpenter (Berkeley: University of California Press, 2006), 188.
5 *My Life in Cinema: Akira Kurosawa* (filmed interview of Kurosawa by Nagisa Oshima in 1993). Included in the Criterion Collection DVD: *Seven Samurai* (2006).
6 See Donald Richie, "Notes on the Film Music of Takemitsu Tōru," *Contemporary Music Review* 21, 4 (2002), 8.
7 Takemitsu quoted in the documentary *Music for the Movies: Toru Takemitsu* (Charlotte Zwerin, 1994).
8 It is interesting to point out that by Japanese music Hayasaka did not mean folk or popular music but high art traditions. In *Rashomon*, Hayasaka's Japanese music of

choice is *gagaku* music, associated with the court and aristocracy, as opposed to folk, or popular, or more contemporary musical forms, even though the central character in the drama, the woodcutter, is a peasant.

9   Timothy Koozin, "Expressive Meaning and Historical Grounding in the Film Music of Fumio Hayasaka and Toru Takemitsu," *Journal of Film Music* 3, 1 (2010), 6.

10   David Neumeyer, "Hayasaka's Music for *Rashomon*," *Proceedings of the XIIIth Congress of the International Comparative Literature Association*, eds. Kawamoto Koji, Heh-Hsiang Yuan, and Ohsawa Yoshiro (Tokyo: ICLA, 1996), 477. See also the brief analysis of the score in James Buhler, David Neumeyer, and Rob Deemer, *Hearing the Movies: Music and Sound in Film History* (New York: Oxford University Press, 2010), 151–53.

11   Kurosawa, 186.

12   Such as Donald Richie in *Focus on Rashomon* (Englewood Cliffs, NJ: Prentice-Hall, 1972), 91.

13   Kurosawa's choice to use Ravel's *Boléro* as a musical model has drawn plenty of criticism from reviewers, critics, and scholars in the West who find its use overly obvious and distracting. It is worth pointing out that in Japan, Ravel's *Boléro* would not have been known to the extent that it was in the West and thus would have functioned differently for Japanese audiences. David Neumeyer likewise notes that "it is only for a Western audience that the boléro seems intrusive." See Neumeyer, 477. For the record, I like the use of this *Boléro*-esque cue, a great example of Kurosawa's disjunctive use of music.

14   Neumeyer reaches the same conclusion: "I am convinced that Hayasaka was making a less plainly defined reference to another, simpler performance style for traditional Japanese music: a solo woodwind carrying a melody to the accompaniment of drums." Neumeyer, 480.

15   Kurosawa, quoted in Yuna de Lannoy, "Happiness and sadness in counterpoint: the psychology of music and image in Eisenstein and Kurosawa's films," in "The View From the Bridge: The Cinemas of Kurosawa and Eisenstein from East to West," unpublished dissertation (2009), 189.

16   See Masaaki Tsuzuki, "Working with Fumio Hayasaka," in *Perspectives on Akira Kurasawa*, ed. James Goodwin (New York: G. K. Hall, 1994), 76.

17   This is not the same "Cuckoo Waltz," incidentally, used by John Ford in *Young Mr. Lincoln* and *My Darling Clementine*—although Kurosawa was a great fan of Ford's work and particularly his westerns—this one is by J. E. Jonasson and it was personally chosen by Kurosawa.

18   de Lannoy, 192–98.

19   The Soviet film generally known in English as *Sniper* has been variously translated in Kurosawa criticism. For instance, the film is translated as *"Sniper"* in both *Waiting on the Weather* (189) and "Working with Fumio Hayasaka" (76), but Kurosawa translates it as "sharpshooter" in his own *Something Like an Autobiography*, trans. Audie E. Bock (New York: Knopf, 1982),163.

20   Parker Tyler, *"Rashomon* as Modern Art," in *Focus on Rashomon*, ed. Donald Richie (Englewood Cliffs, NJ: Prentice-Hall, 1972), 136–37.

21   Donald Richie, *"Rashomon,"* in *Focus on Rashomon*, 90.

22   Thanks to Yuna de Lannoy for pointing this out to me, email correspondence with the author.

23   Kurosawa, 186.

24   de Lannoy, 205.

25   Neumeyer, 481.

26   Neumeyer points this out. See Neumeyer, 480.

27   David Desser, *The Samurai Films of Akira Kurosawa* (Ann Arbor, MI: UMI Research Press, 1981), 71.

28 According to Kurosawa, "As I was writing the script, I heard the rhythms of the bolero in my head over the episode of the woman's side of the story." Akira Kurosawa, *Something Like an Autobiography*, 186.

29 Koozin, 6.

30 Fumio Hayasaka quoted in Tsuzuki, 78.

31 Ritt quoted in Pat McGilligan, "Ritt Large," *Film Comment*, 22, 1 (January 1986), 38–46.

32 North quoted in Sydney Field, "*Outrage*: A Print Documentary on Hollywood Film-Making," *Film Quarterly* 18, 3 (Spring 1965), 34.

33 Howe quoted in Field, 21.

34 Kanin quoted in Field, 14.

35 Lubin quoted in Field, 19.

36 North quoted in Field, 31.

37 Ibid., 32.

38 I wish I knew whether or not North had ever seen Kurosawa's film or had access to Hayasaka's score. To the best of my knowledge, North never mentioned it, in print, if he did.

39 Ritt quoted by North in Field, 33.

40 North quoted in Field, 33.

Part III

The Contemporary Western

Chapter 10

From the Barroom Floor

American Song, Saloon Culture, Stack O'Lee, and *Wild Bill*, or "Did you touch my hat?"

Peter Stanfield

> My lines are women and liquor and rigged games of chance. Are you playing?
> (Cy Tolliver, *Deadwood*)

I argue that the act of inclusion or exclusion of a musical performance in a western is determined by shifting notions of what produces a film's signification of authenticity. By authentic I mean the way in which a film imbues itself with a sense of historical verisimilitude that, in the case of westerns, allows them to declare that they represent the historical West. However, this declaration only has credence, as the art critic Lawrence Alloway has claimed, if the world depicted corresponds to the West that we recognize from comparative representations familiar from other movies and other media:

> The West of the 1880s is enacted in the unchanged present landscape, known to us from post cards, photographs in the *National Geographic* magazine, and state tourist-office literature, or from the bubble on a Vista-Dome train and through an automobile windshield . . . they are part of the correspondence among media which give a film the authority of being real at more than one level as it complies with information derived from other sources. This kind of allusion, characteristic of postwar movies, has an elaborate emblematic quality.[1]

Historical verisimilitude is temporal; it changes over time. The shifting fashions in western hats over the last eleven or twelve decades of film production would attest to that fact, as does the use of music in the western which is equally prone to contemporary fads and trends. One might think here of the use of contemporary musical styles such as B. J. Thomas singing "Raindrops Keep Fallin' On My Head" in *Butch Cassidy and the Sundance Kid* (1969) or the rock group Bon Jovi, who provided much of the music on *Young Guns II* (1990). These two examples will still sound chronologically inappropriate to listeners today, but older films which use contemporary musical styles might not be quite so apparent to anyone but aficionados, and with the passing of time will simply blur into a mix of traditional styles.

Figure 10.1 Frame grab: *Station West.* "Don't you know it's no fun to drink alone?" says the percentage girl. "Not until after the first one," replies the stranger (Dick Powell).

Such a case can be seen and heard in *Station West* (1948). The film opens with a stranger (Dick Powell) arriving in town aboard the night stage; he books himself into the hotel and then sets off to find the saloon. The sound of a piano pumping "Jubilo" (aka "The Year of Jubilo," "Kingdom Coming!") draws him down the boardwalk, past a big sign advertising "BEER," and into "Charlie's Saloon" through swinging doors. With a dance hall girl in the crook of his arm, a miner is high-stepping along to the restless tune. The stranger moves easily past them and others playing cards, pausing to shoot craps. He wins a few throws, but withdraws when someone tries to fix the game by switching the dice. The saloon is large with an ornate mahogany and mirrored bar and the walls are covered in plush drapes. The music changes, and a female singer calms the rowdy element with a torch song—"Sometime Remind Me To Tell You." The song and the singer catch the stranger's attention, pulling him further into the saloon. He then moves to the bar and orders a whiskey. A "percentage girl" joins him and tries hustling him for a drink: "Don't you know it's no fun to drink alone?" "Not until after the first one," he curtly replies.[2] His wisecracking causes a series of confrontations and a fight is only narrowly averted.

The brevity and economy of this sequence is suggestive of how fixed the rituals and dramatic possibilities are in such a setting, with its familiar habitués, its divertissements, and its music, particularly its music. The use of the minstrel tune "Jubilo," much used in other westerns, helps to authenticate the setting, which in turn helps to anchor the anachronistic torch song "Sometime Remind Me To Tell You," which has little in common with popular song from the late nineteenth century and everything in common with contemporaneous pop music. Mort Greene and Leigh Harline, who were prolific songwriters for the movies, composed it. Their composition does not make any concession to historical verisimilitude, but, among all the rituals and conventions the scene foregrounds, its inauthenticity is unlikely to be much noticed.

Alongside costume, settings, props, and historical reference points, Kathryn Kalinak has noted the importance of period song as a means of authenticating the western: "when audiences recognized a song as western (or thought they did), the film seemed more genuine."[3] This is partly why music in the western is so vital, but its vitality is dependent upon misrecognition of its point of origination. The acceptance of popular song as a guarantor of the "real," Kalinak argued, was often in the face of the fact that the songs had little to do with the West, at least directly, drawing most often from minstrelsy.[4] Through endless repetition of minstrel tunes in westerns, a slippage has occurred where now the aural signification of "Jubilo," or "Oh! Susanna" or "Oh! Dem Golden Slippers," for example, have come to represent the West rather than, as they did originally, the South, or perhaps, more specifically, the South *in* the West.

The key site for much of the film western's musical activity is the saloon, and, in its more grandiloquent version, the concert saloon, which incorporates a stage for musical performances alongside the bar and gambling tables. I have argued elsewhere that the western only began to foreground the concert saloon as a dramatic site in the late 1930s as part of an attempt to differentiate class A westerns from series or B westerns.[5] So as not to upset rural and small town picture-goers, who were affronted by depictions of vice and dissolute behavior, series westerns, such as those starring Gene Autry, Roy Rogers, or Tex Ritter, tended not to directly represent drinking cultures.

As a primary setting in late 1930s and 1940s westerns, the concert saloon provided a space for gambling, drinking, sex (with its coded allusions to prostitution), violence (fist-fights and shoot-outs), and musical performance. In grander spaces a small orchestra and a chorus of high-kicking girls might provide the entertainment, or in smaller rooms, a singer and a pianist. The Judy Garland musical *The Harvey Girls* (1946) used a particularly opulent concert saloon, The Alhambra, which has a long bar, a floor covered in gambling tables, a sizeable stage, a piano for more intimate performances and, upstairs, the suggestion of rooms for private entertainments and assignations. The lower range of possible performance spaces is portrayed in flashback sequences in Fritz Lang's Marlene Dietrich vehicle *Rancho Notorious* (1952), where a one time "glory girl's" descent is marked by her performances at ever smaller and seedier places of entertainment and drinking, from grand concert saloon to spit and sawdust barroom.

The western shared the concert saloon location with films with a similar temporal setting but which were situated in the urban spaces of New York,

Chicago, San Francisco, and St. Louis: films such as the Mae West vehicle *She Done Him Wrong* (1933), or *The Bowery* (1933) starring Wallace Beery, or *Barbary Coast* (1935) with Edward G. Robinson, or *San Francisco* (1936) featuring Clark Gable, or *In Old Chicago* (1938) led by Tyrone Power.[6] In these films the concert saloon is depicted as a world away from the home and productive labor; the habitué is a pleasure seeker, and his or her pleasures are at best base and most likely venal. These spaces were the natural home for minstrelsy and hence it is of little surprise to find the same blackface songs also rendered in saloons on the western frontier.[7] But then a sense of *dislocation* was always central to minstrelsy's project. At its height of popularity in the nineteenth century, minstrelsy was predominantly performed in Northern urban areas for an audience of white industrial laborers, yet its subject was the rural antebellum South of slaves and plantations – a world apart from that experienced by its audience.[8]

Asked to put together a musical program for the 1939 World's Fair, folklorist Alan Lomax concocted an extravaganza that would promote America's folk heritage. Jazz historian John Zwed wrote:

> There would be an American folk theater with performances, academic symposia, and performed histories of jazz, popular song, and vaudeville. A giant "main street" would offer a version of the French Quarter of New Orleans; a Pennsylvania Dutch tavern; a Haitian house with cooking, religion, and a history of the Haitian people on display; a Western saloon; a Down East fish house; a Mexican patio with food, music, and a dance; a Hawaiian house; an Acadian dance hall; an Appalachian square dance hall; and an African American church and juke joint.[9]

What music would Lomax have played in the western saloon? Perhaps a selection of cowboy songs collected by his father, John, first published in 1910? If he felt that this would have offered too limited an array of musical styles, then he might have only looked to the movies for inspiration, or to Jelly Roll Morton, the "originator of jazz," as he called himself on his business cards.

Lomax had planned that Morton would take an active part in the World's Fair's musical divertissements but, as things transpired, neither Morton nor Lomax's ideas would be featured. I wonder if it had all come to pass whether Morton would have just played in the New Orleans's section or whether he would have also played his piano in the western saloon. If he had, I wonder too whether he would have played the range of songs and styles he performed for Lomax on the legendary Library of Congress recordings, which represents the richest single source of recorded American song forms, including as it does minstrel tunes, ragtime, blues, folk, hymns, classical, marches, murder ballads, tin pan alley numbers, tangos and of course stomps, swing and jazz. Few musical soundtracks for westerns come close to that kind of eclecticism but one that does is Walter Hill's *Wild Bill* (1995), which was scored and performed by Van Dyke Parks.

Figure 10.2 Promotional poster: *Wild Bill*. Wild Bill Hickok (Jeff Bridges) is the man behind the hat.

Given a limited theatrical run on its release and critically overlooked at the time and subsequently, *Wild Bill* is only now recalled, if at all, as a precursor of sorts to David Milch's critically lauded HBO series, *Deadwood*. Hill directed the first episode in the series, which shared with his film the Black Hills' Gold Rush and a good number of characters including, in its early episodes, Wild Bill Hickok. Adapted from Pete Dexter's novel *Deadwood* and Thomas Babe's play *Fathers and Sons*, Hill's film focuses on the myth of the gunfighter, town tamer, and gambler, Hickok (Jeff Bridges). Milch's series finds its drama in the evolution of American capitalism or, as the character Charlie Utter (Dayton Callie) has it down, "Mr. Amalgamation & Capital," with Hickok and others as no more than bit-players in the trade in body and souls and the lure of gold.[10]

Wild Bill deserves a better fate than a footnote in the history of *Deadwood*, the television series. The film can make a number of claims on our attention, among them its elliptical narrative structure; its thematic conceits; its set designs and costumes; its fulsome primary and secondary characters; the sterling performances from all its actors who give air to Hill's often mordant dialogue; its declamatory formal and stylistic elements; and its redolent musical score, fashioned by Van Dyke Parks, which offers, to my mind, the fullest rendering of traditional American music since John Ford's *My Darling Clementine* (1946). Some of Parks's commercial recordings, such as those on his 1968 debut *Song Cycle*, can conjure up the effect of standing in the midway of a fairground and being struck by the sound of competing attractions, a musical kaleidoscope of clashing and contrasting elements that make up a glorious mélange. The overall effect, I think, is something similar to that imagined by the modernist American composer Charles Ives with "Circus Band" (*c.*1900), which attempts to capture the thrill a child feels at the sights and sounds of the march of a circus troupe down a town's main street.[11] *Wild Bill's* musical moments have the same appeal. With tunes seeping in and out of the listener's consciousness, bleeding into adjoining spaces and across scenes, the music has an often phantasmagoric effect—sometimes barely heard background ambience, other times assaulting and cacophonous, but all of a piece in its effectiveness.

The music in Ford's film, like Hill's, "provides a wash of authenticity for the film's evocation of the historic past."[12] This is how Kalinak describes the work of the songs Ford chose for his film, which she notes comprise seventeen separate pieces of period music. These include traditional Anglo-American songs, minstrel tunes, Spanish Californian folk songs, protestant hymns and a cowboy song written for a Broadway play. She writes: "These uncomplicated arrangements of American music, with their focus on simple and characteristic western instrumentation, are a departure from the typical scoring practices of the era, but they are reassuring signs of the authenticity of the images."[13] The list of songs used in *Wild Bill* is remarkably similar to those in *Clementine*, if not by title then by type.

Parks draws from the deep muddy pool of nineteenth-century American song, notably blackface minstrelsy, including "Beautiful Dreamer," "Jeanie with the Light Brown Hair," "Ring, Ring de Banjo" by Stephen Foster, and "Cotton

Eyed Joe," "Hop High Ladies," "Lorena," "Get Off the Track" (aka "Old Dan Tucker"), and "The Yellow Rose of Texas" by a variety of known and anonymous tunesmiths. Patriotic songs such as "Battle Hymn of the Republic" and "Marching through Georgia," sit alongside tunes with their roots in the British Isles that are given an old-time string band treatment, including "Queen Anne's Reel," "Sweet Genevieve," and "Rosin the Bow," while hymnals "Leaning On Jesus" (aka "Leaning on the Everlasting Arms") and "What a Friend We Have in Jesus" are used up against cowboy ballads such as "The Dying Cowboy" (aka "The Streets of Laredo"), "The Good Indian," "Goodbye, Old Paint," and "I Ride an Old Paint—Leaving Cheyenne." With the exception of the hymnals, which are used in sequences featuring a sermon and at a funeral, the other songs are used almost exclusively in and around saloons.

In *The Long Riders* (1980), director Walter Hill had commissioned a musical soundtrack that has clear parallels with that later used in *Wild Bill*, mixing Foster's and others minstrel songs with patriotic numbers alongside hymnals. Where *The Long Riders* differs from *Wild Bill* is in the way it highlights Ry Cooder's involvement through foregrounding the sound of his slide guitar. As much as anything else, the film is a showpiece for Cooder's talent. The songs are used to stress the notion of community and family, whether in terms of signifying group loyalty to the North or South ("Battle Hymn of the Republic" or "I'm a Good Old Rebel") or string bands playing waltzes at weddings and barn dances (for example, "Seneca Square Dance," or hymnals sung at funerals, such as "Hold to God's Unchanging Hand"). Besides the anachronism of Cooder's signature style of playing, the songs have arrangements that owe much to the modern tradition of bluegrass. Bluegrass might allude to past musical forms, but it is wholly a post-1940s musical innovation.[14] It is at once authentic and fabricated, and as such it is a perfect complement to the western's shifting notions of historical verisimilitude.

Discussing his theory of composition for films, Parks's notes, "A guy who writes pop music is creating a personality. The film composer has an entirely different challenge: to be nobody. There is so much to do to create music that can be felt and not heard. It is the absence of personality that is a hallmark of a real film composer."[15] The arrangements and choice of instrumentation for *Wild Bill* elide any authorial signature or readily discernable contemporary (or at least late twentieth century) musical style. Indeed, the overarching musical motif is played through an automatic piano, or pianola, an instrument that appears prominently in the main setting of the No. 10 saloon, the mechanical piano signifying both the story's historical location and its modernity. And, just as significantly, the music does not have a role in creating any sense of communal cohesion, as in *The Long Riders*, a point made plainly when Wild Bill is shown as an observer looking in on a congregation singing "What A Friend We Have In Jesus." Wild Bill belongs to a community of one and the music he is identified with is elegiac, or one marked with an overwhelming feeling of ennui.

There is another piano in the town of Deadwood, but this one has a black "manipulator" sitting at its keyboard. He provides the music at the Dakota

Dance Hall, or whorehouse, the "preferred site for assignations." We are told by *Wild Bill*'s narrator, Charles Prince (John Hurt) that, "this was no rude crib or flimsy shack. It featured papered walls, comfortable furniture, polished spittoons, and a piano that was actually in tune." In the HBO series *Deadwood*, the arrival of a new piano at the Gem saloon, purchased through a Montgomery Ward catalog, signifies as much the rapid growth of the town as it does its precarious relationship with the world beyond the Black Hills that constantly threatens to impede Al Swearengen's (Ian McShane) entrepreneurial ambitions. Foster's jumping "Oh! Susanna" is the first easily identifiable tune to be played on the new piano, and it contrasts nicely with Foster's sentimental parlor ballad "Beautiful Dreamer" which, in an adjoining scene, is being played at the more flamboyant Bella saloon and brothel.

All of this drama around pianos takes place in episode nine of the first series. Up and until then there has been little in the way of any music featured in any of the saloon scenes, either at the Bella or Gem. Instead, musical interest is reserved for the end credit sequence which, across the course of the three seasons, featured a wide diversity of commercial recordings, but all of which are readily locatable within any given definition of Americana. Episode nine concludes appropriately (and no doubt in good humor) with Jelly Roll Morton's solo piano rendition of "Stars and Stripes Forever"—a patriotic song, but played as if it was for the entertainment of pimps, punters, and whores. This is wholly appropriate in the context of *Deadwood*, a series that locates the birth of the nation within commerce of the most ignoble kind, and certainly not in some abstract high ideal.[16] Music in the saloon scenes carry many of the same connotations found in the films discussed here, but in *Deadwood* the music is always understood to be ornamental, surplus to the core business, in Swearengen's words, of "cunt and whiskey."

In a similar fashion to the use, or non-use, of music in *Deadwood*, the revisionist westerns of the late 1960s and 1970s, which strove for a more authentic representation of the Old West than found in the studio and post-studio era productions, signally refused to indulge in anything that was suggestive of musical performance in saloon scenes, as if it would undermine the historical verisimilitude so carefully rendered elsewhere. Sam Peckinpah's *Pat Garrett & Billy the Kid* (1973), for example, although casting musicians in lead and supporting roles (Kris Kristofferson, Rita Coolidge, Donnie Fritts, and Bob Dylan), and using the latter's music on the soundtrack, notably declines anything resembling a musical performance within the film's diegesis. *Dirty Little Billy* (1972) is almost exclusively filmed inside a ramshackle tavern come brothel, yet nobody is singing any Stephen Foster songs. In *Culpepper Cattle Co.* (1972) the cantinas and barrooms are equally dissolute, and the absence of entertainment is alluded to in campfire talk and tall tales. One cowboy holds his eager and gullible audience by describing his experience of a saloon that was much like any other saloon, only "it had this here glass ceiling. Bunch of Parisian girls living up on it . . . Naked as Jaybirds." This cowboy's concert saloon is a place of outrageous fantasy, but his tall tale also suggests how such

Figure 10.3 Publicity still: *Wild Bill*. Hickok looks at himself in the mirror and performs a shooting trick.

settings in other westerns are not much more than similar acts of fabrication (or at least exaggeration).

Bookended by Hickok's funeral, *Wild Bill* introduces Bill looking at himself in a hand mirror, tidying his long moustache. Holding a pistol over his left shoulder, staring into the mirror, he takes aim at a whiskey glass that sits upon the head of a small stocky fighting dog. "Goodbye Old Paint" plays on the soundtrack. Its plaintive tones will be used again and can be considered the film's melodious theme. At no point in the film does Parks use a vocalized version of the song but, for those unfamiliar with its melody, its sentiment is carried in this version of the song's lyrics:

> Now, when I die
> Take my saddle from the wall
> Put it on the pony
> Lead him out of his stall
>
> Tie my bones to his back
> Head our faces toward the west
> We'll ride the prairie
> That we love the best
>
> Ride her out Old Paint
> I'm a leaving Cheyenne
> And goodbye Old Paint
> I'm leaving Cheyenne

The melancholic cowboy is effectively limning his own elegy. Similarly, in the hop house and saloon in Deadwood, Wild Bill acts as if he is a ghost at his own long drawn out wake. He performs as if he were the principal character in a mournful monody, someone like the narrator in "Goodbye Old Paint," or the dead cowboy in "The Streets of Laredo." Although wrapped in white linen and as cold as the clay, the dead cowboy can still tell his tale.

The shooting trick successfully accomplished, Bill takes his due in money and backslaps from an appreciative audience. This is the first of a sequence of vignettes that provide Bill's back story, which, truth be told, amounts to little more than recognizing his prowess with firearms, fighting, gambling, and drinking, and his wide renown for all of these things. Each vignette provides Bill with a stage of one sort or another, and most have saloon settings. The film's narrator expands on this theme: "The theatre of Bill's life had come to demand that he walk up the centre of a muddy street rather than use the boardwalk. He had discovered being 'Wild Bill' was a profession in its own right."

After the display of trick shooting, Bill is next shown crossing a vast prairie where he encounters a Sioux warrior who challenges him to a duel, of sorts. Facing each other on horseback, the two combatants charge with all guns blazing, replicating the action of a medieval joust between knights. There is no royal court to witness the fight, only Bill's companion, California Joe (James

Gammon). The joust and Bill's regal appearance, suggested by his long curling locks and the sweeping curve of his wide-brimmed hat, recalls the heroes of Owen Wister's essay "The Evolution of a Cow-Puncher" (1895), which took the toiling agricultural worker of reality and transformed him into an Anglo-Saxon figurehead with a lineage that ran back to the cavaliers of the English civil war and further back to the knights of the crusades and the round table. Wild Bill is demotic showman and knight-errant combined, and the stage to tell of Bill's mythic exploits is set. "He fashioned himself as just an ordinary man," announces the narrator, "in no way special, but of course that was just a deception. By luck or by design, it had fallen to him to play the hero's part."

The vignettes that follow the joust sequence are all given dates and place names: Nebraska Territory 1867, Tommy Drum's Saloon Hays City 1870, Abilene, Kansas 1871, Bowery Theatre New York, Kansas City Missouri 1875, Cheyenne July 1876, before the final showground for Bill is reached—Deadwood Gulch Dakota Territory, August 1876. Each brief scene adds a little to the myth of Wild Bill, but in Abilene, after standing down a drunken hoard of cowboys and besting their leader in a gunfight, he accidentally shoots his own deputy. The moment reveals him to be a fallible human being, still an extraordinary man capable of heroic feats of derring-do, but imperfect nonetheless. His next appearance is on an actual stage in New York, where alongside Buffalo Bill Cody (Keith Carradine), Bill plays himself in the production "Scouts of the Plains." The film's narrator, notes that as a "thespian he was, by all reports, simply dreadful." With the stage lights hurting his eyes, Bill fails to stay "in character." In Kansas City, Missouri, Bill is diagnosed with glaucoma, brought on, the doctor tells him, by proximity to "infected females." Bill reports that he had had some trouble ten years back, but "it cleared right up when the local doc stuck a hotwire up my privates." The diagnosis is that he will lose his eyesight, might be in two years might be in ten, but he has certainly lost his libido, as Calamity Jane (Ellen Barkin) sorrowfully recalls at his funeral.

Bill's physical prowess and powers are waning, but not his sense of showmanship, or his mythical status. Charles Prince tells Bill that never mind how many times he has gone bust at cards, he has never known real poverty because everyone wants to buy the great Wild Bill dinner and drinks. Even the Chinese woman, who lights Bill's opium pipe and who speaks no English, has heard of Wild Bill. "A hero to the country," Bill's killer will call him.

In Cheyenne, during the summer of the nation's centennial, in a rather luxurious hotel, richly carpeted, with papered walls and overstuffed leather easy chairs, high ceilings and large windows, Bill is drinking and gambling the day away with his friends when a young girl approaches to tell him an old man is calling him out. Tied to a chair Bill is carried out into the street where he faces Will Plummer (Bruce Dern), a crippled old man in a wheel chair. He had been paralyzed in a fight with Bill, who had also killed Plummer's brother. Charles Prince reports that he "never saw a greater compliment to Bill than that paid by the citizens of Cheyenne. The confidence they showed in his marksmanship was such that none of them ran for cover, but lined up as if they were watching

Figure 10.4 Publicity still: *Wild Bill.* Hickock and Buffalo Bill Cody (Keith
Carradine) on stage, playing themselves: "as a thespian he was,
by all reports, simply dreadful."

some athletic contest." However, with the two men confined to chairs, the gun-fight between them is a parody of a western shoot-out: it contains drama, but it is played in the theater of comedy, not tragedy.

Leaving Cheyenne, Bill and Charles head for the Dakota Gold Rush: "Like a city in the Old Testament, Deadwood had become a place of prophecy and visions." Bill and Charley, along with California Joe and Calamity Jane, will spend their time at the No. 10 saloon, gambling, drinking, and talking the day into night and the night into dawn. In this setting, Bill's friends swap stories of his daring deeds, and although Bill often disputes the detail, he does not interfere in the story telling and myth making. As the stories of Bill's exploits get ever grander, Bill, the man, diminishes. The myth will eventually over-whelm him. At the end of one story telling session, Bill excuses himself and leaves to visit the Chinese quarter where he smokes opium. He dreams, or remembers, an encounter with Cheyenne dog soldiers. He had been following through the snow a fox, or little dog, as he describes it. A dog soldier tells him that the next time the little dog appears before him he will not live to see another moon. The dream ends and the sequence of Bill rousing himself from his opium slumber opens with a close-up on his pocket watch—his time is playing out.

The watch was once lost in a card game to the man who married an old belle of Bill's, and who Bill will kill in order to reclaim its possession and maybe even the woman. Bill's old belle, however, will live out her days in an insane asylum, and her boy will grow up with a fierce hatred of Bill for leaving his mother. He will be Bill's assassin, killing him as he holds a hand of cards made up of the jack of diamonds alongside black aces over eights. The cards came in a box bearing the legend "Brown Fox Playing Card" and carry the image of a fox head. The little dog has returned and Bill has seen his last moon. The figure of the little dog echoes across the film, from a whiskey glass shot off a dog's head at the film's beginning to the pack of cards, and like the bulldog in the alley in the ballad "Stack O'Lee," whose barking prefigures the slaying of Billy Lyons by the bully, it is a portent of death.

Shortly before his death, Bill will shoot dead another five men who had threatened his life, but also showed him a lack of respect, symbolized by their leader flicking the brim of Bill's hat. "You ought to know better than to touch another man's hat," Bill tells them before letting rip with his pistols. This is the third time in the film an act of great violence has followed someone showing disrespect to Bill by touching his hat. The first instance takes place in a dark claustrophobic drinking den and trading post; a snow blizzard howls around the den and four ruffians look to steal the winter pelts Bill has with him. When Bill refuses to buy drinks, one man removes the fur cap Bill is wearing and drops it to the ground. In a single movement Bill turns and hits the man, draws his gun and then kills them all. By way of explanation (if not justification) for the killings, he says, to no one in particular, not the dead, the barman, or the audience: "You oughta understand, you ever touch another man's hat." The implication of the unfinished sentence is clear.

The second instance occurs in Tommy Drum's Saloon. It is a large but not particularly salubrious room; it is raining hard outside and a good number of soldiers sit and stand around the tables. They are here to get revenge on Bill after he had beaten and locked up one of their comrades. Provoked into a fight when a soldier demands he apologize, Bill gives out with what might be his credo: he does not apologize, not for anything. The soldier slams his fist down on the crown of Bill's hat, which lies on the bar. Bill's credo will later grow to include not only a refusal to apologize and a violent response to anyone who would touch his hat without respect, but also that he does not owe anyone anything, nor will he explain himself. Before the fight begins Bill repeats part of his credo: "Shouldn't touch another man's hat." The fight between Bill and the soldiers is vicious, long and bloody.

Wild Bill's wide-brimmed hat was made by the Baron Hat Company of California, who are justifiably proud of their design: "The hat itself seemed to convey everything of the man, and the legend. With its towering extra wide cupola-shaped open crown, to the 'Saturn Rings' brim with its striking open-air pencil roll, all specially dyed in the almost ghostly 'Gray Eye' Slate."[17] The hat makes the man. Bill's violent outbursts at the touching of his hat echoes a story told by jazzman Louis Armstrong when recalling his young life in New Orleans. He describes an evening's entertainment at the notorious Funky Butt Hall:

> At the end of the night, they'd do the quadrille, beautiful to see, where everybody lined up, crossed over . . . Fighting was only to be expected. If a cat wanted to show respect for his chick, which was rare but not unheard of, he would ask her to stick out her elbow, and he would balance his hat on it. The hats were Stetsons, brand new, and very expensive, as much as six months salary. And if anyone so much as grazed that Stetson balancing precariously on a chick's shivering elbow, there would be hell to pay. "Did you touch my hat?" the offended party would demand. And if the other cat admitted he did, which was the manly thing to do, "he hit him right in the chops."[18]

Here the hat is a sign of a man's standing among his peers. Armstrong's story corresponds well to images of black American urban life at the turn of the century, in this particular instance to the myth and ballad of "Stack O'Lee" and his milk white Stetson hat. Armstrong's considerable trick is to turn that ballad and myth into a dance with razor sharp choreography. With *Wild Bill*, Walter Hill has pulled off an equivalent trick, reworking "Stack O'Lee" as a part of the western myth and remaking the ballad as a movie.

The ballad of "Stack O'Lee" (aka "Stag-O-Lee," "Stagger Lee," or multiple variants) belongs firmly in the tradition of the "bad man" songs that first began to appear around the turn-of-the-century. The story centers on a dispute between Stack O'Lee and Billy Lyons which leads to Billy Lyons's murder—justified by Stack O'Lee on the grounds that Billy "dun ruint my Stetson hat, And I'm bound to take [his] life."[19] The historical figure and the myth of Stack

O'Lee was nourished in the underworld of East St. Louis's brothels and saloons, with the myth given voice and form by the area's ragtime piano professors. "You dun stole my Stetson hat and I'm bound to take your life," Stack O'Lee tells Billy Lyons in one version of the song. While not ubiquitous, the Stetson hat forms the centerpiece of most retellings of the tale—"Now what do think of that! Old Stackalee shot Billy Lyons About a damn old hat." Stack O'Lee defines the idea of a "bad hat," the Victorian slang name given to a bully and a rogue.

This is a story cultural critic Greil Marcus said, "black America has never tired of hearing and never stopped living out, like whites with their Westerns."[20] A less racially essentialist reading may claim otherwise. In fact, it may claim that often the western and the ballad of "Stack O'Lee" are telling the same story about local or ward politics and the control of vice and criminal activities. Consider too the overlap in the setting for the two dramas; in East St. Louis, where Stack O'Lee plied his trade, the scene for the shooting of Billy Lyons, as told by the bad-man's biographer, is barely distinguishable from any number of western saloons: "They walked deep into the bar, near the stove. A ragtime band was playing happy, delightful music. There were good-looking belles sitting at the tables. In the back, on a platform, a craps game was in session."[21] As the proprietor of *Deadwood*'s Gem saloon, Al Swearengen ruminates: "Truth is, as a base of operations, you cannot best a fucking saloon."[22]

Literal evidence for the crossing between the ballad of "Stack O'Lee" and the western is not just in the story of Wild Bill and his credo, but it is also there in an obscure B western from Lippert Production, *Rimfire* (1949). Like with *Wild Bill*, much of the film's story is set in a saloon, which alongside all the usual divertissements also offers the attraction of slot machines. An ex-vaudevillian who had long been making his living as a sidekick in westerns and could also be relied upon to produce a musical turn or two, Fuzzy Knight plays Porky Hodges, an addict of these machines. He also plays the saloon's piano. A tight shot looking down on a craps table opens a scene, the camera pulling back away from the table as a piano is heard, the player revealed to be Hodges who draws a small but appreciative audience of saloon girls and cowboys. The song Hodges plays and sings is "Stack O'Lee." His story opens on a dark and stormy night with the rain falling fast, just like the night Wild Bill killed the soldiers in Tommy Drum's saloon. Stack and Billy get to fighting, and Stack says to Billy "tell nothing about your children, tell nothing about your wife, you done broke my Stetson hat and I'm gonna take your life." Stack then draws his .44 and shoots Billy. A rubber-tired hack takes Billy to the graveyard, but it does not bring him back. Stack O'Lee meanwhile is bound for Hell.

Knight performs the song with great gusto and at the appropriate point takes off his own Stetson to underline Billy's indiscretion. It is a song he has obviously performed on numerous occasions; indeed, he had performed it once before in the 1936 version of *Trail of the Lonesome Pine*, a story of feuding Kentucky families. It is essentially the same version here as in *Rimfire*, but with an added verse about barking and howling dogs. The brutish Falin clan demand Knight's

Figure 10.5 Publicity still: *Rimfire*. It was a dark and stormy night . . . Porky Hodges (Fuzzy Knight) sings "Stack O'Lee."

character play the song on guitar as accompaniment to a fight. This use of a performer offering a musical supplement that is complementary to the action, something akin to the use of live music to accompany silent films, is fairly commonplace in saloon scenes in westerns and is indeed parodied in *Rimfire*. Shortly after Hodges finishes his song, and has moved to the bar, a fight breaks out over a game of cards. Within moments Hodges is back at the piano and pounding out a cacophonous stream of notes, no tune, no discernable rhythm but plenty of bass rumble and pinging high notes.

In *Rimfire* the use of the ballad has little, if any, relevance to the film as a whole, but in other films a ballad might be intricately woven into the story and film. This is certainly the case in *Rancho Notorious* where good time girl Altar Keane (Marlene Dietrich) might well have been drawn from folk ballads. The core idea of Altar's character is contained within a scene in which she smokes a cigarette and sings "Gypsy Davey" in some cheap barroom. The song is also known as "Black Jack David," a sixteenth-century English ballad that was one of the many examples of British folk song that had survived in America. It was subsequently recorded by a number of pre-World War Two hillbilly, old-time and folk musicians.[23] The story told in "Gypsy Davey" has direct parallels with events in Altar Keane's life. Given the choice of a cosseted world of luxury or a game of chance with a cowboy, Altar has always chosen the latter. When she is introduced singing "Gypsy Davey" she is already well into the verses, but the essential meaning of the ballad is contained in the few lines we hear: "How could she leave her high-born Lord? / How could she leave her baby? / How could she leave her bed and board / And elope with Gypsy Davey? / Last night she slept in a goose-feather bed / Along with her Lord and baby / Tonight she sleeps . . ." She cuts the song off, it would have continued: "tonight she sleeps on the cold, cold floor / Beside Gypsy Davey." What spell has Gypsy Davey cast that could hold the girl in such thrall? What enchantment could make her leave her feather bed, her child and her master? The belief that the supernatural will explain her actions denies, of course, any agency on the girl's part and any recognition of her desire and lust. Altar's desire will not be denied or suppressed and it will destroy her.

The use of a ballad to add resonance to characterization in addition to working as another level of historical authentication can also be found in the employment of the "Ballad of Jesse James" in a good number of films that feature the notorious outlaw. The song describes the killing of Jesse James by his one time friend turned betrayer Bob Ford.

> Poor Jesse had a wife, a lady all her life
> And three children, they were so brave
> But that dirty little coward that shot Mr. Howard
> Has laid ol' Jesse James in his grave

> It was Robert Ford, the dirty little coward
> And I wonder how he feels
> For he slept in Jesse's bed and he ate o' Jesse's bread
> But he laid Jesse James in his grave

In both Samuel Fuller's *I Shot Jesse James* (1949) and in Andrew Dominik's *The Assassination of Jesse James by the Coward Robert Ford* (2007) the song is performed in a barroom in front of Ford (John Ireland and Casey Affleck respectively), whose presence is not at first known to the singer. In this context the song is less a public rebuke and more an act of voicing Ford's conscience. In the former this is underscored midway through the song when the singer suddenly becomes aware he is singing to Ford and brings things to a premature halt. Perversely, Ford forces him to continue until the story has been sung out. Later the ballad is reprised in another saloon, much to Ford's discomfort, bursting the bubble of renewed confidence that was symbolized by his identification with the Stephen Foster song, "Beautiful Dreamer." "Ballad of Jesse James" brings him back into the nightmare world he now inhabits. In the latter film the setting is a Bowery barroom, which a guitar player (Nick Cave) enters and then starts straight into singing the ballad. A drunken Ford interrupts him by firing his pistol into the floor, announcing that he is "Robert Ford," and then correcting the singer on the song's details; Jesse had two children, not three. In both films Ford had expected to become a hero by killing Jesse; instead he is doomed to replay his role as betrayer on stage (a role Dominik's film tells us Ford acted out on over 800 occasions) and to become a disgraced figure in the long and oft-sung ballad.

Nick Cave and Warren Ellis's score for *The Assassination of Jesse James* is a sparse affair dominated by guitar, cello, viola, and piano, made up of repeated refrains which sound like a music box winding down. Like *Wild Bill*, the film tells the story of a mythic figure in his final days, impotent in the face of the fate myth has decreed he should meet. Just before Bill gets sent to meet his maker, an angry Calamity Jane leaves Bill and friends to their cards and takes herself to the pianola which she manically cranks and then sulkily sits in front of. The music that issues forth, and that plays as Bill's final seconds tick away, is a particularly plaintive version of "Goodbye Old Paint." This die-cut industrially produced rendition played on an automatic piano is redolent with the myth's mechanical retelling, but it is not without its human dimension because the music is steeped in a bitter-sweet invoking of loss.

The melancholia evoked in such moments in the western may be for longgone times when such heroes as Wild Bill existed, or for an era when America was still a story to be told, or for some set of lofty ideals not yet besmirched. Given the setting in which the songs are performed, a Bowery barroom or Gold Rush saloon, I suspect the longing belongs to a more prosaic yearning for authentic yet fantastical spaces that offer base masculine pleasures untrammeled by responsibility to anyone or anything: where respect can be demanded and will be shown to both a man and his hat.

Filmmakers will often talk about the need to be respectful to the history of the West, but in actual fact it is to the history of the western that they are most mindful of. Due regard is paid to how the West has been delineated by previous interpreters and how elements, costumes, settings, props, and music, for example, become conventionalized. These conventions effectively signal a film's historical verisimilitude. But as they become over used, clichéd, and hackneyed, they can work to undermine authenticity, revealing the convention to be no more than a formula. What was once represented as real now appears as fabrication. The shifts and changes in styles of music and its performance used in the western are an index of this complex play between authenticity and convention. Similarly, the western has to deal with the apparently contradictory demand for historical verisimilitude and the need to appeal to contemporary tastes and fashions. That is, for example, between the nineteenth-century minstrelsy of "The Year of Jubilo" and the contemporary pop of "Raindrops Keep Fallin' On My Head." But even a song with a seemingly certain western provenance, such as "Goodbye Old Paint," can turn out to be an anachronism. It was first published in 1909, but in *Wild Bill* it appears wholly credible as a piano roll, which Calamity Jane can crank out on the mechanical piano in the No. 10 saloon in 1876.

Notes

I want to thank Van Dyke Parks for the time he gave in London, June 2010, to discuss his work on *Wild Bill* and the many other aspects of his extraordinary career. He is a true gentleman.

1 Lawrence Alloway, *Violent America: The Movies 1946–1964* (New York: MOMA, 1971), 27. See also, Peter Stanfield, "Maximum Movies: Lawrence Alloway's Pop Art Film Criticism," *Screen* 49, 2 (Summer 2008), 179–93.
2 The description of saloon girls as "percentage girls" comes from the film's source novel, Luke Short, *Station West* (New York: Bantom, 1948).
3 Kathryn Kalinak, "How the West Was Sung" in *Westerns: Films Through History*, edited by Janet Walker (New York: AFI/Routledge, 2001): 151–76.
4 Ibid.
5 Peter Stanfield, *Hollywood, Westerns and the 1930s: The Lost Trail* (Exeter: University of Exeter Press, 2001), 173.
6 For further discussion of these films see Stanfield (2001), 174–75 and the chapters on "Frankie and Johnny" and "St. Louis Blues" in Peter Stanfield, *Body & Soul: Jazz and Blues in American Film* (Urbana: University of Illinois Press, 2005): 44–113.
7 For an in-depth discussion of this, see my chapter on "Dixie Cowboys" in Stanfield (2001), 193-224.
8 See, for example, David R. Roediger, *The Wages of Whiteness: Race and the Making of the American Working Class* (London: Verso, 1991) and Dale Cockrell, *Demons of Disorder: Early Blackface Minstrels and Their World* (Cambridge: Cambridge University Press, 1997).
9 John Szwed, booklet accompanying *Jelly Roll Morton: The Complete Library of Congress Recordings by Alan Lomax* (Rounder Records, 2005), 15.
10 Season two, episode nine: "Amalgamation and Capital"
11 My thanks to Kathryn Kalinak for making this connection between Parks and Ives.
12 Kathryn Kalinak, *How the West Was Sung: Music in the Westerns of John Ford* (Berkeley: University of California Press, 2007), 77.
13 Ibid.
14 For more on authenticity and fabrication see, Robert Cantwell, *Bluegrass Breakdown: The Making of the Old Southern Sound* (New York: Da capo, 1992).
15 Parks is being interviewed in *Variety* "Life supplement" (Dec. 2003): 86.
16 The closing credits music is as follows:

   Season 1
   1 "Hog of the Forsaken"—Michael Hurley
   2 "Creek Lullaby"—Margaret
   3 "Twisted Little Man"—Michael J. Sheehey
   4 "Fallen From Grace"—Mark Lee Scott
   5 "God and Man"—Brownie McGhee and Sonny Terry
   6 "High Fever Blues"—Bukka White
   7 "Old Friend"—Lyle Lovett
   8 "Will the Circle Be Unbroken"—June Carter Cash
   9 "Stars and Stripes Forever"—Jelly Roll Morton
   10 "Hog of the Forsaken"—Michael Hurley
   11 "Snake Baked a Hoecake"—Mike, Peggy, Barbara, and Penny Seeger and their children
   12 "Farther Along"—Mississippi John Hurt

   Season 2
   1 "Song to Woody"—Bob Dylan

2 "Business You're Doin'"—Lightnin' Hopkins
3 "Skin and Bones"—Ann Rabson
4 "The Fox"—Bill Staines
5 "Life Is Like That"—Big Bill Broonzy
6 "Pretty Polly"—Hilarie Burhans
7 "A Prayer"—Madeleine Peyroux
8 "Rattlesnake"—"Spider" John Koerner
9 "Mama's Gonna Buy"—Vera Ward Hall
10 "Calling All Angels"—Jane Siberry & k.d. lang
11 "Hey Willy Boy"—Townes Van Zandt
12 "Stay a Little Longer"—Bob Wills and His Texas Playboys

Season 3
1 "I Got a Razor"—Willie Dixon
2 "Hole in the Wall"—Brownie McGhee
3 "Walking the Dog"—Hans Theessink
4 "Mean Mama Blues"—Ramblin' Jack Elliott
5 "I'm Going Home"—Bama Stuart
6 "Daniel in the Lion's Den"—Bessie Jones
7 "Soul of a Man"—Irma Thomas
8 "O Death"—Alan Lomax, Bessie Jones
9 "Garryowen"—unknown
10 "Dangerous Mood"—Keb' Mo'
11 "Mad Mama Blues"—Josie Miles
12 "O Mary Don't You Weep"—Bruce Springsteen

17 http://www.baronhats.com/aces.htm. Accessed June 21, 2010.
18 Laurence Bergreen, *Louis Armstrong: An Extravagant Life* (New York: Broadway Books, 1998), 39–40.
19 These lyrics are used in Sigmund Spaeth, *Weep Some More, My Lady* (Garden City, New York: Doubleday, 1927), 131–32. In his 1926 autobiography, low-life criminal Jack Black reports hearing the ballad for the first time in a prison cell; it is no more than an authenticating detail, much like a minstrel tune in a western, but I like the fact he makes Stackalee the victim: "Somewhere a colored woman was singing a mournful dirge about 'That Bad Stackalee.' The verses were endless. The point of the song seemed to be that the negro bully, Stackalee, had been killed with a 'big forty-four gun over a damn old Stetson hat. In the most harrowing tones at the end of every verse the singer moaned the sad refrain, 'That ba-a-d Stackalee.'" Jack Black, *You Can't Win* (San Francisco: AK Press/Nabat, 2000), 42.
20 Greil Marcus, *Mystery Train: Images of America in Rock 'n' Roll* (London: Penguin, 1990), 66.
21 Cecil Brown, *Stagolee Shot Billy* (Cambridge: Harvard University Press, 2003), 22.
22 Season one, episode six: "Plague."
23 Readers looking for arcane knowledge on the history and pre-history of "Gypsy Davey" need search no further than the chapter "Orpheus, Gypsies, and Redneck Rock n Roll" in Nick Tosches, *Country: The Twisted Roots of Rock 'n' Roll* (New York: Da capo, 1996), 4–21. Although not listed, the ballad also opens Van Dyke Parks's *Song Cycle* album; he calls the ballad his personal "Rosetta Stone." Interview with author, London, June 18, 2010.

Chapter 11

Musical Worlds of the Millennial Western

Dead Man and The Three Burials of Melquiades Estrada

Claudia Gorbman

This chapter examines two westerns made within five years of either side of 2000—Jim Jarmusch's *Dead Man* (1995) and Tommy Lee Jones's *Three Burials of Melquiades Estrada* (2005)—and the sonic worlds created by their music. While they could hardly be more dissimilar, *Dead Man* and *Three Burials*, both products of independent art cinema, share a consciousness of the mythic legacy of the western, and each updates the genre in its own way to comment on America at the millennium. Both subject American masculinity and the use of violence to a critical re-vision, and also radically reorder the western's traditional conceptualization of the functions of the frontier and of the cultural Other.

The two films share a number of structural, narrative, and thematic traits as well. For example, in each, one man leads another on a journey away from the dubious comforts and achievements of civilization, and through the wilderness toward a state, perhaps, of purity and innocence. In their intimate scale, they take on mythic proportions: *Dead Man*, a postmodern rewriting of the Indian's and white man's quests, this time with the Indian's worldview prevailing; and *Three Burials*, an almost religious parable of redemption from white racism and xenophobia.

In *Dead Man*, a young accountant named William Blake (Johnny Depp) makes the long train journey west from Cleveland in the 1870s, only to find that the job promised to him in the factory that dominates the town of Machine has been filled. Almost accidentally, he shoots to death a man who happens to be the son of the tyrannical boss of the very factory that rejected him. Gravely wounded from the shoot-out, he escapes the town; boss Dickinson (Robert Mitchum) hires various killers and lawmen to hunt him down. An educated Indian named Nobody (Gary Farmer) takes Blake into his protection, and the two travel further westward on horseback through the wilderness. Nobody will lead Blake to the Pacific, "back to the place where all the spirits come from, and where all the spirits return."

As Jonathan Rosenbaum observes, Blake is not so much the agent of the action, but rather takes on attributes learned from those around him. He becomes adept at killing with a gun (although there remains something awkwardly random and inelegant about his use of violence); and when a couple of marshals hunting him confront him and ask if he's William Blake, he answers, "Yes, do you know my poetry?" before gunning them down. Although we continue to focus on the white man rather than the interestingly complex and competent Indian—is it force of habit, our generic expectations, or the drawing power of Johnny Depp?—Blake is a far cry from a western hero. At first garbed in a slightly ridiculous checkered wool suit on his train odyssey to Machine, and coiffed in a dark pageboy (which is later fondled by three trappers of ambiguous sexuality), he jumps when he first hears guns at close range, and certainly does not know how to use one. The competencies of the western hero—horsemanship, moral certitude, masculine decisiveness, using violence with reticence—elude him. His skills develop as if by accident, as he comes ever closer to death. His eyesight sharpens magically as he unknowingly engages in the "vision quest" Nobody has laid out for him. But at his core he remains clueless; the intelligence guiding him to the west coast is unquestionably Nobody's store of western, native, and European knowledge.

Three Burials is a contemporary western that begins with the discovery of a body in a shallow grave in Texas near the Mexican border. In the morgue, the putrefying body is identified by Pete Perkins (Tommy Lee Jones) as Melquiades Estrada (Julio Cesar Cedillo), an illegal worker who was Pete's friend and fellow cattleman. Pete discovers that Melquiades was shot by border patrolman Mike Norton (Barry Pepper). Pete soon breaks through the border police's veil of self-protection, and "with near-demented singlemindedness,"[1] kidnaps Norton, makes him dig up the corpse of Melquiades, and takes him on an arduous journey on horseback to Mexico to bury the corpse of his friend. This film's male couple, then, consists not of a white man and an Indian, but two white men: a multicultural western hero exacting justice from his bigoted captive.[2]

As always in westerns, a vision of contemporary America is central to both Dead Man and Three Burials. Unlike the classical western that tells of the establishment of law and the taming of the wilderness into the garden, conveying the basic notion that the United States is a nation of laws, justice, and opportunity, both millennial films see America as a corrupt and violent place.

Dead Man's town of Machine does not look like any to be found in the classical western. With animal bones everywhere, shifty-eyed characters, blowjobs in alleys, horses pissing in the street, and its monstrous spewing smokestack, it is a soulless industrial nightmare, and its boss, the factory owner, a conscience-free capitalist. On his first night in Machine, Blake ends up in bed with a young woman; when he asks her why she keeps a gun under her pillow, she simply answers, "Because this is America." The wilderness is by no means any less violent. Nor are the Native Americans the peaceful and wise citizens that inhabit other revisionist westerns from Broken Arrow (1950) to Dances with Wolves (1990). They are complex beings—Nobody is by far the most fully realized character in the film, full of cultural contradictions—and in a Makah village at the end of the story (the native counterpart to the town of

Machine at the beginning), no one looks particularly happy, and death appears omnipresent.

In classical westerns, Indians as an antagonistic force of nature stand in the way of Manifest Destiny; they are the foil against which the hero demonstrates his civilizing strength. *Dead Man*, however, does not subject Native Americans to allegorizing. While certainly the film as a whole does not aspire to documentary realism, it depicts Native Americans with loving historical fidelity. Jarmusch included Native Americans in the production and documentation of rites and the Makah village, and was aware of Native viewers as an audience he wished to reach.

> In Hollywood westerns, even in the 30s and 40s, history was mythologised to accommodate some kind of moral code. And what really affects me deeply is when you see it taken to the extent where Native Americans become mythical people. . . . It's really close to apartheid in America. The people in power will do whatever they can to maintain that, and TV and movies are perfect ways to keep people stupid and brainwashed. In regards to *Dead Man*, I just wanted to make an Indian character who wasn't either (a) the savage that must be eliminated, the force of nature that's blocking the way for industrial progress, or (b) the noble innocent that knows all and is another cliché. I wanted him to be a complicated human being.[3]

If it is fair to see the western town as the embodiment of American values in westerns, the Texas town of *Three Burials*, "a border town of stunning poverty of imagination, values and spirit,"[4] is a devastating commentary on present-day society. The local police and the border patrol have forged a fraternity that's more interested in self-protection than in justice, and the sheriff is pointedly impotent in literal as well as figurative ways. Norton's young wife LuAnn (January Jones) has two strategies to relieve her boredom: motel assignations and mall shopping. At the town's center we find not the church but the Sands Café, where Rachel the waitress (Melissa Leo), the eyes and ears of the town, conducts affairs under the nose of her husband who's the cook. Masculinity in this border town is a veneer painted on with guns, cell phones, and sport utility vehicles with all-wheel drive.

While Nobody the Indian represents an intelligence in answer to the hopeless violence and cupidity of America in *Dead Man*, the alternatives to the bleak moral vacuum of America in *Three Burials* are, on one hand, Pete Perkins, who possesses John Wayne's western values and Clint Eastwood's potential for explosive revenge, and on the other, by the relative honesty and gentle humanity of Mexicans. Like *Dead Man*, *Three Burials* is a multicultural film, even more insistently so: the titles that punctuate the narrative appear in both Spanish and English,[5] and there's about as much (subtitled) Spanish-language dialogue as English. But of the two films, *Dead Man* launches a far more radical critique of America. *Three Burials* resembles the classical western more closely in that its hero, Pete, carries moral authority and uses violence only with reluctance (even though numerous critics have described him as a madman). The role traditionally played by good settlers, and later by Indians (e.g. in *Dances with Wolves*), here goes to Melquiades and the Mexicans encountered across the border. *Three Burials* is an outspokenly liberal western that replaces Indians-as-victims by Mexicans-as-victims, and shows Mexicans to be the true hardworking Americans.

What music does the modern western draw on to tell these very different tales of America at the millennium?

Dead Man's Music

Dead Man's overall strategy is to employ generic western sounds and push them to a limit, much as the film both participates in and denatures the western genre itself. It has an essentially monothematic score: aside from one barroom piano in Machine and Nobody's tribal chanting in the wilderness, the film's music consists of just one instrumental song that is repeated, and varied throughout; sometimes just a line of the theme plays, sometimes just a harmonic run. Jarmusch invited Neil Young to watch the film and improvise to it, essentially responding to the film as he went:

> He [went through the rough cut] three times over a two-day period. Neil asked me to give him a list of places where I wanted music, and he used that as a kind of map, but he was really focused on the film, so the score kind of became his emotional reaction to the movie.[6]

Jonathan Rosenbaum's book on *Dead Man* makes the rare and laudable gesture for a non-film music scholar of devoting attention to the music. He provides notes on the production process of the score and insights as to its effects. But in describing the melody itself he characterizes the *Dead Man* theme in a way that might mislead: "Its most often repeated melodic phrase resembles, in both shape and feeling, 'Sometimes I Feel Like a Motherless Child,' pointing to the absolute aloneness of both Blake and Nobody."[7] Rosenbaum's perception of a partial syntactical relationship between the Negro spiritual[8] and the musical theme of *Dead Man* allows him to then suggest that the music highlights the characters Blake and Nobody as "motherless." What his characterization misses is the *feel* of the music as it is performed and recorded. Listen to Paul Robeson or the boy soprano Bobby Breen sing "Motherless Child" on YouTube,[9] then consider the voiceless performance of the *Dead Man* theme.[10] On acoustic guitar and more often on electric guitar, complete with fuzz and feedback, *Dead Man*'s attenuated melodic material comes off, to me, more as an evocation of mythic western masculinity, incorporating the modal seventh (lacking in "Motherless Child") and that *uber*-macho lead-guitar sound (likewise).

I would be more inclined to trace the score's pedigree back to Ennio Morricone and his imitators, to Sergio Leone and Clint Eastwood westerns, but above all to the impulse that produced the wildly popular and much-covered 1960s hit recording, "Apache," by the British surf band The Shadows.[11]

"Apache" fused the minor-modal tradition of some movie western music with the masculine energy of electric rock guitar performance. It includes a rhythmic riff in the lower register that is a cousin to the last line of the *Dead Man* theme, although the latter has far more explosive tension in its fuzzed-out fortissimo.

As a concession to Rosenbaum, we might characterize *Dead Man*'s music as the possible progeny of "Motherless Child" and "Apache." Yet even this verbal formulation is wrong, implying that the song acts as an expression of *Dead Man*'s ideological project of correcting the classical western's mythology of America's origins—to parallel the motherlessness of the white man (Blake) and red man (Nobody) and level the playing field by referring to Indians ("Apaches") through a classically white musical sound. I hear nothing of the sort in the score. Rather, the music conveys to me a postmodern version of western masculinity on steroids. It is the post-war quintessence of the solo western hero— oddly out of kilter as it applies to the only likely figure in the frame, William Blake, who progresses from foppish to clueless to near-dead, weaving in and out of consciousness throughout—hardly the alert, skilled hero that is the masculine paragon of the genre.[12]

To sum up so far: the score features primarily the lone guitar,[13] the minor-modal tonalities and melodic lines that can be heard in any number of westerns, reaching for the heroic quality of man-meets-landscape—but this western music is electrified, fragmented, its pedigree weakened, attenuated, and in the process exaggerated. Since it is the Indian companion, Nobody, who ensures William Blake's passage through the hostile environment and thereby could be the film's real hero, we could imagine Jarmusch and Young opting for a Native American musical sound of some kind,[14] but they did not; they went for a denatured "white" music instead. This decision emphasizes *Dead Man* as a reaction to the white hero movie, rather than a reordering of the white–Indian hierarchy of point of view.

Even before the first full statement of the theme music, the pre-credits opening sequence of *Dead Man* exemplifies the film's formal experimentation with sound-image relations. This is the train journey westward, a sequence of seven minutes. The sequence announces *Dead Man*'s tendency throughout to move in and out of consciousness as it were, through episodic narration punctuated by fades. The three components of image, sound effects, and music are minimal, fragmentary, and mixed. Jarmusch represents the duration of the journey by means of fades-in and -out, alternating among shots of Blake, the train wheels turning, occasional glimpses of the increasingly forbidding countryside through the train's windows, and views of his fellow passengers, whose garb and manner become progressively rougher and dirtier with the progress westward.

The musical component to this mix is hardly music at all: it is an inchoate, fragmentary taste of what will be stated as the central theme once Blake arrives in Machine. An electric guitar spits out some notes, especially when we see images of the train's wheels; mostly what we hear at first, over sparse sound effects of train noise, are the treble G and B open strings, and the bass E string, played as if randomly, scratchily, with no "technique." There seems hardly any distinction between music and sound effects, but since we do hear such noises as the rushing of the wheels during the wheel shots, and squeaking of a lantern as we see it swinging in the train cabin, the guitar notes are marked as clearly non-diegetic by contrast. Blake alternately looks around him at the changing roster of passengers, reads or plays solitaire, and sleeps. The loud, disconnected, arhythmic guitar notes seem to signal his passage into dreaming or sleeping; music serves as a gateway between consciousness and dream. Consciousness itself comes in broken pieces, and these disconnected, scattered open-string guitar notes resemble whiffs of western music, but are not organized into a musical syntax.

This loosely or hardly linear, surrealist, episodic, repetitious structure punctuated by fades, even though most pronounced in the prologue, characterizes the entire film. The music's single theme threads through the film and binds it together, even in its variation and fragmentation. The guitar's often heavy reverb adds to the oneiric sense of denatured space and time.

One odd feature of the score is a motif assigned to only one character, the psychopathic hired killer Cole Wilson (Lance Henriksen). When Wilson appears on screen, doggedly pursuing Blake and Nobody a few hours or days behind them, the score usually marks him with a four-note fragment of the theme. (Rosenbaum might describe this motif as "And She Loves Me, Yeah, Yeah," the missing Beatle "yeah" being the first one on the tonic.) Perhaps Young saw fit to give him prominence musically, since the final terrestrial thing the dying Blake will see from his canoe floating out to sea is an absurd shootout on the beach, where Nobody and Wilson kill each other in short order. Does it make sense to assign a motif to only one character in a film? Perhaps this choice was a casualty of the process of Young's composing in real time to the film as it ran.

Three Burials' Music

The Three Burials of Melquiades Estrada takes a more conventional approach to its music. Like a number of post-classical westerns, and indeed like numerous American films since the 1980s, it deploys both orchestral scoring and pre-existing songs in what is commonly called a hybrid score. The scoring generally complements the emotional tone of the narrative events, and the songs, all of which are diegetic, help constitute the characters' world. The songs additionally work to comment on narrative action and indicate ethnic separations and mixing of characters.

Like Jarmusch, Tommy Lee Jones reveals himself as a *mélomane*—an auteur who loves music and who applies it to his work with great personal investment.[15] Jones talks about the musicality of the film's rhythms and even colors, but more significantly perhaps, he cast musicians in two key roles. The country star Dwight Yoakam plays Sheriff Belmont; and the old blind man is played by octagenarian rocker and country legend Levon Helm. Jarmusch, too, has a history of casting musicians in his films: *Dead Man* has Iggy Pop, the father of punk rock, as the trapper Sally Jenko, who wears a dress and reads Bible stories before his summary death by the campfire.

Marco Beltrami's spare and beautiful scoring gives *Three Burials* its musical coherence. Aside from a melodic mini-motif of a minor third (usually in the key of D minor, moving from D to F), there is no melodic theme per se, and thus *Three Burials* deploys a very different model of scoring from *Dead Man*. But the initial musical statement over the opening credits serves as a kind of *matrix* from which fragmentary motifs, patterns, and textures are subsequently taken and developed. The textures of Beltrami's ensemble range from orchestral strings and guitars to accordion, various drums and flutes, invented instruments, and electronics. The cues' instrumental arrangements freely mix these distinctive timbres to emphasize now the American West, now Mexico and Mexicans, and underneath it all, the Native American. The accordion's contribution often consists of just a few notes, sometimes in sustained dissonance and sometimes in tuneful Mexican-style thirds; similarly, small drums can simulate tense heartbeats or else ethnic rhythms; a flute or recorder or whistle evokes a native or otherworldly voice.

The scoring works in two main modes. First, it helps evoke the adventure of the journey, the feel of the arid landscape and of danger. It draws on rhythmic repetition, often with blocks of guitar, strings, and/or accordion sounds above the rhythm, and often dissonances of half-tones when there is danger. The opening sequence provides a good example of this pattern.

The opening credits unroll over the landscape, where two lawmen will shortly discover a coyote eating a human body. What sounds like electronically phased tones, with pulsing reverberation, gives way to a repeating plucked string note in the bass, the beginning of the score's characteristic insistent rhythm, as the title appears in both English and Spanish. The D minor theme comes in, its dominant motif the upward minor third, played on a mandolin, accompanied by two notes on accordion, joined eventually by small drums and a recorder-like flute. This textured mix of instruments that will be heard throughout the score, joined by various bells, chimes, and strings, allows the music to approximate or even anticipate sound effects; for example, a rattle anticipates the scene late in the film when Norton gets gravely bitten by a rattlesnake. Sometimes the mix is dominated by the drum rhythms; for example when Norton chases illegal immigrants, or later when Norton briefly escapes from Pete on foot in the desert.

The other main sound from the score is the theme for the friendship between Pete and Melquiades. It is a lovely major melody heard in thirds for harmony that give it an appropriately Mexican cast, usually on accordion, with an *andante* $\frac{4}{4}$ plucked rhythm in the lower strings. With one exception, it is heard over the flashbacks that show Pete and Melquiades enjoying camaraderie at work or leisure. In its style and effect, it recalls Jerry Fielding's elegiac major-mode theme in *The Wild Bunch* (1968) that accompanies the flashbacks of the Bunch sharing moments of laughter—so moving since it graces such rough men.

The wonderful surprise comes almost at the end, when Pete decides to designate the ruins between two hills as the hamlet of Jimenez that Melquiades had told him about. Mike Norton, who has learned some humility through his journey in captivity, sees that Pete needs for this place to exist, in order to have made the arduous mission with the festering corpse worth the trip. The two men work to bury the body and restore the "house," making a roof with boughs and mudding the walls. The Melquiades theme plays as they work—giving a touching resonance to the casual way Pete calls Norton "son" at the end. The music eloquently suggests that not only has Norton redeemed himself, but also a harmony has developed between the two men that begins to replace Pete's bond with his lost friend.

The soundtrack is also replete with diegetic tunes—music heard on car radios, in cantinas and restaurants. In the world of the Texas border town, the diegetic popular songs resonate with authenticity. For one thing, just about all the songs we hear are by Texans or about Texas: the Tex-Mex musicians Augie Meyers, Bobby Flores, Flaco Jimenez, and Freddy Fender; and the country standbys Merle Haggard, Dwight Yoakam (who's not from Texas, but the song that appears here is "Fair to Midland"), Hank Williams, Jr., and Roger Miller. This music effectively circumscribes the milieu of Pete Perkins (who himself sings a few notes of Roger Miller's classic "Dang Me" as he and Melquiades take their afternoon dates to the motel). Also note that there is not a Loretta or Dolly or Selena in the batch: the exclusively male performances of all the diegetic tunes help, not so subtly, to define the film's predominantly male subjectivity.

The proportions of "Tex" to "Mex" lend dialectical tension to these tunes. Border patrolman Pete has none of the "Mex" in his musical taste; he patrols the desert roads listening to Haggard's "Working Man Blues." Tex-Mex music plays in the neutral territory of the café. Then, when there is complete harmony of the Mexican and the American (and this is a film about crossing borders), when Pete and Melquiades dance with Rachel and LuAnn in the late afternoon sunlight at the end of a motel assignation, they dance to Freddy Fender's bicultural classic, "Before the Next Teardrop Falls." Both women sing along, first with the verse in English, and they also do as well as they can when the lyrics switch into Spanish. Cultural barriers have fallen. The dialectic between Latin and country-and-western is maintained throughout the film by means of Jones's choices of popular recorded songs.

When Pete and Norton first arrive on the property of the blind man in the desert, the latter is listening to a Spanish-language radio station even though he speaks no Spanish. No surprise, then, that when the Border Patrol arrives later to ask about Pete and Norton, he is at his radio again. This time, Cornelio Reyna's Norteño hit, "Me Cai de la Nube" is playing—quite humorously so, as helicopters descend onto the property "from the clouds," along with a phalanx of squad cars.

But the ethnic signposts of music can yield richness by complicating our cultural categories as well. As Mike gets treated for his rattlesnake bite in

Mexico, Pete drinks at a cantina nearby, where a girl is playing Chopin on an out-of-tune piano. This is a musical moment worthy of a *mélomane*—giving us to hear European classical music ineptly played in the middle of nowhere in Mexico. The Chopin has the effect not of showing the primitiveness of rural Mexicans, but rather that loveliness can arise even from a horrible piano: the strings of party lights in the cantina, the light of the setting sun, and the sound mix as a whole make for one of the film's most heart-rending subjective moments. The scene shows Pete quite drunk, bathed in yellow light. Close-ups help identify the sources of most of the sounds Pete hears, which mix into a truly surreal audio wash: the untuned piano, Spanish-dubbed sci-fi dialogue from a TV, with an unearthly sound effect, probably for a spaceship, that sounds like a cross between an elephant and a siren; tinny wisps of Mexican music coming from nowhere in particular. Onscreen a pan approximates Pete's gaze out over the empty, scrubby landscape. The complex sound mix, replete with reverb, gets even denser with the ring of a telephone, which we take to be one more subjective sound until the bar manager answers a real phone. If the musico-visual mix of *Dead Man*'s opening train sequence approximates an oneiric state and sets the tone for that entire film, music for subjectivity in *Three Burials* is restricted to this scene of Pete's drunkenness, culminating in Rachel's rejection of him on the long-distance phone call and his equally pitiful conversation with the decomposed corpse of Melquiades behind the cantina.

As for the film's recorded diegetic songs, consider two tunes that play in the Sands Café during conversations between LuAnn and Rachel. The music that plays in the café at this point is Hank Williams, Jr.'s "The Cheatin' Hotel"; LuAnn and Rachel look sympathetically at each other, wordlessly sharing their disgust at their married lives. "The Cheatin' Hotel" continues on the soundtrack as the film segues to Pete, Melquiades, and the two women going to the motel, where they will "cheat" for an afternoon of human contact. The song abruptly ends when Pete turns off the radio in his truck—a magical thing films can do with diegetic music.

Later, LuAnn, having learned from Pete that her husband killed Melquiades, comes to the café to tell Rachel she is leaving Mike. "You Can't Roller Skate on a Buffalo Herd" plays on the café's radio—a Roger Miller novelty song whose perky silliness would seem to belie the pregnant significance of the moment of LuAnn's liberation. Jones deploys the diegetic country songs more loosely than does Ridley Scott in *Thelma & Louise* (1991), where every song title bears an intimate semantic relationship to the action on-screen; in *Three Burials*, the songs define a culture, a world. But at least Roger Miller's song is about happiness—the refrain line of each verse being "You can be happy if you've a mind to." LuAnn has gotten her mind back, a monumental change given her acquiescence to her husband's objectification of her as a sexual receptacle at the kitchen counter or as a child to buy a Nintendo for. It is such a lonely marriage; when LuAnn gets a mind to be happy, her leaving is an unheralded moment. With no musical fanfare of any kind, she just boards a bus out of town.

In *Dead Man*, a solo guitar—sometimes acoustic, sometimes electric—enters to attempt to mythify a protagonist who hardly qualifies as a western hero. Still, like all the conventional trappings of the western—the town, the bandits, the Indian sidekick, the wilderness, guns—music is present as a generic signpost. In a western universe where everything is off-kilter, where the frontier town has all the evils of the Industrial Age, the girl is unceremoniously killed at the outset, trappers read from the Bible in drag, and the Indian scout knows British poetry, the music is "wrong" too, by traditional standards. Although it is suitably modal, an electric guitar plays it, harking from a century later; and the fragmentation and repetition are better suited to a Godard film than to the western genre, in a sort of radical formal experiment. *Dead Man* belongs to the small group of films which, ever since *The Wild Bunch*, have been announcing the end of the western. The distinction of *Dead Man* is the fidelity of its details to a history that shows up the Hollywood conventions as artifice. Of course there was industrial production in towns in the West, of course there were Native Americans Europeanized in captivity, of course men who lived in the homosocial conditions of the wilderness had a range of sexualities (a fact finally given full expression in *Brokeback Mountain* in 2005). Neil Young's score supplies music with a single guitar for the most part—an instrumentation more realistic than the orchestras of the 1930s and onward, even though the plugged-in guitar foregrounds its modernity. And as the film progresses, the music no longer sounds wrong at all, but entirely of a piece with its universe.

The Three Burials of Melquiades Estrada shares in the classicism of the best westerns. Its hero Pete Perkins defines masculinity as effortlessly as John Wayne's persona. If this man's mission dissolves in poetic ambiguity at the end, the film is still marked by closure: justice has been served, the body has reached its resting place. Even better in the film's thorough multicultural liberalism, the antagonist is not killed but thoroughly redeemed. Beltrami's score works according to a principle of texture designed for maximum flexibility and mutability while still serving to unify; in so doing, it also unifies the cultures that history and politics have set in such stark opposition.

Notes

1 Jim Kitses, "Days of the Dead," *Sight & Sound* 16, 4 (April 2006), 14.
2 The wilderness where the murderer has deposited the body is its first "burial" site. After the police have taken the body and buried it a second time, Pete forces Mike to dig it up. Pete travels with the rotting corpse and Norton in tow to Melquiades's putative home in Mexico, a deserted place where he makes Norton dig the grave for the final resting place, its third burial.
3 Jarmusch quoted in Jonathan Rosenbaum, *Dead Man* (BFI Publishing, 2000), 47.
4 Kitses, op. cit.
5 The film's French producers disliked the pinks, blues, and greens of the film's credits, but Jones stood his ground on their evocation of Mexican pastel colors.
6 Jarmusch quoted in Rosenbaum, 43.
7 Rosenbaum, 43.
8 The song dates back at least as far as the end of slavery in the US, when it was common to sell children of slaves away from their parents.

9 http://www.youtube.com/watch?v=KiJx1Hbn_KM and http://www.youtube.com/ watch?v=HGMZ1dN7eT8—a scene from the 1939 film *Way Down South*.

10 The music can be heard in numerous clips on YouTube, such as here: http://www. youtube.com/watch?v=n6aCMgy0ES4—although the picture has been re-edited by the poster. On the CD (the version used here on YouTube) and in the film's first scene after the opening credits, in Machine, the electric guitar does not enter until the final line of the first iteration of the verse.

11 http://www.youtube.com/watch?v=pY-rPDwzM9M. Grateful thanks to Daniel Goldmark for this reference. Covers and samples include those of the Incredible Bongo Band in 1973 and the Sugarhill Gang in 1981.

12 For a study that reads William Blake rather as a site of "becoming," of hybridity, neither white nor Indian, see Justus Nieland, "Graphic Violence: Native Americans and the Western Archive in *Dead Man*," *CR: The New Centennial Review* 1, 2 (2001), 171–200.

13 The score also makes occasional use of a pump organ.

14 Leonard Rosenman experimented with a Native American-inflected score for *A Man Called Horse* (1970), wedding traditional tribal song to orchestral and choral scoring that borrows musical qualities of tribal singing and vocalizing.

15 See Claudia Gorbman, "Auteur Music," in *Beyond the Soundtrack: Representing Music in Cinema*, eds. Daniel Goldmark, L. Kramer, and R. Leppert, (Berkeley: University of California Press, 2007), 149–62.

Chapter 12

Mountains, Music, and Murder

Scoring the American West in *There Will Be Blood* and *No Country For Old Men*

Matthew McDonald

There Will Be Blood and *No Country For Old Men* are acclaimed American films released at the end of 2007, each set in the American West and thus inevitably engaging with the tradition of western films. Paul Thomas Anderson's film concerns the oil boom in southern California during the late nineteenth and early twentieth centuries, whereas the Coen brothers' film depicts a nearly lifeless stretch of western Texas in 1980, where financial opportunities arise not from fertile land but from murder and theft. The musical soundtracks of these two films, both of which garnered significant critical attention, amplify and complicate the films' depictions of the West. Jonny Greenwood's score for *There Will Be Blood* is exceptional for the overwhelming intensity established during the opening frames and returned to frequently throughout the film. Carter Burwell's score for *No Country*, conversely, is an extreme example of cinema's unheard melodies: it is virtually unrecognizable as music, consisting of barely audible drones generated acoustically by singing bowls and electronically by sine and sawtooth waves.[1] In each film, a crucial function of the music is to establish and comment upon the physical setting, not merely via stereotyped musical associations (as in the classical cinema, westerns and non-westerns alike), but by investing the locale with a sonic presence, which at times takes on an omniscient quality or in some cases even seems to function as an agent guiding the action. The extreme contrast between these scores reflects two very different ideas about the West and its symbolic meanings in contemporary America.

Dueling Images of the West

Any film set in the American West necessarily engages with the mythology of the region, and these two films are no exceptions. The marked differences in their respective portrayals of the West might be accounted for via the fundamental oppositions upon which its mythology is based. In his 1934 essay "A Plundered Province," the western historian Bernard DeVoto outlined the apparent contradictions in popular characterizations of the "Western Man":

This is the symbolism of the Westerner in our metropolitan press—the national wild man, the thunder-bringer, disciple of madness, begetter of economic heresy, immoral nincompoop deluded by maniac visions . . . And yet there is a queer thing: a mere change of clothes gives him a different meaning on quite as large a scale. Put a big hat on his head, cover the ragged overalls with hair pants, and let high heels show beneath them, knot a bandana round his neck—and you have immediately one of the few romantic symbols in American life. He has ceased to be a radical nincompoop and is now a free man living greatly, a rider into the sunset, enrapturer of women in dim theaters, . . . the only American who has an art and a literature devoted wholly to his celebration.[2]

DeVoto related these images of the westerner to similar ideas about the Western landscape:

[The West] has meant escape, relief, freedom, sanctuary. It has meant opportunity, the new start, the saving chance. It has meant oblivion. It has meant manifest destiny, the heroic wayfaring, the birth and fulfillment of a race. It has, if you like, meant what the fourth house of the sky has meant in poetry and all religions—it has meant Death. But whatever else it has meant, it has always meant strangeness. That meaning may serve to reconcile the incompatibles.[3]

One aspect of this opposition is particularly relevant here: the vast open space of the West has been a symbol both of abundant possibility and of desolation—or, to use DeVoto's words, of opportunity and oblivion. These competing visions of the land have given rise to notions about westerners themselves: DeVoto's Romantic cowboy thrives on the region's limitless opportunity, whereas the barren soul of DeVoto's immoral wild man is shaped by the barrenness of the land.[4]

These views of the West have not, of course, been static over time: as the plentiful resources of the West have been mined and exploited and much of the landscape developed and destroyed, so the balance has shifted from opportunity toward oblivion. Lagging somewhat behind these changes in the region, the views of western historians have evolved as well. The American historian Frederick Jackson Turner's famous frontier thesis, which celebrated American individualism not as a product of the country's European ancestry but of the American frontier itself, dominated the discourse for decades after its introduction in 1893 at the World's Fair in Chicago. But in the 1970s and 1980s, the so-called "New Western historians" challenged this idea as one-sided and insufficiently critical, emphasizing instead the long-standing exploitation of the region's natural resources and indigenous peoples (a critique that was already being advanced in the cinema as well).[5] The two films I am focusing on here can be understood to depict critical stages in this historical trajectory: *There Will Be Blood* portrays an era of unbounded possibility and its decline, whereas *No Country* identifies the end point of this decline, what Mary P. Nichols (drawing on Nietzsche) referred to in her analysis of the film as "the end of history."[6]

Heeeere's Jonny!

Whereas each film's vision of the West is conveyed via narrative and visual means, it is arguably the musical scores that encapsulate the ideas of opportunity and oblivion most vividly. Most of the score for *There Will Be Blood* was composed by Jonny Greenwood, best known as the guitarist of Radiohead. From the opening frames, Greenwood's music identifies the oil business as an opportunity fraught with danger. The opening cue is unmistakably portentous, fitting for a film that seems always to be pointing to the future: there will be blood, and there will also be oil, bubbling and gushing unpredictably from the ground, and there will be harbingers of recent episodes in American history as well. Greenwood borrowed this cue from his concert piece *Popcorn Superhet Receiver*, in which string instruments simulate electronically generated sounds. The fragment heard at the beginning of the film consists of a sustained array of tones, forming a chromatic aggregate; these slowly converge via *glissandi* onto a unison and then reverse course, returning to the original sonority. The outer voices, notated, form an "X" (see Figure 12.1).[7] This music is coordinated with two images: a single exterior shot of three mountains followed by Daniel Plainview (Daniel Day Lewis) repeatedly swinging his pick ax in a mine shaft. The former shot is critical in establishing audiovisual meaning: the foreboding western landscape and Greenwood's score reinforce one another's menacing presence, setting up a mood that will loom, mountainlike, over the entire film.[8]

This opening is rich with film-historical associations that strengthen the connection between Greenwood's cue and the images it accompanies. The opening sustained string harmony is strongly reminiscent of the first sonority from György Ligeti's *Atmosphères*, as heard against a black screen at the beginning of the "Overture" to *2001: A Space Odyssey*.[9] Greenwood's cue is likewise introduced against a black screen that precedes the initial image of mountains. This musical similarity might be understood as part of a larger network of connections with *2001*: Plainview's ax and later his bowling pin are descendants of the bones wielded by Kubrick's apes, and the trapezoidal oil derricks tower over the characters like the monolith of *2001*. Furthermore, like *2001*, *There Will Be Blood* is concerned with the evolution of technology from

Figure 12.1 Opening cue of *There Will Be Blood* (from *Popcorn Superhet Receiver*; transcribed by the author)

its primitive forms and its effect on human behavior. Most important in the present context, however, are the awe-inspiring and sometimes terrifying open spaces with which each film is concerned: There Will Be Blood plays upon associations between the western frontier and the so-called final frontier of space.[10] Indeed, with its subtle balance between the glorification and critique of space exploration, 2001 provides a template for simultaneously deploying and undermining romanticized notions of western frontierism.

Cementing further the bond between music and image in the opening of the film is the Eisensteinian nature of the audiovisual relationship. In his well-known analysis of "The Battle on Ice" sequence from Alexander Nevsky (1938), Sergei Eisenstein outlined individual linear gestures that he understood to underlie individual shots and their musical accompaniment.[11] Among the many types of music-image connections that Eisenstein cited, two are especially relevant here: 1) in the first shot of the sequence, a fade-in is coordinated with an ascending melodic line in the low strings; and 2) in the third shot, Eisenstein related the same melodic line to the contour of the image—an arched cloud formation emerging from behind a cliff follows a similar trajectory in space as the notated melody.[12] The opening of There Will Be Blood seems to draw upon a similar strategy for uniting music and image. The musical crescendo and converging melodic lines are coordinated with the fade-in from a black screen to the opening shot of mountains. Further, the V-shaped contour of the notated upper instrumental line can be linked to the contour of the mountains, which outlines two Vs against the clouded sky (see Figure 12.2), a shape echoed by Plainview's arms and ax in the next shot. The opening cue is reprised six minutes into the film, and here the crescendo and converging melodic lines are coordinated with an upward pan of the camera from Plainview, crawling out of another shaft after breaking his leg, to the very same shot of mountains. These sorts of audiovisual correlations, as identified by Eisenstein, have frequently been critiqued as arbitrary and unlikely to be apprehended in the way Eisenstein imagined. Nonetheless, they are relatively easily perceived at the beginning of There Will Be Blood and thus help—if only subliminally—to

Figure 12.2 Opening shot of There Will Be Blood

establish an immediate link between the western setting and Greenwood's score: the former, immobile and daunting, seems to give rise to the latter. None of this can be taken as evidence that Anderson or Greenwood endorsed or even were aware of Eisenstein's theories. Yet we still might wonder if Anderson, who enjoys embedding film-historic references in his films, was inspired by Eisenstein, and if perhaps the idea to draw upon *Alexander Nevsky* was even triggered by the image of mountains against a clouded sky shared by these films.

Returning to Kubrick, we might discern one more potentially significant cinematic reference in the opening of *There Will Be Blood*. Greenwood's scoring and Anderson's title no doubt are sufficient to impress upon the viewer that Plainview's initial ax blows are omens of violence to come, but further evidence is provided by this shot's apparent mimicking of Jack Torrence's famous bathroom entry in *The Shining*, as shown in Figure 12.3. *The Shining* is also set in the American West, specifically in Colorado, and in this film the Overlook Hotel, built on an Indian burial ground, is the vast and terrifying space shaping Jack's behavior; this site deserves the warning "there will be blood" every bit as much as the looming mountains of Anderson's film.[13]

Plainview's ax takes much longer to find its blood than Jack's, however. About two-thirds of the way through the film, Plainview murders "Henry" (Kevin J. O'Connor), a man posing as his brother. Here, Greenwood's opening cue returns a third time (now extended to include more of the original concert piece), and it continues as Plainview buries Henry's body, once again swinging his pick ax, but now to place something into the earth rather than to extract something from it. In this new context, the music is likely to be heard as deranged and sinister, and thus as a reflection of Plainview himself, as opposed to its less specific and less human associations in the film's opening frames. In other words, the music's connotative function seems to have shifted from the realm of setting to the realm of character.[14] This shift is presaged, however, by the same music's presence at the beginning of the film, where it twice forges a connection between juxtaposed images of Daniel Plainview and the mountains. The inseparability of the land and its inhabitants is thereby established, a demonstration that the nature of the westerner is shaped by the nature of the West. As DeVoto put it his essay "The Anxious West," updating the frontier thesis in terms more fitting for the topic at hand: "The West is plains, mountains, and desert. Its landscape is dramatic, its climate violent. . . . Its inhabitants, products of its landscape, climate, and history, are a volatile, expansive people, energetic extroverts at the base of whose consciousness are tensions and conflicts."[15]

All Quiet on the Western Soundtrack

If the western frontier made a monster out of Daniel Plainview, *No Country For Old Men* shows how things only got worse in the ensuing decades. Save for a few carefully placed moments in which iconic western landscapes are on full display, most of the film is set in trailer parks, seedy hotels, airports and office

Figure 12.3 Stills from *There Will Be Blood* (top) and *The Shining* (bottom)

buildings, bland main streets, and suburban neighborhoods. Areas that remain undeveloped are repositories not of natural resources but of bags of money and drugs. As Joan Mellen has written, the film "is set on a [flat] landscape of West Texas desolation where nature can no longer be enlisted even ironically as a metaphor of transcendence."[16] This setting seems to predetermine the dynamics of the narrative (or, one might say, the lack thereof): whereas *There Will Be Blood* is oriented toward the future and reaches a violent climax in its final scene, the world of *No Country* is static and devoid of possibility or redemption, its story stubbornly resisting any satisfying closure. In keeping with these qualities, no musical score forces itself aggressively onto the viewer, but just the opposite: most viewers are unlikely to realize that there is a musical score at all.[17] The paucity of music suggests a connection with William Butler Yeats's poem "Sailing to Byzantium," whose first sentence, "That is no country for old men," inspired the title for the Cormac McCarthy novel adapted by the film. Yeats's poem repeatedly links music with the young (and, by implication, silence with the old); the poem's aging persona wishes to recapture the "sensual music" of youth. The Coen brothers' film (like the novel) is also oriented from the perspective of the old, personified by Sheriff Ed Tom Bell (Tommy Lee Jones), whose voice-over narration begins the film and whose monologue concludes it. By the film's end, Bell has been rendered inert and irrelevant, and the complete absence in the film of the emotionally charged music heard in most narrative cinema reflects his lost vitality.

The dominant sound throughout *No Country* is wind, a continual reminder of the setting (itself drained of vitality) and a symbol of emptiness: empty space, empty souls, empty meaning. The film ends with Sheriff Bell staring into space while the wind blows and a clock ticks. These sounds continue as the screen goes black; time moves on and nothing happens. The rare moments of music in the film (about fifteen minutes total) seem to be an extension of the wind, both sonically and symbolically. The opening of the film is a good example. The sound of wind and Sheriff Bell's voice-over accompany several long shots of landscape. Eventually, Anton Chigurh (Javier Bardem) enters the frame as he is led into a police car. His presence seems to occasion the first occurrence of Burwell's music, a humming perfect fifth that sneaks in under the wind and only gradually registers (to the attentive listener) as a non-diegetic sound. The other instances of music in the film are similar to this one, although the sonorities are sometimes more complex. Because the first cue is closely synchronized with Chigurh's entrance, it lends an otherworldly and perhaps ominous aura to the character. Sure enough, he is soon revealed to be the very personification of evil, and later instances of music are generally associated with Chigurh as well. But as in *There Will Be Blood*, the music is linked to the physical setting prior to any character. Burwell has said that he wanted the music to "emanate from the landscape,"[18] and its tendency to blend in with the sound of the wind helps to suggest this origin. Furthermore, open fifths often signify nature and the elemental (as in *Also Sprach Zarathustra*, for example), a connotation that is strengthened in Burwell's cue by the fact that this fifth is generated via actual overtones on a vibrating instrument.

Open fifths have of course been associated with the American frontier in the music of many American composers and film scorers, as exemplified in the music of Aaron Copland. But their meaning is by no mean fixed. A useful point of comparison is a scene from *There Will Be Blood*. About twenty-five minutes into the film, Daniel Plainview and his adopted son, H. W. (Dillon Freasier), drive to the Sunday family's farm, acting on a tip from Paul Sunday (Paul Dano). Greenwood's cue consists of a stoic ascending fifth in the low strings, repeated several times with its upper tone sustained. The violins respond to each utterance of this fifth, shimmering above it with clusters from the Dorian mode, and eventually overlay dissonant counterpoint that sounds like it has been imported from a Bartók string quartet. This music is first heard while Paul is identifying the location of his family's property (and its sizable reserve of oil) on a large map, and it continues into the next scene where we see the land itself, empty save for a railroad track receding into the distance and Plainview's automobile, slowly approaching the camera in a parallel trajectory. If the lower strings evoke the vast space in front of us, the upper strings suggest the percolating possibility within it.

Whereas Greenwood's music is anticipatory, however, Burwell's opening cue is static in every respect except volume, an expression of both the Texas landscape and Anton Chigurh, two immutable facts of nature. The intensity of Greenwood's music implies something lurking behind the relatively inert images it accompanies, but Burwell's arises more naturally from the images, matching the visual void with an aural one, a musical extension of the wind that serves as a constant aural reminder of empty space.

As in *There Will Be Blood*, *2001* is an important (and perhaps intentional) reference point for the opening frames of *No Country*, one of the most instructive points of overlap between these two westerns. The link to *2001* is evoked most vividly by the initial succession of images, which almost seem to have been cribbed directly from Kubrick's film.[19] The landscape shots of Earth that begin the "Dawn of Man" sequence in *2001* (directly following the opening title sequence) were shot in Africa but might easily be mistaken for the American West, and there is a striking resemblance between the composition and editing of these shots and those that begin *No Country*.[20] Both sequences are composed primarily of static long shots of barren landscapes, generally about five or six seconds in length. The soundtrack of each sequence features wind, and in each case this sound is introduced over a black screen. Table 12.1 outlines the correspondences between these sequences in much more detail, comparing them shot-by-shot, tracking both the duration and content of shots as well as their overall timing within the sequence (see the column labeled "Time," which locates each shot in relation to the beginning of the sequence, as designated aurally by the sound of wind); similarities of timing are highlighted in bold. Each sequence begins with several shots of the horizon at dawn, with the sun eventually peeking out from behind a mountain on the left side of the screen; the first three shots of *2001* and Shots 2–4 of *No Country* are juxtaposed in Figure 12.4, such that their shared compositional features can easily be seen. Although the first several shots of each sequence are devoid of primates, the telephone poles in Shot 2 of *No Country* and the "Dawn of Man" title in Shot 1 of *2001* allude to their presence; each visual appears six seconds after the onset of the first shot. The primates arrive at virtually identical points in each sequence, as highlighted in bold in the bottom row of Table 12.1. These arrivals are set up in each sequence by camera movement (anomalous in each sequence, where static shots are the rule), as shown in the table. Furthermore, the pan over a cliff and toward the horizon in Shot 10 of *2001* begins at precisely the same juncture as a staggered three-shot "zoom" toward an isolated windmill in *No Country* (each commences 1:01 minutes into the sequence).

These correspondences, evoked at the very beginning of *No Country*, invite us to consider the metaphors and meanings of *2001* in making sense of the film we are about to see. We can hear the Coen brothers' wind and, by extension, Burwell's music, in relation to the wind of *2001*, which accompanies much of

Table 12.1 Shot-by-shot comparison of dawn sequences in No Country and 2001

No Country				2001			
Shot	Time	Duration	Description	Shot	Time	Duration	Description
—	0:00	16 secs	wind (+ narration) over titles and black screen	—	0:00	3 secs	wind (+ bird and insect sounds) over black screen
1	0:16	6 secs	mountain at dawn	1	0:03	6 secs	mountain at dawn
2	0:22	8 secs	telephone poles; see Figure 12.4		0:09	8 secs	"THE DAWN OF MAN"; see Figure 12.4
3	0:30	6 secs	see Figure 12.4	2	0:17	5 secs	see Figure 12.4
4	0:36	12 secs	see Figure 12.4	3–4	0:22	10 secs	see Figure 12.4
5–6	0:48	13 secs		5–9	0:32	29 secs	
7–11	1:01	27 secs	zoom on windmill (shots 7, 10, 11)	10	1:01	25 secs	camera pans over cliff
12	1:28	11 secs	camera pans	11–12	1:26	12 secs	skeletal remains
	1:39	9 secs	Chigurh enters frame	13	1:38	8 secs	apes eating

No Country, Shots 2–4   2001, Shots 1–3

Figure 12.4 Comparison of opening shots from *No Country* and *2001*

Kubrick's opening sequence and is heard again during the famous jump cut into the space age that occurs at the end of the "Dawn of Man" sequence. In *2001*, just as the barren landscape seen early in the film is a corollary for outer space, the wind is a direct corollary for the silence that later dominates the scenes in space. The film highlights these open spaces both visually and aurally in order to set up one of its basic concerns: what happens when humans are inserted into new environments. Understood in relation to *2001*, then, we can interpret the opening sequence of *No Country* as a brief view of the West as it would be without the overdevelopment and corruption that are on display during the rest of the film, just as Kubrick began *2001* with a glimpse of Earth before the monolith. But whereas *2001* shows us the precise moment that violence is introduced into the environment, *No Country* reveals little about the source of the societal violence and nihilism embodied by Chigurh. There is only the ambiguous suggestion, once again, that the man is a product of his environment, that a vacant land has begotten a vacant soul. And this idea is suggested most strongly by the nearly imperceptible music, emanating from the land but attaching itself consistently throughout the film to Chigurh.

Coda: Westerns in 2007

There Will Be Blood and *No Country For Old Men* were not the only prominent westerns to arrive in theaters at the end of 2007. The fall of that year also saw the releases of *3:10 to Yuma* and *The Assassination of Jesse James by the Coward*

Robert Ford, two period westerns whose musical scores help to bring into relief what is striking and noteworthy about the scores of *There Will Be Blood* and *No Country*. In *3:10* and *The Assassination of Jesse James*, an important role of the music is to position the film efficiently and unequivocally in relation to contemporary genres. As *3:10* is essentially an action-movie set in the West (Arizona), the central functions of its score are to create a mythic aura, enhance the action, and generate suspense. These functions are established during the opening title music, which begins with violin drones and an upright piano manipulated by fishing wire; the latter evokes the sound of a tack piano or, as the composer Marco Beltrami has suggested, a mandolin.[21] These instrumental sounds gesture toward the western,[22] but the soundtrack quickly enters the world of contemporary action films, featuring the sort of rhythmic hammer blows that seem to be ubiquitous as accompaniment to the frenetic montages of contemporary action-movie trailers. Such music punctuates the staggered rendering of the title "3:10 to Yuma," the words appearing one by one as though a series of bullet shots. In the opening scene that follows, Dan Evans (Christian Bale) and his family are awakened from their sleep by an ambush, and the soundtrack is loaded with sounds that double as conventional signifiers of the western and suspense-generators: we hear not merely the wind (as in *No Country*), but approaching riders on horseback, agitated cattle and dogs, and a creaky barn door. Where the music and sound design of *No Country* and *There Will Be Blood* seek to defamiliarize our filmic experience of the West (albeit in very different ways), in *3:10*, the soundtrack pulls us into a more familiar and comfortable world of cinematic convention.

In stark contrast to *3:10*, the prologue of *The Assassination of Jesse James* unmistakably brands what we are about to see as an art film. As in *No Country*, the opening sequence begins with the sound of wind over a black screen and soon after introduces voice-over narration. The voice-over and montage reflect upon the growing despondency and detachment of Jesse James (Brad Pitt) in his final months, establishing the film's temporal focus.[23] Unlike in *No Country*, however, the sound of wind is joined by music. The opening cue (composed by Nick Cave and Warren Ellis) is played by vibraphone, piano, and glockenspiel, and is characterized by minimalist oscillations between tonic and submediant in the minor mode; in other words, any expectation of hearing a typical western score is quickly eliminated. The brittle and glistening instrumental timbre here and elsewhere is decidedly wintry, in keeping with the film's primary time frame, September 1881 to April 1882 (Missouri is blanketed in snow through much of the film, a less familiar aspect of the foreboding western climate), and the first shots of the film, coordinated with the opening cue, feature dense layers of winter clouds filmed in fast motion. Tellingly, however, images of winter are abandoned in the montage that follows, suggesting that the music is fundamentally a manifestation of the film's concern with the "winter" of James's life and his lack of purpose during this time: Cave and Ellis's score attaches itself firmly to the human element of its story and functions throughout the film as a musical expression of James's ennui.[24]

The scores of *There Will Be Blood* and *No Country*, on the other hand, are bound equally to the characters and the land they inhabit, contributing to the powerful suggestion in each film of an inseparability between the West and the Westerner, between habitat and inhabitant. If environment provides a window into the murderous souls of men such as Plainview and Chigurh, perhaps the eight-year shooting spree of another lone gunman is the best explanation for the re-emergence of the western as a genre and the West as a metaphor in cinema in the year 2007. The four films considered here address the need to write new narratives and mythologies of the West in the waning years of the Bush era, which so cynically co-opted images from the Romantic half of DeVoto's dualism: the big-hatted rider ready to take on the unknown in gleeful isolation. However backward-looking these films might appear to be in their preoccupation with American history, directorial giants from past generations of the cinema, and an aging film genre, they are in a deeper sense films of, and about, their own time. Yet, whatever their political motivations may be, perhaps *There Will Be Blood* and *No Country* ultimately suggest that George W. Bush cannot be blamed for his role in creating an image of the United States as the world's misguided cowboy: like Ben Wade, Jesse James, Daniel Plainview, and Anton Chigurh, Bush is a craggy outcropping of a mythic national geography, inexorably bound to the violence of its history. By directly confronting this violence within unfamiliar narrative structures and audiovisual environments, *There Will Be Blood* and *No Country* offer possibilities for reimagining the West and re-examining America's cultural heritage.

Notes

1 Carter Burwell, "Carter's Notes," at http://www.carterburwell.com/projects/NCFOM.html. Accessed October 11, 2010.
2 Bernard DeVoto, "The West: A Plundered Province," *Harper's Magazine* 169 (August 1934), 355–56.
3 Ibid., 356.
4 And so it is in western films, as has been noted by John G. Cawelti:

> The moral character of the hero also appears symbolically in the Western setting. The rocky aridity and climatic extremes of the Great Plains complement the hostile savagery of Indians and outlaws. On the other hand, the vast openness, the vistas of snowcovered peaks in the distance, and the great sunrises and sunsets ... suggest the epic courage and regenerative power of the hero. In every respect, Western topography helps dramatize more intensely the clash of characters and the thematic conflicts of the story.

> See Cawelti, *The Six-Gun Mystique Sequel* (Bowling Green, Ohio: Bowling Green State University Popular Press, 1999), 24.

5 For an enlightening historiography of western studies, see Margaret Walsh, *The American West: Visions and Revisions* (Cambridge: Cambridge University Press, 2005), particularly Chapter 1, "The Frontier and the West: Realities, Myths and the Historians," 1–18.
6 Mary P. Nichols, "Revisiting Heroism and Community in Contemporary Westerns: *No Country for Old Men* and *3:10 to Yuma*," *Perspectives on Political Science* 37/4 (Fall 2008), 207–15.

7   The score has recently been published by Faber Music but was not easily available.
8   Such might well have been the intent of director and composer, as suggested when
this volume went to press by the following exchange:

> Anderson: "[W]hen I heard 'Popcorn,' I just loved the sounds of it, and I
> just couldn't put my finger on what I liked about it. Because I would always
> hear it when it wasn't on, like a phantom limb, just the strange sounds of
> it. I had been listening to it over and over again, and then when not
> listening to it, would feel like I had left the stereo on in the other room or
> something."

> Greenwood: "That's mad, because that's exactly why I wrote that! . . . The
> whole [conceptual] idea was about when you think there's some music
> playing, and there isn't. You know, like when you're doing a Hoover or a
> vacuum cleaner and you think there's a radio playing as well, and you turn
> it off, but there isn't any music on. That was the starting-off point for that
> piece, anyway."

Chris Willman, "There Will Be Music," *Entertainment Weekly* (November 8,
2007), http://www.ew.com/ew/article/0,,20155516_20155530_20158721,00.html.
Accessed October 11, 2010.
9   On music in *2001*, particularly Kubrick's use of *Atmosphères*, see Michel Chion,
Kubrick's Cinema Odyssey, trans. Claudia Gorbman (London: BFI, 2001), and
David Patterson, "Music, Structure and Metaphor in Stanley Kubrick's *2001: A
Space Odyssey*," *American Music* 22/3 (Fall 2004), 444–74.
10 Anderson, in an interview about the film, acknowledged his debt to Kubrick:

> Well, it's so hard to do anything that doesn't owe some kind of debt to
> what Stanley Kubrick did with music in movies. Inevitably, you're going
> to end up doing something that he's probably already done before. It can
> all seem like we're falling behind whatever he came up with. "Singin' in
> the Rain" in *Clockwork Orange*—that was the first time I became so aware
> of music in movies. So no matter how hard you try to do something new,
> you're always following behind.

Willman, 2007.
11 S. M. Eisenstein, "Vertical Montage," in *Selected Works, Vol. II: Towards a Theory
of Montage*, eds. Michael Glenny and Richard Taylor, trans. Michael Glenny
(London: British Film Institute, 1991), 378–99.
12 See the folded insert between pp. 396 and 397 of Eisenstein 1991 for Eisenstein's
graphic analysis of the sequence, including still shots and a reduction of Prokofiev's
score.
13 Greenwood cited *The Shining* as a musical influence for his score: "Sometimes Paul
would describe the thing as kind of close to the horror-film genre. And we talked
about how *The Shining* had lots of Penderecki and stuff in it" (Willman, 2007).
Given Kubrick's influence on Anderson (as cited above), we might wonder
whether *The Shining*, in addition to *2001*, was an important point of reference
for *There Will Be Blood*. Could the fortuitous casting of Jack Nicholson as Jack
Torrence, for instance, have inspired Anderson's invention of Daniel Plainview
(loosely based on characters from Upton Sinclair's novel *Oil!*), a character to be
played by Daniel Day Lewis? (Both directors carried this name game further:
Danny Torrence was played by Danny Lloyd and Paul Sunday by Paul Dano.)
14 Jan Swafford has offered a more reductive view: "That opening creepy glissando of
strings and dissonant buzzing returns after our antihero Plainview has killed a man
for no discernable reason. So all along the music has represented [Plainview's]

madness." This conclusion seems to have been predetermined by Swafford's assessment that, unlike the Coen brothers, who "have always worked well with landscapes," Anderson "has been more interested in the inner landscapes of his characters." See "Silent, Spooky: The Soundtracks for *No Country for Old Men* and *There Will Be Blood*," *Slate* (February 19, 2008), http://www.slate.com/id/2184698/. Accessed October 11, 2010. Alex Ross reached a similar conclusion about the meaning of Greenwood's opening cue: "although ['Popcorn Superhet Receiver'] wasn't composed for the film, it supplies a precise metaphor for the central character. The coalescence of a wide range of notes into a monomaniacal unison may tell us most of what we need to know about the crushed soul of the future tycoon Daniel Plainview." Yet Ross seems to have been unable to make up his mind as to whether or not Greenwood's score also tells us something about the land Plainview inhabits: in the same short essay, he referred to Greenwood's music as both "unearthly" and "the music of an injured Earth." See "Welling Up," *The New Yorker* (February 4, 2008), http://www.newyorker.com/arts/critics/musical/2008/02/04/080204crmu_music_ross. Accessed October 11, 2010.

15 Bernard DeVoto, "The Anxious West," *Harper's Magazine* 193/1159 (December 1946), 481.

16 Joan Mellen, "Spiraling Downward: America in *Days of Heaven, In the Valley of Elah,* and *No Country for Old Men*," *Film Quarterly* 61/3 (Spring 2008), 28.

17 As Michel Chion has recently observed, citing *No Country* as an example, "films that contain very little or no diegetic or extra-diegetic music . . . are often linked to the idea of the end of the world or of some catastrophe." See "Without Music: On *Caché*," in *A Companion to Michael Haneke*, ed. Roy Grundmann (Oxford: Wiley-Blackwell, 2010), 163.

18 Dennis Lim, "Exploiting Sound, Exploring Silence," *The New York Times* (January 6, 2008), http://www.nytimes.com/2008/01/06/movies/awardsseason/06lim.html. Accessed October 11, 2010.

19 Another important point of reference is the Coens' first feature film, *Blood Simple* (1984), whose opening sequence is remarkably similar, consisting of several long shots of Texas landscape accompanied by a voice-over and the sound of wind.

20 Although I have no concrete evidence that the Coens were directly inspired or influenced by this particular sequence in *2001*, a direct connection seems entirely plausible: the presence of cinematic references and borrowing in the Coens' films is well established. In the case of *No Country*, consider the scene in which Llewelyn Moss (Josh Brolin) prepares his ammunition in the first hotel room in which he stashes his money, a scene whose content and editing is obviously indebted to Martin Scorsese's *Taxi Driver*.

21 Video *3:10 to Score*, produced by David Naylor (executive) and Karolyne Oak (Lions Gate Films Inc, 2007), http://music.lionsgate.com/301/. Accessed October 11, 2010.

22 As Beltrami has remarked, "It's more of a gritty, Sergio Leone type western. . . . As such, the music had to reflect that" (*3:10 to Score*). Beltrami's emulation of Ennio Morricone's score for *The Good, The Bad, and The Ugly* is particularly evident.

23 Like the prologue, the entire film is decidedly past-oriented, as set up by its title, which follows *The Man Who Shot Liberty Valance* in spoiling the fate of its hero and goes further by killing the suspense surrounding the culprit.

24 Roger Deakins's cinematography serves a similar purpose, particularly in its use of "Deakinizer" lenses to create vignetting effects evocative of nineteenth-century photography; see Stephen Pizzello and Jean Oppenheimer, interviewers, "Western Destinies: Q&A with Deakins," *The American Society of Cinematographers* (October 2007), http://www.theasc.com/ac_magazine/October2007/QAWithDeakins/page1.php. Accessed October 11, 2010.

Contributors

Ross Care is an independent scholar and a composer. As a scholar, he has published extensively on classic film music of the studio era. As a composer, he has written for concert, film, and theater, most recently a score for two West Coast revivals of Tennessee Williams's *The Glass Menagerie*. His current writing project is a monograph on Hollywood film music, 1950 to 1965, based on one of his essays for the Library of Congress.

Corey K. Creekmur is an Associate Professor of English and Film Studies at the University of Iowa, where he also directs the Institute for Cinema and Culture. He has published on American film genres, popular Hindi cinema, comics, and representations of race, gender, and sexuality in popular culture. Among other publications, he is the co-editor of *The International Film Musical* (2011), *Cinema, Law, and the State in Asia* (2007) and the general editor of the *Comics Culture* series for Rutgers University Press.

Yuna de Lannoy received her PhD in Film Studies from Birbeck College, University of London, in 2009. She has taught Japanese cinema and manga at Oxford Brookes University, Antwerp University, and elsewhere. Her article, "Revisiting Akira Kurosawa's *The Idiot*: A Comparison with Sergei Eisenstein," appeared in *Journal of Japanese and Korean Cinema* in 2011.

K. J. Donnelly is Reader in Film at the University of Southampton. He is the author of *British Film Music and Film Musicals* (2007), *The Spectre of Sound* (2005), *Pop Music in British Cinema* (2001), and is the editor of *Film Music: Critical Approaches* (2001). He is currently working on a book on sound and image synchronization to be published by Oxford University Press.

Caryl Flinn is the author of *Strains of Utopia: Nostalgia, Gender and Hollywood Film Music* (1992); *Brass Diva: The Life and Legends of Ethel Merman* (2009); *New German Cinema: Music, History, and the Matter of Style* (2003); and co-editor of *Music and Cinema* (2000). She has been teaching at the University of Arizona since 2000, where she currently is Head and Professor of Gender and Women's Studies and an affiliate in Media Arts and the LGBT Institute.

Claudia Gorbman is Professor of Film Studies at the University of Washington at Tacoma, and an adjunct faculty member in UW-Seattle's Cinema Studies and Women's Studies programs. She is the author of *Unheard Melodies: Narrative Film Music* (1987), has translated six books including five by the French critic Michel Chion, and has published more than fifty articles on film and film music. She received the UWT Distinguished Scholar Award for 2009.

Kathryn Kalinak is Professor of English and Film Studies at Rhode Island College. She is the author of *Settling the Score: Music in the Classical Hollywood Film* (1992), *How the West Was Sung: Music in the Westerns of John Ford* (2007), and *Film Music: A Very Short Introduction* (2010). Her next book project, with Mervyn Cooke, is a reader in global film music, a collection of essays by composers and filmmakers around the world about the craft of film composition outside Hollywood.

Charles Leinberger is Associate Professor of Music at the University of Texas at El Paso, where he teaches various classes in music theory and film musicology. He is the author of the Scarecrow monograph *Ennio Morricone's The Good, the Bad and the Ugly: A Film Score Guide*. He has presented lectures on Ennio Morricone's compositional techniques in the United States and England. He is also a freelance trumpet player.

Matthew McDonald is Assistant Professor of Music and member of the Cinema Studies faculty at Northeastern University where he teaches courses in music theory, music history, and film music. His articles have appeared in the journals *19th-Century Music*, *Music Analysis*, *The Musical Quarterly*, and the *Journal of the American Musicological Society*. In 2010, he was awarded an ACLS Fellowship to complete his book on the music of Charles Ives.

Peter Stanfield is a Reader in Film Studies at the University of Kent. He is the author of two studies of the western, *Horse Opera: The Strange History of the 1930s Singing Cowboy* (2002), and *Hollywood, Westerns and the 1930s: The Lost Trail* (2001), and a singular study of American's gutter songs and the movies, *Body and Soul: Jazz and Blues in American Film, 1927–63* (2005). His latest book is *Maximum Movies—Pulp Fictions: Film Culture and the Worlds of Sam Fuller, Mickey Spillane, and Jim Thompson* (2011).

Mariana Whitmer directs special projects at the Center for American Music at the University of Pittsburgh where she also teaches a course on music and film. She is currently working on Jerome Moross's score for *The Big Country* for Scarecrow's Film Score Guide series and is executive director of the Society for American Music.

Ben Winters is a Stipendiary Lecturer in Music at Christ Church, University of Oxford, and has published articles on film music in journals such as *Music and Letters*, *Music, Sound, and the Moving Image*, *Brio*, and the *Journal of the Royal Musical Association* and is the author of *Erich Wolfgang Korngold's The Adventures of Robin Hood: A Film Score Guide* (2007). Current film-related research projects include a study of concert performance in screened fiction.

Index

2001: A Space Odyssey (1968) 216–17, 221
3 Godfathers (1948) 38, 40
3:10 to Yuma (1957) 23
3:10 to Yuma (2007) 223–24

A westerns: folk songs in 30–31; scoring conventions of 131, 173; songs in relation to gender 100, 101, 103; songs in relation to setting 97, 185
Adorno, Theodor 34–35n
Aeolian mode 139, 141, 143–44, 145
aerophones 138, 139, 143
Alamo, The (1960) 83
Alamo, The (2004) 122
Albarn, Damon 149, 151–54, 158, 159–60
Alexander Nevsky (1938) 217, 218
Alloway, Lawrence 183
Also Sprach Zarathustra (Strauss) 220
Altman, Robert 36n
Ames, Ed 29
Anderson, Lindsay 37, 39–40
Anderson, Paul Thomas 214, 218
anempathetic music 156–57, 159
Annie Get Your Gun (1950): masculinity and femininity in 95–96; musical and western genres, combination of 97–98; novelty and tradition in 94–95, 103, 112–13; vocal style 106–7, 108
Annie Oakley (1860–1926) 94, 104
Annie Oakley (1935) 94, 104
Annie Oakley (1954–1957) 103
Antheil, George 54
Anthology of American Folk Music 31
"Apache" 206–7
Appalachian Spring (Copland) 52
Armstrong, Louis 196
Arnold, David 10

art music 3, 30, 112, 149, 150, 172
As Man to Man (1967) *see Death Rides a Horse* (1967)
Assassination of Jesse James By the Coward Robert Ford, The (2007) 199, 224
Atmosphères (Ligeti) 216
authenticity: musical conventions of 200; gender roles and 110–12; historical verisimilitude and 121, 122–23, 168, 169, 177, 183; period songs and 30–32, 45, 188, 210; saloon sets and 184–86
Autry, Gene: B westerns 3, 5, 41, 97, 185; songs and film promotion 32–33, 103, 131

B westerns: audience for 2–3; decline due to television 41, 103; gender roles, mixing of 100–101; singing cowboys 30–33; songs in relation to setting 97, 185; inclusivity 111
Back in the Saddle (1941) 32–33
Bad Sleep Well, The (1960) 168
Bale, Christian 224
"Ballad of Jesse James" 199
ballads 198–99
banjo 108, 120, 144, 154–55, 159, 160
Bardem, Javier 220
Barquero (1970) 143
Barry, John 6–7, 204–5
"Battle Hymn of the Republic" 88, 189
"Beautiful Dreamer" 188, 190, 199
Beckerman, Michael 10
Behlmer, Rudy 35n
Beltrami, Marco 209, 212, 224
Berkeley, Busby 105
Berlin, Irving 94, 98, 106
Bernstein, Elmer 22, 39, 54, 112, 165, 173
BFI Companion to the Western 9

Big Country, The (1950): "Americanness" of 51, 121; score as model for *Chambara* westerns 119–21; Death of Buck Hannassey 64–69; opening scenes 55, 119; The Raid 57–63; synopsis 56–57
Billy the Kid (Copland) 38, 53
Bird, Antonia 148–50, 153, 161
"Black Jack David" *see* "Gypsy Davey"
Blazing Saddles (1974) 34
Blood Simple (1984) 227n
"Blue Shadows on the Trail" 46, 47
bluegrass music 189
Boléro (Ravel) 167
Bonanza (1959–1973) 33
Boone, Richard 33
Branded (1965–1966) 33
Bridges, Jeff *187*, 188
Brill, Lesley 79, 88
Broken Arrow (1950) 4
Brolin, Josh 227n
bromance 47, 48
Bronson, Charles 137, 173
Brooks, Mel 34
Bucking Broadway (1917) 2
"Buffalo" Bill Cody 38, 94, 95, 104, 193, *194*
Burch, Noël 166
Burke, Martha Jane Cannary *see* Calamity Jane
Burwell, Carter 221, 223
Buscombe, Edward 24, 25, 26, 78, 80, 85
Butch Cassidy and the Sundance Kid (1969) 183
Butler, Frank 95–96, 104

Calamity Jane: depiction in *Wild Bill* (1995) 193, 195, 200; real cowgirl 94, 103–4
Calamity Jane (1953): gender roles, mixing of 96, 99, 110–11; musical and western genres, combination of 97–98; novelty and tradition in 94–95, 99–100, 103, 112–13; vocal style 106–7, 108–10
Canyon Passage (1946) 29
Cardinale, Claudia 137
Care, Ross 11
Carey, Harry 93
Carey, Harry Jr. 40, 100
Carmichael, Hogey 29
Carroll, Jidge 29–30
Cash, Johnny 33
Cat Ballou (1965) 34

Cave, Nick 200, 224
Cawelti, John G. 161n, 225n
chambara westerns 117–24
Charro! (1969) 23
Cheyenne (1955–1963) 33
Cheyenne Autumn (1964) 6, 39
Chion, Michel 156, 227n
Chisum (1970) 131
"Chuckawalla Swing" 41, 42, 43
Cinema Paradiso (1988) 145
"Circus Band" (Ives) 188
Clarida, Bob *see* Tagg, Philip
Clockwork Orange, A (1971) 226n
Cochran, Alfred 9
Cody, William *see* "Buffalo" Bill Cody
Coen, Ethan 214, 220, 221, 227n
Coen, Joel 214, 220, 221, 227n
Cohen, Leonard 8, 36n
Cole, Nat King 34
"Columbia, The Gem of the Sea" *see* "O Columbia"
"Come, Come Ye Saints" 42–43, 45
concert saloon 184–86, 190–91, 197
contemporary westerns 205–6, 214, 216–21, 223–25
Cooder, Ry 153, 189
Cooke, Mervyn 22–23
Cooper, Gary 26
Copland, Aaron 3–4, 30, 38, 51–55, 56
Costa, Don 83, 90
"Cotton Eyed Joe" 188–89
country and western music 3, 31, 119, 210
Covered Wagon, The (1923) 2
cowgirls 12, 94–95, 101, 103
Crain, Edward L. 31
Crawford, Joan 100, 103
Creekmur, Corey K. 10–11
Crucified Lovers, The (1954) 167
Culpepper Cattle Co. (1972) 190
Cumbow, Robert 138

Dances With Wolves (1990) 6, 204–5, 206
Danly, Linda 9
Dano, Paul 220
Darby, William 9
Day, Doris 94, 98, 106–8
de Lannoy, Yuna 13, 170
DeVoto, Bernard 214–15, 218, 225
Dead Man (1995): character traits and music 206, 212; experimental score 207–8; storyline 203–4

Deadwood (2004–2006) 188, 190
Deakins, Roger 227n
Dean, James 108
Death Rides a Horse (1967) 142
"Degüello" 122, 133
Depp, Johnny 204
Desser, David 118
Destry Rides Again (1939) 100
Dickinson, Angie 132
Die Dreigroschenoper see Threepenny Opera, The
diegetic: scores 121–22; songs 97, 210, 211
Dietrich, Marlene 100, 185, 198–99
Dirty Little Billy (1972) 190
Disclosure (1994) 145
Disney, Walt 37, 45–47
"Do Not Forsake Me, Oh My Darlin'" 8, 22, 55, 83
Dodes' ka-den (1970) 166
Donnelly, K. J. 10, 13–14
Dorian mode 139, 145, 220
"Down in the Valley" 85
Drummond, Phillip 24, 26, 28
Drunken Angel (1948) 168
Duck You Sucker (1971) 142
Duel in the Sun (1946) 5
dulcimer 154–57, 155
Duning, George 23
"Dying Cowboy, The" 189
Dylan, Bob 8, 190

easterns 7, 13
Eastwood, Clint: Dollars Trilogy 136, 138, 140; as film director 8; as masculine hero 101, 128, 142–43; *Rawhide* (1959–1966) 33
Eckstein, Arthur M. 79–80
Ehresmann, Patrick 137, 138
Eine Kleine Nachtmusik (Mozart) 142
Eisenstein, Sergei 217–18
Eisler, Hanns 34–35n
El Salon Mexico (Copland) 176
electronic music 154
Ellis, Warren 200, 224
Evans, Dale 101

Fantasia in C minor K. 475 (Mozart) 84, 86
Fantasia in D minor K. 397 (Mozart) 85–86
Fielding, Jerry 5, 209
Fighting Fists of Shanghai Joe, The (1972) 144

Fistful of Dollars, A (1964) 7, 136, 138, 141, 144
Fistful of Dynamite, A see Duck You Sucker (1971)
Five Card Stud (1968) 23
Flinn, Caryl 12
folk song 31–32, 151
Fonda, Henry 137
For a Few Dollars More (1965) 7, 136, 141, 150–51
Ford, Dan 37, 118
Ford, John: Akira Kurosawa, influenced by 118; *Iron Horse, The* (1924) 38; *My Darling Clementine* (1946) 188; *Rio Grande* (1950) 40; *The Searchers* (1956) 1, 24–27; Sons of the Pioneers and 41, 45; *Stagecoach* (1939) 4, 38; Stan Jones and 40–41; traditional music, use of 4, 38–39; *Wagon Master* (1950) 37, 39–40
Ford, Tennessee Ernie 24, 27
Fort Apache (1948) 39, 43
Forty Guns (1957) 29–30
Foster, Stephen 152, 160
Frayling, Christopher 133–34, 135
Fried, Gerald 54
Friedhofer, Hugo 53, 54
Frontiere, Dominic 143
frontier, musical images of 216–17, 218, 220–21, 223
Fuller, Samuel 29–30

gagaku music 54, 167–68
Garland, Judy 94, 105, 185
Geronimo: An American Legend (1993) 153
"[Get Along Home] Cindy, Cindy" 121
"Get Off the Track" 189
geza music 167
"(Ghost) Riders in the Sky" 40
"Girl I Left Behind Me, The" 4, 39
Gish, Lillian 5, 77
Goldsmith, Jerry 39
Good, the Bad and the Ugly, The (1966) 136, 137, 138–39, 140, 141, 142
Good, the Bad, the Weird, The (2008) 144
"Good Indian, The" 189
"Goodbye, Old Paint" 189, 192, 200
Gorbman, Claudia 9–10, 14–15, 108, 153
Great Train Robbery, The (1903) 2, 47
Green, Douglas B. 10
"Green Leaves of Summer, The" 83

Greene, Lorne 33
Greene, Mort 185
Greenwood, Jonny 216–18, 221
guitar: folk songs and 151; perceived
    authenticity of 5, 32, 122, 132–33
guitar, electric 138, 150–51, 207–8, 212
Gun Glory (1957) 27
Gunfight at Red Sands (1963) 137–38
Gunfight at the O.K. Corral (1957) 28
Guthrie, Woody 31, 137
"Gypsy Davey" 198–99

Hageman, Richard 37, 38, 39, 40, 42–45
Hammond, John 150
Hang 'Em High (1968) 143
Hardy, Phil 9
Harline, Leigh 185
harmonica 5, 32, 132–33, 151
Harris, Roy 30
Harvey Girls, The (1946) 185
hats, western 183, 195–96, see also
    stetsons
Have Gun Will Travel (1957-1963) 33
Hawks, Howard 117, 127, 131
Hayasaka, Fumio 165, 167–68, 170, 173
Hellbent (1918) 2
Hepburn, Audrey 77, 78
Herrman, Bernard 51
Hickok, "Wild" Bill: Calamity Jane and
    104; depiction in Calamity Jane
    (1953) 96, 108, 110; depiction in
    Wild Bill (1995) 187, 188, 191,
    192–96, 194, 200
Hidden Fortress, The (1958) 168
High Noon (1952) 22–23, 24
High Plains Drifter (1973) 143
Hondo (1953) 4
"Hop High Ladies" 189
House Un-American Activities
    Committee (HUAC) 92n
Houston, Cisco 31
Howe, James Wong 174
Huston, John 78, 81, 91
Hutton, Betty 94, 105–9
hybrid score 208–11
hymnody 3, 4, 5

"I Ride an Old Paint-Leaving
    Cheyenne" 189
I Shot Jesse James (1949) 199
"I'll Take You Home Again, Kathleen"
    39
"I'm an Old Cowhand" 41
Indian music 6–7, 39, 108

Indianerfilms 7
Inglourious Basterds (2009) 144
Iron Horse, The (1924) 2
Italian westerns 133–35, 150–51
Ives, Burl 27, 57, 122
Ives, Charles 65–66, 160, 188

James, Joni 23, 30
Jarmusch, Jim 205, 206
jaw harp 151, 154
"Jeanie with the Light Brown Hair" 160,
    188
jidaigeki 170
Joe Kidd (1972) 143
"John Brown's Body" 93n
Johnny Guitar (1954) 27, 94, 100
Jones, Stan 37, 40, 41–45
Jones, Tommy Lee 208
"Jubilo" 184, 185

Kalinak, Kathryn 10, 14, 30–31, 40–41,
    86, 88, 122, 150, 174–75, 178, 185,
    188
Kaye, Stubby 34
Keel, Howard 94, 107–8
Khannanov, Ildar 10
Kill Bill Vol.1 (2003) 144
Kill Bill Vol.2 (2004) 144
Kitses, Jim 150
Kobayashi, Atsushi 129n
Koozin, Timothy 167, 172
Kristofferson, Kris 190
Kubrick, Stanley 216–17, 218
Kurosawa, Akira: musical inauthenticity
    122–23; chambara westerns 117–18;
    disjunction of music and image
    168–69, 170; impact of films 13, 128;
    influence of Modernism 169–70;
    Rashomon (1950) 165–66; relations
    with composers 166; Sanjuro (1962)
    124–27; Seven Samurai, The (1954)
    173; Yojimbo (1961) 117–24

Lack, Russell 22
Laine, Frankie 22, 23, 28, 33
Lancaster, Burt 28, 77
L'Arlesienne (Bizet) 166
"Leaning on Jesus" 189
"Leaning on the Everlasting Arms" see
    "Leaning on Jesus"
Lee, Peggy 27, 100
Lehman, Peter 145n
Leinberger, Charles 10, 122, 129n
leitmotif 136, 138, 170

LeMay, Alan 77, 79, 80, 85
Leone, Sergio 7–8, 135–42
Lerner, Neil 22, 25, 56
Levy, Beth E. 10
Lewis, Daniel Day 216
liberal western 6, 206
Life and Legend of Wyatt Earp
    (1955–1961) 33
Little Big Man (1970) 150
Lomax, Alan 52, 186
Lomax, John A. 31
Lonely Man (1957) 27
Lonesome Gun see My Name is Nobody
    (1973)
Long Days of Hate see This Man Can't Die
    (1967)
Long Riders, The (1980) 189
"Lorena" 189
Love Me Tender (1956) 23

"Mack the Knife" 81
MacRae, Gordon 107
Magnificent Seven, The (1960) 165,
    173–74
Man Called Horse, A (1970) 6, 150
Man in the Saddle (1951) 24
Man Who Shot Liberty Valance, The
    (1962) 99, 102
man with no name, the 128, 136, 137,
    141
mandolin 5, 209, 224
"Marching through Georgia" 189
Marcus, Greil 197
Martin, Dean 8, 23, 103, 121, 132
masculinity: challenging of 101, 102–3,
    207, 212; expression of 121, 123, 197,
    205
Maverick Queen, The (1956) 23
Maynard, Ken 31
McCabe and Mrs. Miller (1971) 8, 36n
McCarthy, Cormac 219
McDonald, Matthew 15
McGuire Sisters, The 83, 90
McLintock! (1963) 4
Mellen, Joan 219
melodic material 64–68, 72–73
Melody Ranch (1940) 32–33
Melody Time (1948) 37, 45–49
mélomane 208, 210–11
Mercer, Johnny 41
Merman, Ethel 105
Mexicans: musical stereotyping 122, 173,
    174, 177; traditional instruments 119,
    176

Michael Nyman Orchestra 152, 154
Mifune, Toshiro 120, 121, 171, 173
minstrelsy, minstrel song 86, 88, 185,
    186, 188–89
Mitchum, Robert 5, 23, 203
Modernist film music 169, 175
"Moonlight" Sonata (Beethoven) 85
"Moriat von Mackie Messer" *see* "Mack
    the Knife"
Moross, Jerome: *The Big Country*,
    approach to 12, 51, 54–56, 73–74;
    The Big Country, conveying emotion
    59–63, 69–70; *The Big Country*,
    deleted music 69; *The Big Country*,
    reiterated melodic material 64–68,
    72–73; *The Big Country*, theme music
    150; influence of Charles Ives 65–66;
    relationship with Aaron Copland
    51–53; syncopated rhythms, use of
    58–59
Morricone, Ennio: aerophones 138;
    characterization through timbre 138;
    contribution to film music 144–45;
    influence on Western scores 143–45,
    206; six-note scale, use of 138–39,
    139, 143; spaghetti westerns and 8,
    34, 150–51; title song, use of 137;
    trumpet, use of 141–42
Morton, Jelly Roll 186, 190
multiculturalism 204, 210, 212
musical stereotyping: Mexicans 173, 174,
    177–78; Native American Indians 2,
    6–7, 39, 44, 84–85, 108, 150
My Darling Clementine (1946) 34, 188
My Name is Nobody (1973) 142
My Name is Shanghai Joe (1972) *see*
    Fighting Fists of Shanghai Joe, The
    (1972)
"My Rifle, My Pony, and Me" 8, 121

Native Americans: musical
    representation of 102, 204–5; musical
    stereotyping of 39, 44, 84–85, 108,
    150
Native American music 149, 153–54
Navajo Joe (1966) 142
"Need for Love, The" 81–82
Nelson, Ricky 119, 121, 133
Neumeyer, David 170
New Western history 215
Newman, Alfred 39, 54
Newman, Paul 174
Nichols, Mary P. 216
Nicholson, Jack 219, 226n

Niehaus, Lennie 5
Nietzsche, Friedrich 27, 216
No Country For Old Men (2007): *2001: A Space Odyssey*, links with 221, **222**, 223, 223; opening scenes 220–21; setting for 218–19
North, Alex 39, 165, 174, 175–76
novelty and tradition 94–95
Nyman, Michael 149, 151–53, 159

"O Columbia" 152, 155, 160
Oakley, Annie 94, 104
O'Brien, George 40
"Oh! Dem Golden Slippers" 185
"Oh! Susanna" 44, 160, 185, 190
"Old Dan Tucker" *see* "Get Off the Track"
Once Upon a Time in America (1984) 145
Once Upon a Time in the West (1968) 137, 140, 141, 142, 151
ostinato 58, 157
other, the 6, 78, 174
otherness 6, 84–85, 109, 122, 173, 178
Outlaw Josey Wales, The (1976) 5
Outrage, The (1964) 7, 165, 173, 176–78

Paint Your Wagon (1969) 100
Pale Rider (1985) 5
Palmer, Christopher 78
Paramount Decision 102
Parks, Van Dyke 186, 188, 189
Pat Garrett & Billy the Kid (1973) 8, 190
Peck, Gregory 56, 70, 75n
Peckinpah, Sam 36n, 190
"Pecos Bill" (*Melody Time*) 11, 37, 41, 46–48
"Pecos Bill" (song) 47, 48
period music 3, 13–14, 149, 152, 188
piano 84–86, 184, 189–90, 197, 200, 211
pianola 189, 200
Pisani, Michael 2, 6, 9–10, 49n
Pitt, Brad 224
Popcorn Superhet Receiver (Greenwood) 216, *216*, 226n
popular music: Akira Kurosawa and 167; country and western music 30–31; Ennio Morricone and 8, 137; Jerome Moross and 56, 59; star performers and 98, 103; western title songs and 21, 22, 23
post-classical western 208
post-modernism 172, 203–4, 207
Prats, Armando José 79–80
Presley, Elvis 23

Previn, Andre 4
Pursued (1947) 5, 102

"Queen Anne's Reel" 189
Quick and the Dead, The (1995) 144, 145
Quiet Duel (1949) 166
quijada 125, 128

Raimi, Sam 144
"Raindrops Keep Falling on My Head" 183, 200
Raitt, John 107
Raksin, David 54
Rancho Notorious (1952) 28, 185, 198
Rango (2011) 144
Rapée, Erno 2, 38
Rashomon (1950): *Boléro*-esque theme 167, 170, 172; *gagaku* music, incorporation of 168; international art film and 165–66; Modernism, influence of 169–70; subjectivity/objectivity in 171–72
Ravenous (1999): central character *149*, *151, 157*; European approach to westerns 148–50, 158, 160–61; experimental music 151; Native American music 153–54; principal theme 154–56, *155*; repetitive, additive musical structure 155–60
Rawhide (1959–1966) 33
Red Beard (1965) 128, 166
Red Pony, The (1949) 38, 53
Red River (1948) 4, 5, 8, 78, 100
red westerns 7, 168
Republic Pictures 38, 40, 97, 100
revisionist westerns 5, 7–8, 34, 135, 150, 190
Rhapsody in August (1991) 168–69
Rhythm on the Range (1936) 41
Richie, Donald 117–18
Riders in the Sky (1949) 40
Rimfire (1949) 197–98, 198
"Ring, Ring de Banjo" 188
Rio Bravo (1959) 5, 8, 119–24, 132–33
Rio Grande (1950) 4, 40
Rite of Spring, The (Stravinsky) 143
Ritt, Martin 165, 173, 176
Ritter, Tex 3, 22, 23, 29, 83
Robards, Jason 137
Rodeo (Copland) 38
Rodgers, Jimmie 3
Rogers, Roy 3, 33, 41, 46–47
"Rollin' Dust" 41, 43

Rosar, William 10, 75n
Rosenbaum, Jonathan 203–4, 206
Rosenman, Leonard 6, 150
"Rosin the Bow" 189
Ross, Alex 227n
Rozsa, Miklos 54
Ryan, Robert 108

Salter, Hans 29
Sanjuro (1962) 118, 125–26
Sato, Masaru: American scores, inspired by 118–21; Chambara Westerns, scores for 117; quijada, use of 125, 128; "Sanjuro's Theme" 120–21, 126–27
Scheurer, Timothy 6–7
Searchers, The (1956) 1, 6, 24–27, 132–33
"Secret Love" 94, 98, 111
Seeger, Pete 31
series westerns see B westerns
Seven Samurai, The (1954) 7, 165, 170, 173
sexuality 109, 111–13, 212
"Shall We Gather at the River" 4, 5
shamisen 122–23
Shane (1953) 118
Sharrett, Christopher 78–79
She Wore a Yellow Ribbon (1949) 4, 39
Sherk, Warren 9
Shining, The (1980) 218, 219
silent western 2
Sinclair, Upton 226n
singing cowboys 30–31, 32, 33
Slye, Leonard see Rogers, Roy
Smith, Harry 31
Smith, Jeff 10, 22, 83
Smith, Paul 48
Smoky (1946) 35n
"Sometime Remind Me to Tell You" 184, 185
"Sometimes I Feel Like a Motherless Child" 206
"Song of the Wagonmaster" 41, 42
Sons of the Pioneers: career of 11, 40–41; John Ford films 24, 42, 45; Melody Time (1948) 46–47
sound effects 32, 207–8
spaghetti westerns 134–35
"Stack O' Lee" 195, 196–97
"Stag O' Lee" see "Stack O' Lee"
Stagecoach (1939) 4, 34
Stagecoach (1966) 39
"Stagger Lee" see "Stack O' Lee"

Stanfield, Peter 5, 10, 14, 100–101, 103, 111
Stanwyck, Barbara 29, 30, 104
Station West (1948) 184, 184
Steiner, Max 1, 132–33
stetsons 196–97
Stevens, George 118
Stone, Sharon 144
Straw, Will 23, 25
"Streets of Laredo, The" see "Dying Cowboy, The"
Sturges, John 24, 118, 136, 173
Sukiyaki Western Django (2007) 144, 145
Swafford, Jan 226–27n
"Sweet Genevieve" 2, 189

Tagg, Philip 10, 15n, 139
Takemitsu, Toru 166
Tarentino, Quentin 144
Taxi Driver (1976) 227n
television westerns 33
Tennessee Ernie. see Ford, Tennessee Ernie
Tevis, Peter 137
There Will be Blood (2007) 5, 9, 215–17, 217, 218
They Died With Their Boots On (1941) 6
This Man Can't Die (1967) 143
Thomson, Virgil 3, 150
Three Burials of Melquiades Estrada, The (2005) 204, 208–12
Threepenny Opera, The 81
timbres and character traits 150, 151, 209
Tiomkin, Dimitri: classical formal structure, use of 132–33; "Degüello" 122, 133, 133, 141; "Do Not Forsake Me, Oh My Darlin'" 8, 22, 55; Gunfight at the O.K. Corral (1957) 28; musical stereotyping of Indians 6; "Need for Love, The" 81–83; television westerns 33; Unforgiven, The (1960) 78–79, 81–83, 90–91
title songs 10–11, 22–28, 33, 34
Toho Studio 120, 125
Tompkins, Jane 98–99, 101
tom-tom rhythm 2, 6, 39, 84, 108
Tornatore, Giuseppe 145
True Grit (2010) 5, 9
trumpets, mariachi 140–41, 143, 150
Tulsa (1949) 27–28
"Turkey in the Straw" 86–88
Turner, Fredrick Jackson 27, 215

Two Mules for Sister Sara (1970) 8, 142, 143
Tyler, Parker 169

Ugetsu (1954) 167
Ulzana's Raid (1972) 102
Unforgiven (1992) 8
Unforgiven, The (1960): central theme reflected in score 79–81; ending, music in relation to 90–91; marketing of 82, 83, 90; Matthilde's controlling influence reflected in score 83–86, 89–90; musical representation of character in 12; race and identity in score 77–79, 86, 88; Rachel's theme 83–84

Van Cleef, Lee 136, 138, 142
Vaughan-Williams, Ralph 167
verisimilitude 38, 94, 102, 183, 185, 189–90
Viva Zapata (1952) 175
Volanté, Gian Maria 136

Wagner, Richard 132, 168
Wagon Master (1950) 8, 37, 39–40, 41–45
"Wagons West" 41, 42, 43
Wagstaff, Christopher 151
Walk in the Sun, A (1945) 35n
Wallach, Eli 138
War Wagon, The (1967) 29
Washington, Ned 22, 23, 28, 29, 33, 81–82
Waxman, Franz 54
Wayne, John 97, 107, 122, 131–32, 205

Weill, Kurt 81
Western, Johnny 33
"What a Friend We Have in Jesus" 189
Whitmer, Mariana 11
Wichita (1955) 23, 29
Wild Bill (1995): depicted life 192–93, 200; hats, importance of 195–96; period songs and authenticity in 186, 188, 192; publicity material for *187, 191, 194*
Wild Bunch, The (1968) 5, 209
Wills, Chill 28
Winters, Ben 12
Wood, Robin 131
world music 153
Wyler, William 53–55, 70

Yamamoto, Shugoro 124
"Year of Jubilo", "Kingdom Coming" *see* "Jublio"
Yeats, William Butler 219–20
"Yellow Rose of Texas, The" 189
Yojimbo (1961): composer's input 118–19; influence of *Rio Bravo* (1959) 119–22; inspired by *The Big Country* (1950) 119–21; reason for making 117–18
Yoshimoto, Mitsuhiro 118
Young, Neil 206–8, 212
Young, Victor 23, 39, 40
Young Billy Young (1969) 23
Young Composers' Group 51, 53, 56, 74
Young Guns II (1990) 183

"Zip Coon" 86, 88, 89
Zwed, John 186